BRANDS HATCH

The definitive history
of Britain's best-loved
motor racing circuit

BRANDS HATCH

Chas Parker

To JP and Will

First published in February 2008

A catalogue record for this book is
available from the British Library

ISBN 978 1 84425 334 0

Library of Congress catalog card no 2007922005

Published by Haynes Publishing, Sparkford,
Yeovil, Somerset BA22 7JJ, UK
Tel: 01963 442030 Fax: 01963 440001
Int. tel: +44 1963 442030 Int. fax: +44 1963 440001
E-mail: sales@haynes.co.uk
Website: www.haynes.co.uk

Haynes North America Inc.,
861 Lawrence Drive, Newbury Park,
California 91320, USA

Printed and bound in Great Britain
by J. H. Haynes & Co. Ltd, Sparkford

Jacket illustrations
Front: The start of the parade lap for the 1985 Grand Prix of
Europe *(Michael Hewett)*
Rear, clockwise from top left: The start of the 1970
British Grand Prix *(LAT)*; Touring cars race around the Indy
circuit at Brands in 1995 *(LAT)*; Bernie Ecclestone drives his
Cooper-JAP around the anti-clockwise circuit in 1951 *(LAT)*; a
huge crowd at the 1989 Brands Hatch Trophy race for World
Sports Prototypes *(LAT)*; (centre) a present-day aerial view of
Brands Hatch circuit *(MSV)*

ACKNOWLEDGEMENTS

It is a mark of the affection in which Brands Hatch is held that so
many people have been willing and eager to assist me in my
research. I am deeply indebted to all those who gave up their
time to talk to me or helped source information and
photographs.

Kathy Ager (LAT), Ray Allen, Peter Anderson, Simon Arron,
Rob Bain, Jeff Bloxham, Robin Bradford, Kirstin Brimsted
(MotorSport Vision), Martin Brundle, Ron Chandler, Fred Clarke,
Gareth Crew, Bernie Ecclestone, Jackie Epstein, Emerson
Fittipaldi, Robb Gravett, Stuart Graham, Nicola Green (née
Foulston), Martin Hadwen (Motor Racing Archive), Johnny
Herbert, Michael Hewitt, Peter Higham (LAT), Jim Holder, Matt
James (*Motorsport News*), Doug Jennings, Brian Jones, Max Le
Grand, Chris Lowe, Tony Lovett, Colin Mann, Nigel Mansell,
Derek Minter, Stirling Moss, Simon North, Jackie Oliver, Jonathan
Palmer, Jason Plato, Andy Priaulx, Stuart Pringle, Brian Redman,
Anthony Reid, Allan Robinson, Jody Scheckter, Colin Seeley,
Christine Smith (Haynes Publishing), Jackie Stewart, John
Surtees, Gerald Swan, John Symes, James Thompson, Ian
Titchmarsh, Jill Todd, Alan Wilson, Kevin Wood (LAT), Stan
Woods, Mick Woollett.

Special thanks to John and Angela Webb, without whose help
and support this book would not have been possible; to Mark
Hughes and Steve Rendle at Haynes for their help and
encouragement; to Simon Hearn at Chaters for planting the seed
of an idea and to Quentin Spurring, for his invaluable help in
editing and adding information.

Thanks also to Joe and Sue Pemberton and to Bobbie
Pearman, for being the latest custodians of my peripatetic
collection of *Autosport* magazines.

No thanks to Scrabble and Dib-Dib, two black cats who
respectively sat on my keyboard and cried to be fed all the time.

Contents

Foreword

Brands Hatch has always been a bit special for me. I began my racing career there in motorbike 'scrambles' meetings when I was just 15 years old, and then raced on the grass track. I took part in the

first race when the track was surfaced and then went into 500cc Formula 3 racing.

In those days, a lot of the superstars of the time were competing at Brands in grass track racing – people like Eric Oliver and John Surtees. And then in the car world there was Stirling Moss and other people who turned into very good drivers.

Brands was always a challenge, particularly in the early days when the races were run in an anti-clockwise direction. I enjoyed some success there but I had an accident. I was running quite a successful business at the time, so I thought I had better make a choice. I could have finished up in hospital for a long time, so I thought I had better stop.

A lot of people who were real, genuine stars in those days are regretfully no longer with us. People like Bill O'Rourke and Don Gray. I do not know how I survived. I think it was because I started younger. Lots of guys were about 30, so I had a 10-year advantage on them. If I had been 30, I probably wouldn't be here now.

I think it's true to say that Brands Hatch is the country's best-loved circuit. In its heyday, it was the heart of motor sport in England and was always one of those nice places to go to. There are a lot of places today that people are in love with and others where they say – 'We haven't got to go back there, have we?' Brands was always a pleasure to visit.

It is high time that the full history of Brands Hatch was written and I am delighted to see that Chas Parker has been able to talk to so many people who have been involved with the circuit over the years, both working and racing there, and has encouraged them to tell its story in their own words.

It is also pleasing to see the circuit undergoing a revival under Jonathan Palmer's stewardship, making it particularly apt that its history should now be written. I've always thought that Brands is one of those magical places and I think that this comprehensive account, packed as it is with fascinating illustrations, helps to capture some of that magic.

BERNIE ECCLESTONE

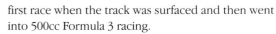

Introduction

It was only after undertaking to write a full history of Brands Hatch that I began to realise the magnitude of the task I had set myself. Brands, as indicated in the sub-title of this book, is Britain's best-loved motor racing circuit and anybody attempting to write the 'definitive' history of the place was always going to risk being shot down in flames if they didn't get it right.

I didn't want to make this book a list of race results, strung together into sentences, but rather to relate the tale of the circuit as told by the people who worked and raced there over the years. Race reports and results can be obtained from a number of sources, so I set out to approach the history from a different standpoint, rather than just re-hashing contemporary accounts.

However much detail you go into, however many people you interview and race reports you read, there is always something you are going to miss or that has to be left out for reasons of space – and you can guarantee that it will be one fan's special memory that you have omitted. To all those who can't find their favourite Brands moment in this book, I sincerely apologise.

Brands Hatch isn't just about car racing either. There are the bikes, the trucks, the karts, the rallycross, the racing schools, the corporate days – where do you stop? And what about the marshals' tales, or the people from the press office, or the man on the gate? Every one has a story to tell about the circuit which is unique in some way but it is just not possible to include everything.

The circuit has always held special memories for me too. It was only an hour's drive from my parents' home in East Sussex, and in the seventies many a Sunday afternoon was spent standing at Druids hairpin with a group of friends, enjoying a good afternoon's racing in the sunshine.

The weather wasn't always kind, though. My first visit had been in December 1969 to a small club meeting. It snowed and a gale blew through the canvas back of the old grandstand at Paddock. Not the most inspiring introduction. It was my next visit in April 1970 that got me hooked. The BOAC 1000 km sports car race was held in atrocious conditions but

provided a truly memorable event, which you can read about further on in this book. That day, despite the weather, I fell in love with the circuit and walked round it many times during the six and three-quarter hours it took to complete the race.

From then on, I returned whenever time and finances allowed. In latter years I was able to take my sons, Jonathan and William, along and they too became enchanted with the place. These are special visits which we still share to this day and the three of us get just as excited at the spectacle of A1GP cars on the Grand Prix loop, or of flame-spitting DTM and panel-bashing BTCC cars on the Indy circuit as I used to watching sports-prototypes or Formula One cars when I was younger. But then Brands Hatch has that sort of effect on you. It has been a privilege and an education to be able to research and write its history.

CHAS PARKER

ABOVE *Bernie Ecclestone takes his 500cc Cooper-JAP around the anti-clockwise circuit during the 9 September 1951 meeting. (LAT)*

Early Days

BRITAIN'S FINEST TRACK IS BORN

The story of Brands Hatch is inextricably linked with the career of one man. Not only will the name of John Webb forever be synonymous with the Kent track, but his vision, enterprise and sheer hard work moulded the structure of British motor racing over nearly four decades.

John Webb was born on 10 February 1931 in Caversham, near Reading, the son of an accountant. His hips were dislocated at birth, and he walks with a distinctive, rolling gait. "The medics couldn't do anything," he recalled. "It was even suggested that I would be in a wheelchair at the age of 25."

The young Webb was "nuts about aeroplanes and railway engines", but not about cars, as he remembered: "All through the war, I inveigled my way onto footplates, and I can drive a locomotive. I used to tell myself in those days: 'I'm going to drive a train, I'm going to be a pilot, and I'm going to be a racing driver.' And I achieved all those things."

Educated at a private school, he showed an aptitude for mathematics and history, but not science. His father wanted him to join a bank – "Because you get a pension". Instead, he ran away to London at the age of 16 to pursue a career in press and publicity work for the aircraft industry.

His working life had already started at Miles Aircraft, an aeroplane manufacturer based at Woodley, in Berkshire. "I just walked in and asked for a job," Webb recalled. "They asked me what I wanted to do, and I saw a sign for the publicity department, so I said I wanted to be in that. I didn't know what publicity was."

Nevertheless he immediately showed a flair for the work, and also became a freelance aviation journalist. Unfortunately, Miles Aircraft was one of the first British companies to go broke after the war, and Webb ended up the last employee left in the publicity department: "I was forced in adverse circumstances to learn an awful lot very quickly."

RIGHT *Eric Oliver and his sidecar passenger accelerate up Paddock Hill Bend in 1946. The circuit ran anti-clockwise in those days and was marked out by white pegs.*
(Mick Woollett)

On leaving Miles, Webb headed for London and got a job with the Royal Aero Club. He became the assistant press officer for the Farnborough Air Show and then took over press work for Silver City Airways, which was the first company to fly cars across the Channel commercially. Generating publicity about such a glamorous subject came easily to Webb: "It was so novel. Every time we flew cars across to France, we were dealing with famous personalities.

"I was reasonably successful in the airline publicity business and, as a result, a number of other companies came to me with offers. I decided to take them all. In September 1953, I formed my own press and PR company. At that stage, somebody suggested that I went to see the people at Brands Hatch. So I did. With effect from 1 January 1954, I initiated their press relations as an external consultant. I had never seen Brands Hatch until the late autumn of 1953 and my only

BELOW *John Webb's career at Brands Hatch endured for 36 years. (LAT)*

awareness of it was from the *Daily Telegraph* sponsorship of the 500cc racing."

At the time, the circuit was managed by John Hall, an accountant appointed by the shareholders. "As I understand it," Webb explained, "it was owned by 55 different shareholders, among whom nobody had more than 10 per cent. The leading light up until then had been a man called Joe Francis, a motorcycle trader and who had previously raced on the Isle of Man. He, I believe, was the person who

got Brands Hatch going after the war – but perhaps not with a great deal of commercial success. That was why an accountant had been put in as the managing director, to keep an eye on things.

"John Hall was a very convivial gentleman, but he wasn't a motor racing person. He was very much safeguarding shareholders' interests by spending as little as possible. You couldn't really call him a motor racing promoter."

Webb's first impression of the place was not exactly favourable. He remembered: "Apart from the fabulous viewing, it was an absolute dump. It had a poor reputation for amenities. But that didn't concern me yet. I was purely involved with publicity then – not advertising, but gratuitous publicity. My job was to write and send out press releases detailing forthcoming meetings and to turn up on the day and run the press box. Although it wasn't really a press box – it was a couple of deckchairs in a hut opposite the start-finish line. Fairly soon afterwards, we did build a press box, which was a hut with a couple of windows in it. My first specific job, in February 1954, was to announce the Druids loop extension."

In those days, the circuit was used about equally by cars and bikes, many of the former being the very popular F3 cars, powered by 500cc Norton or JAP motorcycle engines. These were very numerous, and a typical car meeting consisted of a number of heats and finals. In total, the track was probably used about 20 times a year, with occasional midweek use for general practice days.

Up until this point, Webb's personal interest had been almost exclusively in aircraft. As a result of his Brands Hatch involvement, however, he also acquired the PR account for the Connaught Formula One team, and began to take more of an interest in motor racing. "The first motor race I ever saw, I think, would have been in 1952 or 1953 at Goodwood," he said. "I just decided to go there one day. Mike Hawthorn won in a Cooper-Bristol.

"I became much more involved in 1957. I acquired a Jensen 541 and entered it for a sprint at Crystal Palace. I did reasonably well – and got bitten by the bug. I started entering the Jensen in various races, sprints and hillclimbs and found myself with the Brands Hatch saloon car lap record and one or two hillclimb records. You couldn't keep me away from motor racing then. I even won at Silverstone."

One of Webb's first innovations at Brands Hatch was the 1954 Boxing Day race meeting. "Silver City Airways were still my clients and we had an opening party for Ferryfield Airport in Kent, which is now Lydd Airport," said Webb. "Chris Jennings, who was the editor of *The Motor* at that time, said to me: 'I suppose the next thing you'll be doing is running racing on Boxing Day.' I replied: 'That's a good idea! We'll do it!'"

Webb put the idea to John Hall, who in turn asked the BRSCC (British Racing & Sports Car Club) for its views. The outcome was that some 20,000 spectators turned up on 26 December for a seven-race meeting which included an ox-roast and Stirling Moss dressed up as Father Christmas. "That's 20,000 people on a day when people had never, ever been motor racing before," smiled Webb. "To me, the great fun in life is making things happen which wouldn't have happened if I hadn't made them."

And it is fair to say that, without John Webb, much of what is contained in this book would never have happened.

Almost 30 years before John Webb had ever cast his eyes on Brands Hatch, the natural bowl in the Kent countryside had caught the attention of another man. Ron Argent was the proprietor of five bicycle shops in Kent and was well known within the cycling community. One day in 1926, while leading a group of cyclists on a 125-mile tour, Argent stopped to look at a sloping mushroom field lying next to the main A20 London to Dover road.

The fields belonged to Brands Hatch Farm. The name could be very ancient. Some sources believe it to be derived from 'Brondehach', which they describe as a Gaelic term – 'bron' meaning 'wooded slope' and 'hach' meaning 'entrance to the forest'. However an Anglo-Saxon derivation seems more likely: 'brant' meant 'steep' and 'hæth' (as now) 'untilled land'. The ground was chalk-based and steeply sloped, so heavy rain would quickly wash away the thin topsoil, making it unsuitable for arable or grazing use. Mushrooms and rabbits were about

the only things that thrived there. The fields had been used for military training for a number of years and, when Argent enquired of the farmer, Bert Cornwall, if he and his fellow cycling enthusiasts could make use of it, Cornwall's attitude was: "If you want to use it, go ahead."

Over the next few years, cyclists from the London area converged on the field at weekends to practise and hold time trials on the dirt tracks created by the farm machinery. An old army hut, a relic of the First World War, was converted for use as a café and, in 1928, the first actual race was held. It was run over four miles as a contest between cross-country runners and the cyclists. The runners, whose numbers included the World Cross-Country Champion, Australian Jackie Hoobin, were the victors.

In the same year, informal grass track racing was started by motorcycling enthusiasts, who had already been using the surrounding woodland for scrambles. Initially a straight strip was laid out, corresponding approximately to what became Bottom Straight, and then a three-quarter-mile circuit was mapped out. It was this kidney-shaped course which became the basis for the track as we know it today.

In 1932, the Bermondsey, Owls, Sidcup and, initially, West Kent motorcycle clubs joined forces to become the Brands Hatch Combine, and organised their first meeting on 28 March. The popularity of the BHC events grew quickly. During the rest of the 1930s, crowds in excess of 30,000 would enjoy watching the likes of Jack Surtees (father of John), Eric Oliver (later four-times the Sidecar World Champion) and Harold Taylor, a 'demon' one-legged sidecar racer. With the increase in the performance of the bikes, the grass track was extended to one mile in 1936.

During the Second World War, the Brands Hatch site was requisitioned by the Army as a transport base, being at a strategic location on the way to Dover. Soon after hostilities ceased, the Army departed, and it was not long before the motorcycling fraternity returned.

Max Le Grand, who would become an accomplished Grand Prix photographer, was six at the time. His parents had been involved with the pre-war motorcycle meetings. "After the war," said Le Grand, "my parents went to a meeting in a café known as the Pavilion. This was a converted sports pavilion at the back entrance to Brands Hatch, on the left-hand side as you go in from Scratcher's Lane, where the paddock was eventually located."

As a result of that meeting, racing was soon under way again on the well-worn grass track, the line of which was marked out by small white pegs. At that time, the paddock was located in the centre of the track. "It was considered a convenient spot

because they had no way of controlling spectators and stuff was getting stolen left, right and centre," explained Le Grand. "So the paddock was isolated in the middle and you had to cross the track to go in and out.

"It was just motorcycles in those days. There was a path up to the start-line, where there was a little timekeepers' box on the infield with a commentary box on top of it. Everything was done from there.

"This was a time when everyone who owned a motorcycle or car was heavily rationed on fuel, to about two gallons a week. Apparently, questions were asked in Parliament as to how it was that Brands Hatch was racing every Sunday. Where were they getting this fuel?

"When the Army had operated a depot there during the war, for storing trucks and cars and other equipment, they obviously had fuel there as well. The place was bombed quite often and the Army decided to distribute the fuel drums around the site. Many of these drums were pushed into the bomb holes in the woods and camouflaged. When the war finished, and the Army left, they were forgotten.

"One day, some people were riding trials bikes in the woods at the back of South Bank and somebody disappeared into a bomb hole. They pulled the camouflage away and there were these drums of petrol, dozens of them. They didn't tell a soul – but they used the petrol to go racing. Even though the question was asked in Parliament, no answer was forthcoming. And that was how Brands Hatch was reconstituted after the war."

The person in charge in those immediate post-war days was Joe Francis, a Kent-based former TT motorcyclist, who had bought the land from the farmer, Bert Cornwall. In 1947, Brands Hatch Stadium Ltd was formed with Francis as the principal shareholder and managing director.

Tony Lovett, then a member and later to become the chairman of the Greenwich Motor & Motorcycle Club, explained: "When the farmer put it all up for sale, Sidcup, Bermondsey and the Owls, the three clubs which had formed the original Brands Hatch Combine before the war, had the option to buy the land. They had the money, but they wouldn't speculate. So Joe Francis, who was a speedway rider at New Cross Speedway and the proprietor of a main AJS and Matchless dealership in New Eltham, stepped in bought it over their heads.

"Those three clubs were upset that the track had been sold to someone else, and the fact that they had had the first option but hadn't taken it. So they stopped running meetings. But my club, Greenwich, and the Gravesend and Rochester clubs formed a new Brands Hatch Combine and that ran for years and years."

The new owner operated everything from the Pavilion, in which he also lived. "There were living quarters behind the counter in the Pavilion where everything was served," remembered Max Le Grand. "It was a notorious den of iniquity, really! Not only did it serve up cups of tea and suchlike, but it also served as a venue for many social occasions, one of which was the Tramps' Supper. All the members of the motorcycle clubs used to come as tramps, drink themselves under the table and dance. It was always held in November and was great fun.

"The administration was run from the Pavilion as well and the offices were there. A man called George Pennington, who was the track manager and responsible for the maintenance of all the facilities, moved in there with his wife and two sons."

The track was soon a popular venue again for motorcycles and sidecars, and in September 1947 Joe Francis even persuaded the BBC to televise a grass track meeting from the circuit: it was the first time a motorcycle event had been seen on British screens. Familiar pre-war figures were back at the track, as well, including Jack Surtees, whose son acted as his passenger in sidecar races.

"John cut his teeth being passenger to his dad," remembered Max Le Grand. "He was invariably thrown off and was given a thorough clouting by his father for not hanging on. There was also a team called the Blue Boys, who I think were brothers and who always wore black leathers with blue polo neck jumpers over the top. Then there were the Grey brothers from Chatham and Eric Oliver, who went on to become a Sidecar World Champion. All kinds of people used to race there, including Bernie Ecclestone."

The young Ecclestone had started riding at Brands Hatch in scrambling events, at the age of 15, and developed an affinity for the place. He recalled: "It was a grass track when I was racing bikes there and it was a bit basic, but never mind – it's one of those magic places, Brands Hatch."

Ecclestone liked it so much that, a few years later in 1949, still only 19 but already a successful businessman, he tried to buy the track for £46,000 from Joe Francis. "We agreed and shook hands but it just didn't happen in the end," explained Ecclestone. "I would have liked to have improved it much quicker than they did, but don't forget I was a kid in those days. I would have done what they did, made it a proper hard track, built grandstands, done all the things that seem so obvious today, but didn't seem obvious to people in those days. Anyway, it didn't happen. Joe decided not to sell to me and that was it."

In those days, the circuit ran in an anticlockwise direction. This suited Ecclestone. "I've got a bit of a

RIGHT *In 1949, the Moto
Cross des Nations took
place at Brands Hatch.
Here Belgian rider
F. Thomas leaps through
the air at the 'Bomb
Hole' during the second
beat. (Mick Wollett)*

problem," he explained. "I don't see too well out of
my right eye, something I was born with, and so left-
hand corners always seemed better to me than
right-handers. There was a big left-hander before we
went up the hill, so it suited me better than the
other way round."

From the start-finish line, the bikes would roar off
towards the long, sweeping left-hander at Clearways
and then flick right onto the Bottom Straight and
past a St John Ambulance Brigade hut. Then it was
left into the steep, uphill climb of Paddock Bend,
where the riders really piled on the power.

"There was one well-worn inside track at
Paddock but those who really wanted to make up
ground could go right round the outside," said Max
Le Grand. "The spectacle of Paddock Hill was always
lost, though, especially on dry, dusty days. No one
could stand there because the noise was full-on –
the riders really had the throttle fully open going up
the hill, and there were showers of dust and muck
and flintstones flying around. You couldn't stand
there. But it was a great spectacle and then they'd
barrel down the top straight again."

During the winter of 1947–48, the infield
paddock was relocated to the outside of the track.
"There came a time when they got fed up carting
food, urns of hot water to make coffee and crates of
ginger beer down to the paddock," said Le Grand.
"Competitors were complaining because, if they'd
had their races, they had to wait until the end of the
meeting before they could go home. The paddock
was moved so it was adjacent to the Pavilion, where
all the facilities were."

The racing season ran from April until September
or October, at which point the track was given over
to scrambling events. A scrambles course ran
through the woods behind South Bank, utilising the
bomb holes left over from the war and a chalk pit
around Dingle Dell. "The scrambling and
motorcycle trials had been going on for quite a long
time in the woods," said Le Grand. "It was a winter
pastime. It was a very hilly terrain in those woods
and there were very many paths used by people
shifting cattle from one field to another."

In 1949, an international motocross event was
held in the woods – the 500cc 'Moto Cross des
Nations'. Led by Harold Lines, the British team
narrowly beat the Belgian and Swedish teams and
the event made a huge impression on the nine-year-
old Le Grand.

"When this huge meeting arrived, with top riders
from all over Europe, it was the biggest thing that
had happened up to that time," he said. "The team
leader for the Belgians was a huge mountain of a
man called Augustus Mingles. That man was
responsible for me falling off the wagon – he taught

me to smoke and drink wine. They were all camped
in the paddock with their bikes beside their tents –
it was a wonderfully happy atmosphere. It was the
first time I'd heard so many different languages.

"The meeting used part of the circuit. I think
they used the start-finish line and then veered off,
across Bottom Straight, up over a hump and then
off into the woods. And then they reappeared and
came down across the line. It was a long course and
a tough course. The foreigners used to say it was
one of the toughest of the whole European series.
We all thought that was a real accolade."

Spectator facilities at the fledgling circuit were
almost non-existent. People watching had to endure
clouds of dust if it was dry, a mud bath it was wet.
"Somebody found about 1000 iron bucket seats and
had the idea of terracing the bank in front of the
startline," Le Grand recalled. "These green bucket
seats were laid out and spectators charged a bit
more to sit, rather than stand round the fence. But
the viewing facilities were very sparse at that time,
and very dangerous, because there was a paling
fence around the perimeter of the circuit and a
protective barrier which was really large stakes in
the ground every few yards, with a bit of wire
threaded through them. And that was supposed to
retain an errant motorcycle. That was how primitive
it was. There were a few marshals' posts and the St
John Ambulance had their hut on the outside of the
circuit on Bottom Straight."

The first major development of the Brands Hatch
circuit came about during the winter of 1949–50.
The 500 Club had been formed by a group of
enthusiasts in Bristol in 1946 to develop low-cost
motorsport, and a specification was drawn up for a
national 500cc single-seater formula. The following
year, the club moved to London and a new
committee was elected, including Earl Howe, S.C.H.
(Sammy) Davis, Laurence Pomeroy, Raymond Mays,
John Cooper and Dick Caesar. In 1948, the new
formula supported the international race for Grand
Prix cars at Silverstone and, over the next couple of
years, the 500cc drivers began to compete across
Europe. The FIA, the governing body of world
motorsport, adopted the 500 Club's British national
rules in 1950 to create a new international Formula
3. At the end of that year, the club formally changed
its name to the Half Litre Club and later, in 1954, it
became the British Racing & Sports Car Club
(BRSCC), based in London near Trafalgar Square.

It was still the 500 Club when it persuaded Joe
Francis in 1949 that the future of Brands Hatch lay in
road racing, rather than grass track events, and
jointly funded the laying of a one-mile tarmacadam
surface, at a cost of £17,000. The scene was set for
the first racing cars to appear on the track.

1950s

ROAD RACING BEGINS

The surfacing of the one-mile Brands Hatch track was completed by February 1950 and it was tried out by some of the leading 500cc Formula 3 drivers of the day, including Stirling Moss, Ken Carter, Stan Coldham, Bill Whitehouse and Eric Winterbottom, with a number of demonstration runs.

That March, the first motorcycle race meeting was held on the new circuit, with over 150 riders competing in a 29-race programme. The event was organised by the Greenwich Motor & Motorcycle Club and the first-ever road race, a four-lap heat for 250cc machines, was won by Harry Pearce riding a Triumph, appropriately enough wearing the No.1 plate. Behind him was the Excelsior of Geoff Daniels and in third place John Surtees on another Triumph. One of the starters at this opening meeting was motorbike TT winner Les Graham, whose son, Stuart, would compete successfully at the track on both two wheels and four in years to come.

The first car race ever run at Brands Hatch took place on Sunday 16 April 1950, a week after Easter. Practice was held the day before amid squalls of hail, but race day dawned bright and sunny for 7000 spectators who turned up to watch a 10-race programme. The honour of victory in the first event, which was a 10-lap race for amateur-built cars, went to Don Parker, driving his JAP-engined Parker Special. Both cars and drivers found the new course hard going, especially the steep climb of Paddock Bend. A contemporary report stated: "By the end of the day, the really healthy motor cars still running could very nearly be counted on the fingers of one hand."

Further car race meetings were run that year in June, July, August, September, October and November, when the Maidstone & Mid-Kent Motor Club tried running sports cars for the first time at the circuit and also experimented with using the track in a clockwise direction. This proved popular with competitors who found that, although Paddock

RIGHT *'Big Bill' Whitehouse in his Cooper-Norton on 16 April 1950. (LAT)*

RIGHT *A competitor's car is prepared during the very first car meeting on 16 April 1950. (LAT)*

OPPOSITE *A large crowd eagerly awaits the start of one of the races at the 7 August 1950 meeting. The line of the track from Bottom Straight into the uphill Paddock Bend can be clearly seen in the distance. (LAT)*

BELOW *Just as today, in 1950 cars gained access to the infield of the circuit through a tunnel beneath the track. (LAT)*

now became a rather daunting, downhill right-hander, it was easier to place the cars more accurately on the track.

The half-litre cars brought along their own brand of stars. Stirling Moss had already made a name for himself in 500cc racing and his superiority was quite evident, the 20-year-old winning all five of his races in the June meeting. Other big names of the time included Bernie Ecclestone, Bob Gerard, Don Parker, George Wicken, Pop and Stuart Lewis-Evans, and 'Big Bill' Whitehouse.

"George Wicken had a beautiful, maroon-coloured Cooper," recalled Max Le Grand, "and Don Parker was another, tiny little man who was very successful with a Keift. Albert Zains was an outrageous character – didn't know what he was doing, but raced and always came last. There were great characters around. It was just the greatest fun. I got more excited by 500cc racing than motorcycles."

The race meetings in those days normally comprised an 'Open Challenge' event in three or four heats plus a final, a 'Junior Championship' with three heats and a final, the 'Brands Hatch Championship', again two or three heats and a final depending on the entry, and finally, to round off the day, the 'Championship of the Meeting' race. This was made up of the 14 drivers who had driven the fastest laps during the whole race meeting.

Lured away from two wheels onto four, Bernie Ecclestone competed in his first car race at the opening meeting of 1951, in April. At the time, Ecclestone held the two-wheel lap record at the circuit and was described by *Autosport* as "a former Brands motorcycle expert". He certainly made the transition easily, winning the Junior Championship race and coming fourth in the Championship of the Meeting event in a Mk5 Cooper-JAP prototype. He went on to win seven races at the circuit during the

BELOW *The sloping paddock was a hive of activity on 8 April 1951.* (LAT)

Stirling Moss

"The 500s were quite competitive, pretty evenly matched around Brands. You could go round corners side-by-side, more or less, and Brands lent itself quite well to it.

"Before they changed to racing clockwise, Paddock was upwards, which made it quite easy, but when they changed it the other way it became a lot more difficult. I would say that, for its length, the circuit was quite tricky. It was certainly a lot easier anti-clockwise. Going up the hill was quite a doddle. Going round the back, you had a few tightening corners, but it was nowhere near as difficult as it is now.

"Although you wouldn't tell the others what gear ratios you were using, they might come along and try and work out how many cogs you had, and you'd help the other people out if

anything went wrong – share fuel, share oil – and there were a lot of more likeable people. We were really quite a tightly knit group because, being Formula 3, we were the bottom formula and fairly noisy, but we were fairly close to each other really.

"The people were pretty friendly there and the drivers were thrown together in quite a small paddock. I was never that taken with the extension, in truth, but I suppose it was an improvement because you could have more cars round it.

"I had one particularly good day there. I think I won five races, which was very good."

Stirling Moss guides his 500cc Kieft around the track in 1952. (LAT)

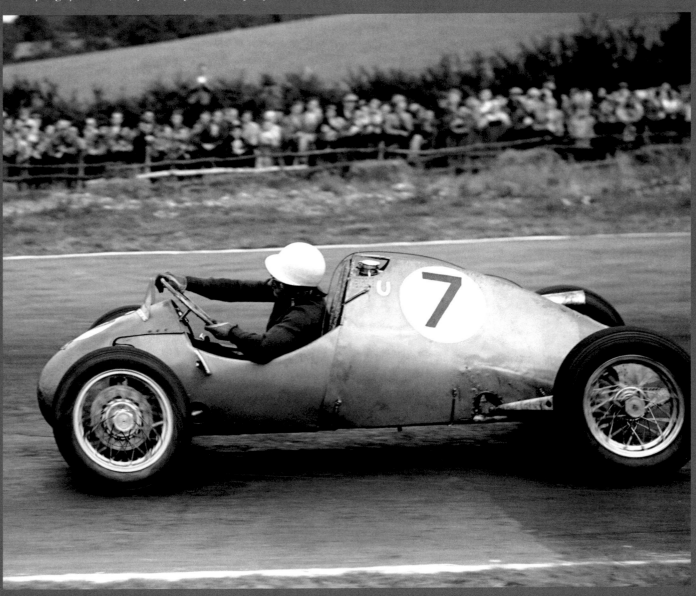

season, making him the third most successful driver there in 1951.

"I moved into driving 500cc cars, I think when the first Cooper came out," Ecclestone remembered. "I drove for Cooper as a semi-works thing. I don't know whether I was the third most successful driver or not. I used to win or fly off the road, one or the other."

This was borne out later in the year when, in order to cut down on reckless driving, the Half-Litre Club (as the 500 Club was now known) instigated a 'no spin' rule for its September meeting. Anyone who spun more than 180deg or completely left the track was automatically disqualified. One of the first to be black-flagged for grass-cutting in the Championship Race was Ecclestone, who claims to have no recollection of the incident. "I don't remember that and I don't know how anyone could introduce a rule to stop people spinning," he said. "It's a matter of you either do or you don't."

The dangers of the sport became apparent on 21 October when Ian Pelling's Emeryson crashed at Clearways, injuring four spectators, and Harry Parker was killed when his Cooper crashed and overturned near the same place later in the day. Ironically, amid calls in the motoring press for safety standards to be improved, the track was completely resurfaced over the winter of 1951–52, making it much quicker.

Safety was also becoming an issue for the motorcyclists, and an alarming number of accidents occurred at Paddock Bend. As a result, from July 1952, all solo bike races were run in a clockwise direction. The honour of winning in the last-ever anti-clockwise motorbike race fell to John Surtees.

In 1953, the Universal Motor Racing Club was formed, which was the forerunner of the car racing schools of today. This was a private enterprise, run by a man called Gordon Thornton, which operated at the circuit on Wednesday afternoons and gained some 350 members. The cost – five shillings (25p) for each lap.

Max Le Grand remembered one particular driver who turned up and paid a pound for four laps: "One day, among all the Hooray Henrys, a working class guy turned up. He definitely wasn't someone who was using daddy's money to race around the circuit. This dishevelled figure paid his few bob for a lesson and promptly went round very, very fast. He was a very unconventional driver – not a natural, but fast. He manhandled a car around a course, he didn't just let it flow. He didn't know any other way. He came in sweating like a pig and red in the face. And that was my first sighting of Graham Hill."

The outcome of this first encounter with a racing car was that Hill, who was to go on to become a double World Champion, began to help out at the school in return for some more laps. But the school stopped operating at the end of the year due to financial problems. Undaunted, Hill found another backer and the Premier Motor Racing Club was formed, with him as both the chief instructor and the mechanic.

Also in 1953, raised earth banks were erected all around the circuit to protect spectators and then, over the winter of 1953–54, a major change was made to the circuit layout. In order to accommodate larger racing cars, the length of the track was extended by the addition of a loop. This ran from the bottom of Paddock Bend, up the other side of the 'bowl' through the trees on a 1:9 incline which was named Pilgrim's Rise, to a tight, 180deg, right-hand hairpin known as Druids Hill Bend, and then

back down the 1:10 hill to rejoin the original track. The extension increased the circuit length to 1.24 miles. At the same time, the width of the whole track was increased from 30ft to 35ft.

Car racing was also now run clockwise. Because of this, the old link between Bottom Straight and Paddock Bend was sealed off. With the direction of the circuit reversed, it was felt that the use of a tight, right-hand bend at the bottom of Paddock Bend would be too dangerous.

The first event on the new layout was a sprint, rather than a race, and the fastest time of the day was set by 19-year-old Jackie Epstein in a borrowed 2-litre Alta sports car. "I held the lap record the present way round for a week, because the sprint was the first event of any sort that ran clockwise," said Epstein, who was to play a major role in the development of the circuit in the seventies.

It was Stuart Lewis-Evans, driving a Cooper Mk8 Norton, who won the first actual race on the 1.24-mile circuit, a heat for 500cc cars. He also won the final and the main event of the meeting, the Senior 500cc race. Making his racing debut that day, in a Cooper Mk4 JAP, was Graham Hill. Not only was it the first race in which he had competed, but also the first he had ever seen. Despite his inexperience, he managed to finish second in his heat and fourth in the final.

According to Max Le Grand, the growth of the circuit reflected a certain amount of ambition among interested parties. "The ambition of a lot of

BELOW *The 19 April 1954 meeting marked the first use of the new Druids extension at the track. (LAT)*

John Surtees

"I would have been taken to Brands before the war, not that I remember that part of it. But I do remember racing restarting after the war and, of course, my father was competing at that time. I first rode round the circuit in his sidecar in 1948, but that was not competing in a race. I was just 14 at that time.

"When the circuit was tarmaced, I took part in the first road race, which in fact was also my first. I'd done one or two grass tracks but I hadn't ridden on the road before. I rode a little

The first race on the new road circuit took place on 9 April 1950. One of the competitors that day was 16-year-old John Surtees (23) on a 250 Triumph. This was his first-ever road race, but he finished third. (Mick Woollett)

Triumph. In that early part of the fifties, I rode solo and I rode in the sidecar with my father. I went on to have a very successful time at Brands Hatch on various bikes I rode and then obviously I drove cars on it. So I've got memories of winning on two wheels, winning on three wheels, and winning on four wheels!

"One of my best memories was the time in 1955 when I was just coming up and I was challenging Geoff Duke. We'd had an event at Silverstone where I'd beaten him for the first time in a straight race, me riding my Norton and him a Gilera. When he came to Brands Hatch, we had an enormous crowd turn up and there was a traffic jam back to Swanley, as usual. I think it was the biggest crowd they'd ever had, and I beat him again on that day."

people, not just the management at Brands, was that the circuit had to grow," he said. "It was the Half Litre Club being ambitious to race cars other than 500s around there. They could envisage saloon cars, sports cars, even Formula One cars. Even at that stage, there was talk of one day getting the Grand Prix. John Hall could see the potential for growth and said: 'Let's do it one step at a time'. Some of the trees in the wood were cut down, a path was made through, and the track extension was laid. I remember standing there and thinking: 'This is really going to put us on the map.'"

By this time, John Hall was the managing director of Brands Hatch Circuit, as the company was now known. It was at this point that John Webb made his appearance on the scene, publicising the new extension to the track being his first task after taking over the press and PR work.

The racing having been switched to a clockwise direction, spectators were treated to the now famous sight of the cars or bikes plunging down the daunting Paddock Hill Bend. It stuck firmly in the memory of Max Le Grand: "Paddock suddenly became much faster, because you weren't going round a continuous bend into Bottom Straight. So you could accelerate down Paddock and up the hill towards Druids, and if you got that wrong you ended up in the boondocks. The bottom of Paddock Bend was out of bounds to spectators. To get to Druids, they had to go round and then up. Even with an earth bank, if a driver got it wrong the car could go over and into the crowd."

During this time, 500cc Formula 3 was still the heart of motor sport in England. With the extended circuit, however, small and medium capacity sports machinery began to appear, and later out-and-out

BELOW *With the opening of the new Druids extension on 19 April 1954, racing changed to being run in a clockwise direction around the circuit. (LAT)*

'Formule Libre' cars and sports cars became regular fixtures on the programme.

In 1956, a telephone system was installed, linking the Race Control centre with all the marshals' posts, and a modern trackside hospital, with a fitted-out operating theatre, was also completed. Even so, Max Le Grand recalled that the facilities at the circuit in those days were fairly basic: "The PA system – the 'tannoy', as it was called – just consisted of tin horns on poles, and they were strung around the circuit. Sometimes they were so loud they were louder than the motorbikes themselves. These tannoys reverberated around the place and the acoustics were terrible. Unless you were right underneath one of them, you could hardly understand what the commentator was saying.

"The crowd on South Bank were a special kind of people," Le Grand continued. "They wanted to park their car within sight of the circuit, so they could either sit in it or beside it and watch the racing. They started hooting their horns as the winner did a lap of honour with his trophy. This became a tradition – the whole of South Bank would erupt into a cacophony of car horns, acknowledging the winner. It happened at every meeting and was unique to Brands Hatch. Nowhere else in the country did that. John Bolster, the commentator, encouraged it. 'Come on, give them a right rouser down there on South Bank,' he would say. It was a great sound – a motor racing sound."

The commentary box and timekeepers' hut, which had previously been on the inside of the track, was moved to the rear of the green bucket seats into a tall wooden tower, known as 'the black box' because it was painted with creosote. The structure only stood for two or three years, though, because in 1955 Brands Hatch acquired its first grandstand.

"The stand, for which my father became responsible, was taken from the Northolt pony racecourse in north London," explained Le Grand. "The course was closed down and the stand was left. We thought: 'This will really put us on the map – we're going to have a permanent grandstand'. So it was bought to supplement the green bucket seats and subsequently the timekeepers' and commentators' box was built into that.

"The grandstand had a café, which replaced the corrugated iron huts along the top straight behind where the grandstand is now. There were corrugated iron toilets for ladies and gents and half the time some people couldn't tell the difference between them and the catering huts, because these green effigies were all around the course. At this time, the Pavilion catered for the paddock only – the riders, mechanics and competitors would

congregate there and there was a bar at the far end. It also housed the administration of the circuit. George Pennington, the track manager, lived with his family at the far end, overlooking the paddock area."

In October 1956, a landmark of sorts was reached when Brands Hatch staged its first Formula One race. In truth, it was a low-key affair, contested only by the British teams and run over only 15 laps, but it attracted a crowd of 37,000. Archie Scott-Brown won driving one of four works Connaughts.

In February 1957, a new racing school opened at the track, operated by the Cooper Car Company. The school was run by Ron Searle until he was killed at Monza that October, when Ian Burgess took over. The Cooper Racing Drivers Training Division, as it was called, operated for two days a week on Tuesdays and Thursdays, with an average of 10 pupils per day. Pupils were offered three familiarisation laps in a two-seater Cooper-Climax, driven by Burgess, then a maximum of 12 laps solo in a Formula 2 single-seater at £1 per lap. In 1958, Motor Racing Enterprises, later

to become Motor Racing Stables, began operating at the circuit with two 500cc cars and a sports car. For a fee, people could attend a general practice day and drive one of the school's machines.

By the end of the decade, the 1.24-mile Kent track was firmly established as a major motor sport venue. It had hosted its first non-championship Formula One race and regularly drew huge crowds, particularly at a Bank Holiday meeting. Going into the sixties, though, major changes were about to take place.

ABOVE *A large crowd on South Bank watches the racing at the 12 May 1951 meeting. (LAT)*

1950

■ Victory in the first-ever car race at the circuit on 16 April went to Don Parker, driving a JAP engined Parker Special.

■ Stirling Moss won all five of his races at the 25 June meeting.

■ On Bank Holiday Monday, 7 August, George Wicken took his Cooper Mk4 JAP to victory at the *Daily Telegraph* International 500cc meeting – but only just. He spluttered across the finish line in the 35-lap final, out of petrol. Betty Bolster, wife of commentator John, became the first woman to start, and finish, a race at Brands, driving a 1910 Standard in the Edwardian event.

■ 'Twenty-One Today' was sung over the loudspeakers for Stirling Moss, whose birthday it was at the 17 September meeting. Moss won his heat but came second to JBS driver Alf Bottoms in the final of the Open Challenge event.

■ Alf Bottoms dominated the 14 October meeting as well, winning the Championship of the Meeting race driving the JAP engined JBS

he had designed and built with his brother and father. The same car won the ladies' race, driven by Elizabeth Store.

■ On 5 November, the Mid-Kent Car Club tried running sports cars at the circuit. A five-lap scratch race was won by Guy Gale in a Healey Silverstone. As an experiment, running clockwise was also tried and proved popular.

BELOW *Competitors run anti-clockwise along Bottom Straight towards Paddock Hill Bend at the first car meeting on 16 April 1950. (LAT)*

RIGHT *Cars exit Clearways onto Bottom Straight during the 7 August 1950 meeting. (LAT)*

BELOW RIGHT *Stan Coldham's Cooper (36) leads off the grid from Paul Emery's Emeryson in the first heat of the 17 September 1950 meeting. On the second row are Don Truman (24), Eric Winterbottom (6) and eventual winner Ken Carter (34). (LAT)*

1951

In February, the Aston Martin Owners' Club hired the circuit to test 1.5-litre sports cars, in preparation for the forthcoming season's long-distance races. They practised pitstops and giving trackside signals, as well as running into dusk with headlights on.

On 8 April, the Half-Litre Club's opening meeting of the year drew a large crowd. Eric Brandon in a Cooper-Norton equalled the lap record of 67.67mph, which was jointly held by Alf Bottoms and Stirling Moss, and defeated Bottoms in the Championship of the Meeting event.

At the 21 April event, four 500 drivers broke the lap record – Eric Brandon, Alan Brown, Don Parker and Bob Gerard became the joint lap record holders at 68.44mph.

In May, the first-ever Grand Prix car appeared at the track – a 1908 Itala driven by Bob Hewitt, which averaged 49.18mph during a demonstration of Edwardian racing cars.

The *Daily Telegraph* sponsored three International meetings during the season. At the first, on Whit Saturday, 12 May, motorbike rider Don Gray, in his first outing in a Cooper-JAP, beat the established stars in their Norton powered cars, while Harry Schell set a new lap record at 59.00sec, 69.23mph.

Don Gray also won the second *Daily Telegraph* Trophy on 23 June but the very wet Bank Holiday event on 6 August was won by 'Big Bill' Whitehouse in his Cooper-Norton. It was a popular victory and Whitehouse did a lap of honour accompanied by "a symphony of motor horns". The Half Litre Club had ploughed up part of the grass verges to form a 'safety barrier' (the forerunner of today's run-off areas). These helped to prevent accidents, even though many cars slid off the track in the slippery conditions, and eventually the meeting had to be abandoned due to torrential rain and a flooded track.

The August meeting was the first car event to be broadcast by the BBC, with John Bolster providing the commentary for the radio as well as for the track public address system.

BELOW *Eric Brandon spins his Cooper-Norton on Bottom Straight during the 8 April 1951 meeting. (LAT)*

RIGHT *Cars enter the fast left-hand sweep of Clearways on 12 May 1951. (LAT)*

1952

1953

■ The International London Trophy on Easter Monday, 14 April, provided a win for George Wicken – the 'Flying Milkman' – in his brand new Cooper Mk6 Norton in front of a large crowd.

■ On 18 May, Norman and Don Gray finished first and second in the Senior race, both driving Cooper-JAPs.

■ On 22 June, Les Leston set a new outright lap record of 50.6sec, 71.15mph, in a Cooper Mk6 Norton. Leston emerged the victor of the Senior Race after a titanic duel with Paul Emery in his Emeryson-Norton.

■ The highlight of the year was the *Daily Telegraph* Trophy on Bank Holiday Monday, 4 August. The largest Brands Hatch crowd ever saw veteran racer Don Parker take the £250 prize in his Kieft-Norton after Stirling Moss's similar car broke a conrod. Moss had the consolation of setting a new lap record at 50.4sec, 71.41mph.

■ Parker won again in September and October. At the latter meeting, he jointly lowered the lap record to 49.2sec, 73.17mph, with Les Leston in his Norton powered Leston Special.

■ Don Parker won the national F3 championship for the second year in succession. On Easter Monday, 6 April, he won both major races and followed this in May with three wins out of three. He lost out to Les Leston in the Coronation Trophy at the end of May, but beat both him and Stuart Lewis-Evans in front of a record 50,000 crowd on Bank Holiday Monday, 3 August, to win the *Daily Telegraph* International Trophy.

■ At the final meeting of the year on 4 October, Don Parker set a new lap record of 48.4sec, 74.38mph, on his way to victory in the Senior Final.

■ The Brands Hatch Racing & Social Club held its first social function in the Pavilion on Saturday 17 October.

BELOW *The distinctive 'kidney' shape of the circuit can be clearly seen in this aerial view from the 1950s. (www.fotoflite.com)*

1954

At the Easter Monday meeting on 19 April, an 11-race programme was held on the newly extended track. Stuart Lewis-Evans took two wins in his Cooper and set a new lap record at 62.4sec, 71.54mph. Peter Gammon won the first-ever sports car race at the track in a Lotus Mk6.

Peter Gammon went on to win the Performance Cars Trophy, a championship for 1600cc sports cars that year, despite strong opposition from the Lotus Mk8 of Colin Chapman and the Lister of Archie Scott-Brown. Unfortunately Gammon crashed at the August Bank Holiday meeting, and this accident was to curtail his motor racing career.

Don Parker was disqualified from the 1 May meeting for 500cc cars after a small amount of nitromethane was discovered in his fuel. Parker went on to win the 7 June and 4 July events, however.

Jim Russell won the top 500cc race of the year, the fifth running of the *Daily Telegraph* International Trophy on Bank Holiday Monday, 2 August, in front of a 40,000 crowd. Don Beauman, driving a 2-litre F2 Connaught A-type in the Formule Libre race, took the lap record to 60.6sec, 73.42mph.

On 5 September, a 'benefit' meeting was held with no prize money awarded and all profits going towards future circuit improvements. John Hall announced plans for another extension to the circuit, to increase its length to 2.5 miles.

The inaugural Christmas Trophy, held on Boxing Day, was won by Ivor Bueb in his Cooper Mk8 Norton, ahead of Les Leston's similarly powered Cooper Mk9.

BELOW *Competitors climb the hill from Paddock towards the new Druids corner on 19 April 1954. (LAT)*

OVERLEAF *Charles Headland in his Martin-Headland (64) and Ivor Bueb in a Cooper (67) round the new Druids hairpin. The pair duelled fiercely in two of the day's races at the 19 April 1954 meeting. (LAT)*

1955

■ The opening meeting of the season was held on 11 April in glorious sunshine. The 500cc runners competed in four heats, the first five from each going forward into the main final. There was a subsidiary final for the second five in each heat and a consolation race for the also-rans. Jim Russell won the main final in a Cooper.

■ Ivor Bueb won a thrilling 1500cc sports car race in his Cooper-Climax at the 1 May meeting, beating Les Leston's Connaught on a streaming wet track.

■ A grandstand, at that time the only permanent one at a British circuit, was erected in time for the Bank Holiday meeting on

1 August. It had been purchased from the defunct Northolt pony-trotting course.

■ On 9 October, Ivor Bueb broke a new outright circuit record which had recently been set by motorbike racer John Surtees, with a time of 59.8sec, 74.65mph.

■ During the Boxing Day event, Tony Brooks ran demonstration laps in his F1 Connaught B-type, fresh from his win in the Syracuse Grand Prix. Don Parker won the 500cc event in his Kieft-Norton after Jim Russell had crashed in practice and broken a rib.

1956

■ Public race meetings were organised by clubs other than the BRSCC. The 750 Motor Club joined with Club Lotus on 10 June for a mixed meeting which included, for the first time, saloon cars.

■ The Bank Holiday International on 6 August, which was blighted by storms and torrential rain, included the first race at the circuit for the new 1500cc Formula 2. Five works teams were entered and Roy Salvadori won in a Cooper T41 Climax. Over 140 cars and drivers took part in the meeting, with everything from the latest Grand Prix Connaught to a 1911 Renault. Mike Hawthorn won his first-ever race at the track in a Lotus-Climax.

■ On a warm and sunny 14 October, Brands Hatch hosted its first F1 race – a non-championship event to which the BRSCC attracted none of the European teams, but a strong entry from Connaught. Stuart Lewis-Evans made his F1 debut for the team and took pole position for the race. He slipped to fifth at the start but eventually finished second behind team leader Archie Scott-Brown, with Roy Salvadori third in Gilby Engineering's Maserati 250F ahead of Les Leston and Jack Fairman in the other Connaughts. Scott-Brown set a new lap record, at 59.0sec, 75.66mph.

■ The Boxing Day meeting was cancelled due to the petrol rationing brought about by the Suez crisis.

1957

■ Despite gloomy forecasts, the fuel crisis faded and the 1957 season ran according to schedule. Car events now regularly comprised a mixture of 500cc single-seaters, sports cars, production sports cars and saloons.

■ On 9 June, John Webb broke the saloon car lap record in his Jensen 541, with a lap in 63.4sec, 60.82mph.

■ Jack Brabham, driving a Cooper T43 Climax, won the F2 races on Whit Sunday, 9 June, and Bank Holiday Monday, 5 August.

■ More than 25,000 people attended the Boxing Day meeting, which featured seven races and a firework display to finish. Despite the cold temperatures and a damp track, Jack Brabham broke the lap record on his way to winning the Formule Libre race in Rob Walker's Cooper T43 Climax. The record, previously held by Archie Scott-Brown, was raised from 75.66mph to 75.92mph.

BELOW LEFT *Pupils receive instruction on 20 April 1957 at the new racing school operated by the Cooper Car Company. (Getty Images)*

BELOW *John Cooper was on hand to provide instruction to trainees at the racing school. (Getty Images)*

1958

■ A 40,000 crowd braved a biting east wind at the BRSCC Easter Monday meeting on 7 April. During practice, an F3 Cooper-Norton, driven by David Dunnage, crashed at Paddock, killing the driver. The first heat of the Chequered Flag Trophy for 1100cc sports cars marked the debut of the new Elva racing team, and one of its Climax engined cars finished second, driven by Mike McKee.

■ The highlights of the 8 June meeting were two closely fought F2 races in which the existing lap record, set by Jack Brabham with an F1 Cooper on Boxing Day 1957, was equalled or beaten by at least five cars. Both these races were won by Stuart Lewis-Evans with the British Racing Partnership's Cooper T45 Climax. Scrapping over second place in the second race, Dennis Taylor (Lotus) and Syd Jensen (Cooper) shared a new record lap of 58.2sec, 76.70mph.

■ The Bank Holiday meeting on 4 August was one of the biggest events on the BRSCC calendar and 35,000 spectators watched six and a half hours of almost uninterrupted racing.

■ The track record fell again when Stirling Moss drove Rob Walker's F2 Cooper at the Kentish 100 International on Saturday 30 August. Moss won the Kentish 100 Trophy, run in two 42-lap parts, with aggregate times deciding the winner. Moss, driving car No.7, left the record at 77.77mph. The meeting was covered live on television by ITV, resulting in a smaller crowd than usual.

■ Jack Sears was crowned the first-ever British Saloon Car Champion after winning a two-car match race with Tommy Sopwith on Sunday 5 October. The pair had tied in the BRSCC-run championship, Sears driving an Austin A105 Westminster and Sopwith a 3.4 Jaguar. The pair were loaned two rally-modified Riley 1.5s by the BMC Competitions Department and each ran five laps of the course in each car. Sopwith won the first part by 2.2sec. The pair exchanged cars and set off again. This time Sears led and, after two laps, had cancelled out the 2.2sec deficit. He won by 3.8sec, taking the victory by 1.6sec on aggregate. Not bad after an entire season's racing. Despite lashing rain, a partly flooded track and poor light, according to *Motoring News*, the race was a highlight of the last BRSCC Brands meeting of the 1958 summer season and rounded off the wettest Brands meeting for a long time.

■ The 1958 Boxing Day meeting was televised live on the BBC but still attracted a large crowd for the noon start. A Green Line coach (service 703) ran from Victoria Station to the circuit and a

ABOVE *Ian Burgess, in a Cooper, leads the similar car of George Wicken through Paddock Hill Bend during the Kent Trophy race for Formula 2 cars on 4 August 1958. (LAT)*

special bus service ran from Swanley train station. Admission cost 5s (25p) for adults and 2s (10p) for children. Grandstand seats were an extra 12s 6d (62.5p) and 7s (35p) respectively. Parking cost 5s (25p) for cars, 2s 6d (12.5p) for motorbikes and 1s (5p) for cycles.

■ Mike Hawthorn dropped the flag to start the Formule Libre Silver City Trophy race at the Boxing Day meeting. It was the new World Champion's final public appearance – he would lose his life a few weeks later on 22 January 1959, when he crashed his Jaguar 3.4 on the Guildford by-pass in Surrey. The race was won by Graham Hill in an F2 Lotus. Lotus boss Colin Chapman won the sports car class and also the GT event from Jim Clark and Mike Costin, all three driving Lotus Elites. Graham Hill won the Christmas Trophy race driving a Lotus Seven.

■ *Motoring News* reported that the meeting closed at 3.30pm and that the light was failing already. It was pitch-black, apparently, by the time the circuit's tractor had pulled the last spectator's vehicle from the quagmire of the car parks.

1959

■ Despite a clash with a big International meeting at Goodwood, there was a good entry for the Easter Monday meeting on 30 March. The feature Formule Libre race was won by Tony Skelton with an F2 Cooper-Climax. The World Sports Trophy for F3 cars was won by Don Parker in a Cooper-Norton, while Ian Walker (Willment-Climax) triumphed in the Easter Trophy for sports cars under 1500cc.

■ Driving rain and strong winds deterred both spectators and competitors at the Martini Trophy on 25 April, and there were many non-starters for the event, which was jointly organised by the Aston Martin Owners' Club and the Jaguar Drivers' Club. Although the track was waterlogged in places, and the rain affected the circuit's intercom and telephone equipment, the 10-race programme was completed on schedule. Bruce McLaren drove a Cooper Monaco to victory in the feature race, the Martini Trophy, for racing cars up to 2000cc.

■ There was an enormous crowd for the Bank Holiday meeting on 3 August, which featured 13 races. The main event was the John Davy Trophy for F2 cars, won by Chris Bristow's BRP Cooper-Borgward. Tim Parnell's Cooper overturned at Druids on the first lap of the first part of the event, the driver suffering broken ribs. Graham Hill won the Kingsdown Trophy with a works Lotus.

■ Jack Brabham was in devastating form, leading the Kentish 100 on Saturday 29 August from start to finish in a works Cooper-Climax. Graham Hill was second in both parts of the two-part event in his Lotus-Climax and Stirling Moss was third. Jeff Uren scored a class victory in his Ford Zephyr, securing the 1959 BRSCC Saloon Car Championship title.

■ The last meeting of the year before Boxing Day was the BRSCC meeting on 4 October, held during an autumn heatwave. The saloon event was won by Graham Hill in a Speedwell Austin A35 and was described by *Motoring News* as one of the most thrilling races seen at the circuit for a long time.

■ Lola and Lotus used the annual Boxing Day meeting to debut their 1960 Formula Junior cars, driven respectively by Peter Ashdown and Alan Stacey. Four of the six races were shown live on BBC television and the highlight of the meeting was a 10-lap FJ event for the John Davy Trophy. The race, affected by heavy rain and strong winds, finished amid great excitement as Peter Arundell used the superior power of his Elva, equipped with a three-cylinder, two-stroke Auto Union engine, to pip Ashdown on the finish-line. Commentator John Bolster said: "If that's Formula Junior, then I'm not missing a single race throughout 1960."

■ Also at the Boxing Day meeting, Graham Hill established a lap record that is unlikely ever to be beaten. He drove a three-wheeled, 125cc Vespa powered bath, built by students at Kingston Technical College, around the track in a time of 2min 59.7sec, an average speed of 24.84mph.

BELOW LEFT *Graham Hill achieved a lap of 2m59.7s in his three-wheeled enamelled bath, powered by a 125cc single-cylinder two-stroke Vespa engine, at the 1959 Boxing Day meeting. (GPL)*

BELOW *Alan Stacey gave the new Formula Junior Lotus 18 its debut at the Boxing Day meeting in 1959. (LAT)*

1960s

CREATING A GRAND PRIX VENUE

In January 1960, almost 10 years after car racing had started at Brands Hatch, Kent County Council awarded planning permission for an extension to be made to the circuit. This would follow the route of an old scrambles course on existing tracks through the woods. It would double the length of the lap to 2.65 miles, enabling a choice of long or short circuits on which to race. Work on the extension, leaving the existing track at Kidney Corner and rejoining it a few yards away at Clearways, began on Tuesday 26 January.

"The Grand Prix loop was started by John Hall," explained John Webb. "We said it was surfacing a pre-war scrambles track. Planning laws had come into effect in the UK in 1948 – they hadn't existed before then. But they included a provision that said, in effect, that if something had been in use before the war, it didn't need new planning permission. So one of the reasons for surfacing that old scrambles track was to preserve the planning right. It was never built with the Grand Prix in mind. I was the guy who saw that possibility."

This process was confirmed by Tony Lovett, the chairman of the Greenwich Motor & Motorcycle Club, which used to organise the scrambles in the woods. "When Brands put in for planning permission to lengthen the circuit, we had a hell of a do," he said. "I had to go to the planning meeting and swear on oath that I had run meetings on all these pathways through the woods for 15 years. By me doing that, Brands got planning permission for the long circuit because it had proven use, so they couldn't stop it. But it wouldn't have happened if it hadn't been for us running the scrambles on it for years.

"The local inhabitants were up in arms," he continued. "They didn't want it to go through the woods, because they were just building houses around the back of Brands. That had all been fields in the early days, but they lost the case and we got

RIGHT *Jim Clark in his Lotus 25 on his way to winning the first British Grand Prix held at Brands Hatch, in July 1964. (LAT)*

the long circuit. But of course, once that was achieved, we lost the scrambles course."

In addition to the extension, it was announced that new pits were to be built on the inside of the circuit, opposite the grandstand, and that the track width was to be 30ft all round. The entrance to Paddock Bend was to be improved by removing a bump at the approach and raising the level of the track all the way from the start-finish line. The alterations were expected to cost between £35,000 and £40,000.

By this time, Max Le Grand was living with his family close to the run up to Druids. "My parents were invited by John Hall to live 'grace and favour' in Kingsdown Park House," he said. "This was to take the pressure off the Penningtons, so there would be two sets of people living at the circuit and they could fill in for each other and people could have holidays. So we moved in to John Hall's flat and occupied the top two floors. I could see the circuit through the trees from my bedroom window."

Living this close enabled Le Grand to follow the progress of the new extension closely. "Because the track followed the original scrambles circuit, it incorporated what used to be the scrambles chalk pit. But although this was all right for motorcycles, it was too steep for cars, which would just bottom out. So the two valleys where the road circuit was going to go had to be filled. I used to come home from college each day and go to see how everything was progressing. One day, after the road had been laid, one of the workmen said: 'You're going to roll Hawthorn Hill.' I got up into the steamroller with the driver beside me and I went up and down and round and round, rolling Hawthorn Bend. It's a very special memory for me."

Le Grand is also privy to a little secret about the track which not many people know about: "There is a time capsule at Brands Hatch, and I'm one of only a few surviving people who know where that is. Even John Webb doesn't know, because he wasn't told. I went to watch it being buried when the Grand Prix circuit was laid. That was in about spring 1960. I don't know what's in it – it was a metal box that was buried under the track."

In June, details were announced of the first car race meeting to be run on the extension. Scheduled for the August Bank Holiday Monday, the main event would be a 50-lap, 132.5-mile Formula One race. The German Grand Prix was scheduled for the day before, but it was to be a Formula 2 event, so it would not affect the F1 entry. It did mean, though, that some drivers would have to hurry back and learn the new circuit the morning of the race.

In mid-July, a group of drivers, journalists and observers were invited to witness the first laps on

the new track, which was likened to a 'mini Nürburgring', the famous 14-mile circuit in Germany. The honour of driving the first officially observed lap went to Tony Brooks in a Formula 2 Yeoman Credit Cooper, who set a fastest lap of 1m49.4s, 87.20mph.

The new extension left the old course by continuing the left-hand swerve of Kidney Bend uphill into the woods, the new tighter part of the curve being crossed by a vehicle bridge to take spectators' cars to the banked area opposite Bottom Straight. After an uphill climb for about a quarter of a mile, there was a slight right-hand kink, and then the extension went under another vehicle bridge (sited close behind Druids Bend on the old circuit) to Pilgrim's Drop, a short straight-line dip leading to the equally short Hawthorn Hill. From here, the track turned right through a climbing 90deg turn onto the almost-level Portobello Straight. Westfield, another right-angled right-hander, followed, taking the cars sharply downhill into Dingle Dell and through a climbing right-hander where sight of the track ahead was lost, only the tops of the trees being visible. A marker board warned that a sharp right turn was sited at the top of the hill and, after a short straight, the tightest of the four new corners, Stirling's Bend, took the cars through more than 90deg to the left. This lined them up for a fast downhill exit from the new extension, under another vehicle bridge and onto the existing course halfway round Clearways, which now became a dipping, 100mph right-hand swerve.

It was noted in *Motoring News* that the entrance to the pits could cause a problem, because a car slowing for the pit-lane would be invisible to a driver emerging from the new section. The position of the marshalling posts was also to be looked at. For the first post on the new loop to be in sight of the post on the outside of Kidney, it had to be positioned exactly where a car might run wide on exiting the corner. If the Kidney Bend post could be moved a few yards, then the next post could be positioned another 30 yards beyond the bridge. As the newspaper said: "These and other small problems can only be solved effectively after drivers have had an opportunity of practising in Grand Prix cars."

It was said that the new circuit, the capacity for which was now 25 cars or 32 motorcycles, would only be used for "high days and holidays" and practice confined to official sessions for specific meetings. Routine general practice would be held on the original track, now to be known as the Club circuit.

There were many other alterations and improvements to the circuit which, it was claimed, would now hold 100,000 spectators. A new 750-

FAR LEFT *Kidney Corner and the rear of the pits, July 1960. (LAT)*

LEFT *The bridge over the track at Kidney Corner, leading out onto the new Grand Prix extension in July 1960. (LAT)*

FAR LEFT *A view towards Hawthorn Bend on the new Grand Prix loop in July 1960. (LAT)*

LEFT *The Portobello Straight as seen from Westfield Bend, July 1960. (LAT)*

FAR LEFT *The newly completed Stirling's Bend on the Grand Prix loop, July 1960. (LAT)*

LEFT *The new track between Stirling's Bend and Clearways, July 1960. (LAT)*

BELOW LEFT *The pits and grandstands in July 1960. (LAT)*

seater grandstand, called *Little Britches*, was built on the exit of Clearways and another, the Portobello Stand, was situated at Hawthorn Bend, on the outside of the track. The valley between Pilgrim's Drop and Dingle Dell was to be used as a car park, and an additional car park was located on the outside of Paddock Bend.

Other changes to the venue included improved toilets and a new tunnel from the paddock to a metalled slip road, which led to new permanent pits. In addition, the paddock itself was resurfaced, part of it levelled, and a partially covered scrutineering bay built in what used to be the marshalling enclosure. Meanwhile, the covered section of the press stand was doubled in size, so that it could accommodate up to 50 journalists.

The inaugural event to be held on the full circuit was for motorbikes. On Saturday 9 July, about 40,000 people turned up to see Mike Hailwood dominate the meeting. Hailwood switched between a Ducati, an AJS and a Norton, and won all four solo races.

The first car meeting was the non-championship Formula One race for the Silver City Trophy, held on Monday 1 August. There was an excellent entry with 23 F1 cars in total, including Phil Hill and Richie Ginther in works Ferraris, Jack Brabham and Bruce McLaren in works Coopers, Graham Hill in a works BRM, Innes Ireland, Jim Clark and John Surtees in works Lotuses, Tony Brooks, Dan Gurney, Bruce Halford and Henry Taylor in Yeoman Credit Coopers, and Roy Salvadori in Tommy Atkins's Cooper. The support races were the 10-lap Kingsdown Trophy for saloons, the 10-lap Wrotham Trophy for GTs, the 20-lap Raffles Club Trophy for sports cars, and the 20-lap John Davy Trophy for Formula Juniors. The entry for every race was oversubscribed.

On race day, the roads around the circuit were jammed as 60,000 spectators – a record crowd for a race circuit in the south of England – made their way towards Brands Hatch for the first-ever car meeting on the new Grand Prix course. There was

Jim Clark

A lap of Brands Hatch with Jim Clark, who won the first British Grand Prix there in 1964, taken from the programme

"I shall be coming past the pits in fourth and approaching our 'point of interest', the approach area before Paddock Hill Bend. Here I shall be braking heavily at a point where there is quite an undulation in the surface, and with the brakes still on I shall be going down to third and then possibly second before accelerating through the second part of the bend. I come in from perhaps a bit left of centre to clip the inside edge just before the final drop into the dip. Here there is a sudden change in camber which has to be watched if the car is not to 'grass' on the left side coming out of the bend. When going really fast at Paddock you feel quite a bit of G loading at the bottom of the dip. It is one of the trickiest corners on a British circuit.

"Assuming there is no-one trying to come up on my right side, I keep well over to the left going up the hill, then brake hard and simultaneously drop down to first for Druids Hill Bend. By keeping in reasonably tight coming out of the turn, I can reduce the amount of 'S' bending necessary to be properly lined up for the first part of Bottom Bend. For this, I have to be well over to the right side of the track, and I take second gear before making the left-hand turn. There are black and white marker stones on the apex of the bend, and I aim to keep close to these, giving me plenty of track to the right for accelerating on to the Bottom Straight.

"This part of the course is badly named for, as any Brands Hatch driver will confirm, it is really a long left-hand curve, and you cannot see the first part of South Bank Bend until you are about half-way along it. I should get third briefly here before going down to second again when braking for South Bank. The line here is quite different from that used for racing on the short club circuit. We have to keep over to the right much later so as to flatten out as much as possible the second half of the bend as it doubles back uphill under the foot bridge. Anyone who fails to cut right back across to the left side for the second apex usually finds themselves running out of road on the right, and of course this loses valuable time on the climb up into the new loop.

"Now I am entering the fastest part of the course, and I shall be up into third again by the time I take the right-hand kink just before the brow of the hill, and fourth as I drop down again under the second bridge. You get a curious sensation here on a grand prix car because at one point it seems as though the bridge has fallen on to the track and you are driving straight for it, but of course the track drops away in time! With the car well over to the left I have to brake quite hard and drop down to third for the fairly fast uphill right-hander, Hawthorn Bend, for which I try to cut across comparatively late so that I do not stray out too far as I come out of the bend. This is a corner which gives me a lot of satisfaction when I take it well, and where valuable tenths of a second can be saved.

"The next right-hander, Westfield Bend, is slower than Hawthorn, although not as slow as it looks as you approach it. By keeping well over to the left in the braking area, I can drop down to second and then cut across to go through quite fast, remembering that there is a rough patch coming out which needs watching when accelerating hard. Speed builds up quickly now as the gradient is sharply downhill, and I am back in third before I clip the right-hand edge of the track in the dip at Dingle Dell. By holding my line here, the Lotus automatically comes back on to the left side of the track as we go uphill again towards Dingle Dell Corner. This needs a lot of concentration, first because you approach it blind, second because you have to brake heavily, and third because the track suddenly flattens out as you are still braking and the back end tends to become a bit light. I drop down to second for this one, and the short straight from here to Stirling's Bend becomes in effect an 'S' bend as I pull the car back from the left to the right side of the track before braking heavily again.

"Stirling's Bend is one of those tight left-handers that seem to go on for ever, and it is essential to turn in late for this one if you are hoping to come out at any speed and still stay on the track. It is a borderline case between first and second gear, and even if I use first I need second again immediately I am out of the turn and heading slightly downhill towards the third foot bridge just before rejoining the short circuit at Clearways. This is another tricky point, because on the GP circuit Clearways becomes a fast corner, for which I hold the car in third, and if you run too wide on the entry you have to fight to keep the car from taking to the grass on the outside. The big problem here comes in matching your speed and braking as you emerge from under the bridge to the precise moment when you have to lock over from the left to the right of the track. I aim to be pretty close in going over the 'hump', then let the car come out again towards the centre for the next part of the bend where I am back on full throttle.

"Even on the run-in to the start-finish line there is no time for relaxation because there is quite a pronounced dip just at the start of the pit area (where I get fourth), which can unsettle a car if it is not correctly placed. Finally, just to let me know that one more lap has been completed, I get another 'dip' just across the line as I accelerate through another undulation."

Jim Clark in his Lotus 25 was on pole position for the first Grand Prix at the circuit, on 11 July 1964. Clark went on to win the race. (LAT)

ABOVE *Innes Ireland (76) and Roy Salvadori go wheel-to-wheel in their Ferrari 250GTOs in the Peco Trophy race on 6 August 1962. (Michael Hewett)*

chaos on the A20 London–Maidstone road as racegoers mingled with holidaymakers heading for the coast, and many spectators missed the start of the first race. They were still queuing to get out of the circuit at 9.00pm, as well.

The opening event on the new circuit was the 10-lap Wrotham Trophy, won by Jack Sears in an Aston Martin. Practice for the main event had been held on the Wednesday beforehand, to enable drivers competing in the F2 German Grand Prix on the Sunday to qualify. Clark took pole with a 1m39.4s lap, with Brabham, Ireland and Graham Hill sharing the front row of the 4-3-4 grid. However Brabham went straight into the lead, and stayed there.

Salvadori won a rain-soaked Raffles Club Trophy in a Cooper Monaco and also the event-closing Kingsdown Trophy in a 3.8 Jaguar, while Clark won the Formula Junior event. It rained during the sports car race, but otherwise the spectators basked in warm sunshine.

Less than a year after the opening of the full circuit, another major event occurred in the form of a complete change of ownership. John Webb explained: "In 1960, John Hall said to me: 'We've got all these shareholders and they don't particularly

like each other and they don't want to see any money spent. The only future is for the place to be taken over. You know more about that than I do (which I didn't) – have a go.'"

An initial approach to Lombank, the finance company, looked promising for a while, but this ultimately failed due to uncertainties over new government legislation covering the company's core business, which was then hire purchase. Then Webb's accountant introduced him to John Danny, who headed a company called Grovewood Securities Ltd.

"He was running this fairly small, general investment company whose assets were fairly boring, so he was immediately attracted by the thought of getting Brands Hatch," explained Webb. "He realised that it would put a more popular image on Grovewood's activities. The numbers crunched quite well and so Grovewood bought Brands Hatch at my instigation for £112,000, which included £20,000 cash in the bank. I was asked to join the new board. The following year, I was asked to join as a full-time executive director, which I did."

In view of the acquisition by Grovewood Securities, it was perhaps inevitable that rumours would fly around about Brands Hatch being turned into a housing estate. These rumours were stopped when, at the end of 1961, a 10-point improvement scheme was announced. This was to include a 300-seat restaurant behind the main grandstand, a 100-seat restaurant in the paddock, a startline control tower with a winner's gallery, modern toilet blocks, a television tower, 12 lock-up workshops and six lock-up shops. In addition, a testing circuit/kart track was to be built, and the safety banks around the circuit were to be strengthened and raised.

"The initial reaction to Grovewood getting involved, on the part of motor sport spectators, was one of misunderstanding," explained Webb. "Somewhere they were referred to as 'money-grabbing, sticky-fingered Grovewood', which was the complete opposite of what they were doing. In all the time I was involved with them, they always put whatever they made out of motor racing, plus more, back into the sport. What they wanted out of it was favourable publicity – an indication that they were closely allied to major national events like the Grand Prix."

This point was reinforced by Max Le Grand. "There was a lot of suspicion when people found out it was Grovewood buying the place," he said. "The feeling was that, if they felt it wasn't making money, they would close it and build a housing estate. So when John Webb was put in charge of developing the circuit on behalf of Grovewood, he had to reassure a lot of people that this was not the case. It gradually became known that John Danny did genuinely want to develop the circuit."

The first year of operation under the new regime was a success, prompting Grovewood to look at acquiring other circuits. "Profits came in well above budget," explained Webb. "John Danny was very happy and he said: 'If you know of any other circuits, go after them for me.' So I jumped on a train to meet Mirabelle Topham, who owned Aintree. I think she wanted £400,000 at that time. I set up a meeting between her and John Danny and, rather sadly, they couldn't get together on price, so that didn't happen. But it nearly did.

"So the first other circuit we bought was Mallory Park. I used to drink with Reg Parnell, who was a top racing driver and also a team manager for Aston Martin. He was a great friend of the owner of Mallory Park. He told me it was for sale, and offered to introduce me to the owner. We bought it for £150,000 in 1962, with about 300 acres. At the time we bought Brands Hatch, it was about 250 acres, but we subsequently bought what is now the airfield from a local farmer, Farmer Baggot, adding another 100 acres.

"I then heard that Snetterton was a bit short of money, so I went to see Oliver Sear, who was then

the owner, and we bought that for £35,000 in 1963 with about 330 acres.

"Oulton Park was a different kettle of fish, in that it wasn't on the market and they didn't really want to sell, but we made a takeover bid and got it for about £150,000 with about 275 acres. That was in 1964. So we acquired three other circuits quite quickly and fairly cheaply and, with the exception of Oulton Park, the others were in difficulty.

"We were building them up as we went along. It wasn't too much of a problem but I could see that, by having a number of circuits, we also controlled an almost infinite number of race meetings. Therefore, we could start our own championships. We could even start our own formulae and make them work automatically without having to eat humble pie with other circuits and promoters. It gave one immense power and opportunity to get things done."

It certainly did. With four circuits on its books, Grovewood – or more particularly John Webb, who was given free reign to run the circuits on a day-to-day basis – was now in the position of being able to control over 50 per cent of UK motor racing. "From my point of view, Grovewood were the perfect people to work for," he said. "Only rarely did we suffer from any lack of understanding of the detail of motor racing. I was invited to put up budgets, which I did, and as long as I operated within those budgets, they were more than happy. Every now and then, I did something silly and got bollocked for it, but that was the learning curve."

BELOW The line-up for the first British Grand Prix to be held at Brands Hatch on 11 July 1964. Back row (left to right): Tony Maggs, Jim Clark, Giancarlo Baghetti, Jo Bonnier (sitting), Dan Gurney, Phil Hill, Jack Brabham, Jo Siffert, Lorenzo Bandini (hidden), Mike Spence, Bruce McLaren, Peter Revson, Chris Amon, Graham Hill. Front row: Richie Ginther, Bob Anderson, John Taylor, Mike Hailwood. (Michael Hewett)

RIGHT *Lorenzo Bandini brings his Ferrari 156 into* parc fermé *during the 1964 British Grand Prix meeting, as Jim Clark walks past the nose of his Lotus 25. (LAT)*

BELOW RIGHT *Team personnel monitor the race from the BRM and Lotus pits during the 1964 British Grand Prix. (Phipps/Sutton)*

BELOW *The packed grandstands and scoreboard can be clearly seen in this shot, taken from Clearways during the 1964 British Grand Prix. (LAT)*

In May 1966, a separate company, Motor Circuit Developments Ltd, was formed. Its purpose, as the coordinating company, was to provide a unified corporate name and image, with Webb as its managing director in charge of planning and policy.

While the Brands Hatch business was undergoing the expansion that would lead to the creation of Motor Circuit Developments, there was the jewel in the crown to go for. John Webb wanted the British Grand Prix at Brands Hatch. In those days, Britain's round of the Formula One World Championship alternated between Silverstone and Aintree.

"One of the first things I did when I joined Brands was come up with the idea that we could have the Grand Prix," he said. "I negotiated it with the RAC. Dean Delamont was the competitions manager and I'd known him since the early days of Brands Hatch, because he used to write for a magazine called 'Motor Racing', with which I'd been connected. One day, I asked Dean how much Aintree and Silverstone paid to have the Grand Prix, and he replied: 'Nothing at all.' So I said: 'Wouldn't the RAC like to make some money out of it?' I suggested he might like to get his board to allocate the Grand Prix to Brands every other year for £5000.

"Unfortunately, John Hall upset John Danny by trying to keep Grovewood out of our first contractual meeting with the RAC. The chairman of the RAC in those days was a chap called Wilfred Andrews, who was a very powerful and much feared man. Delamont set up a meeting, he thought, for Danny to meet

Andrews, and he asked Hall to arrange it. What Hall set up – through lack of experience, I suppose – left Grovewood completely out of it. It was silly, because they were not only going to have to put up the £5000, which was relative peanuts, but pay for a lot of circuit improvements, which they were willing to do. That led to the fairly prompt suggestion that Hall should take a golden handshake, which he did in the autumn of 1963."

The outcome was that Aintree relinquished the Grand Prix, and a deal was done for the race to alternate between Brands Hatch and Silverstone. Brands was to host the 1964 event.

"There was no controversy over Aintree losing the race," said Webb. "It was a fairly peaceful thing. Aintree had run it for the first time in 1955 and their race was financially supported by the *Daily Telegraph*. It was always my understanding that it cost the 'Telegraph' a lot of money and that they hadn't been that impressed with the results. So Mirabelle Topham got to the point where she didn't have a sponsor and therefore she didn't want to go on with it. So it wasn't actually stolen from her – it was coming to a natural conclusion, anyway."

Work immediately got under way to prepare Brands Hatch for the 1964 British Grand Prix, which was also to be bestowed with the title 'Grand Prix of Europe'. "We didn't have to do much to the circuit itself, maybe add a few more safety banks," said Webb. "The great safety crusade hadn't started yet. The most important thing from the RAC's point of view was to build what would become the

Grovewood Suite, a hospitality centre which they didn't have at Silverstone, where they could entertain their guests to a new standard. And I think we had to put up about 20,000 additional temporary grandstand seats, scaffolding ones around Paddock, at the top of Druids, all around Clearways and along the Top Straight. We put some out on the Grand Prix circuit, as well, but they weren't anything like as popular.

"We also put in six or eight new catering points and a dozen toilet blocks. They were pretty archaic by today's standards but they were a start. They were made out of secondhand military buildings – Arcon buildings, they were called.

"That first Grand Prix lost money," Webb continued. "We planned it on the basis that we would get 100,000 people, which is what Silverstone and Aintree always said they got. We now know that this hadn't been the case at all. We were shattered when we only got 42,000, and we lost £20,000. In those days, the starting money and prize money bill was only £25,000 – I hear it's £10 million now.

"From then on, though, the Grand Prix always made money. At that first race, I was the first evil bastard ever to charge a pound to come to a British motor race meeting. Prior to that it had been 12s 6d (62.5p). The second year we kept it at £1, but included a free programme.

"We didn't doubt for a moment that we were going to get the crowds and we were very worried about what the traffic situation was going to be. BEA [British European Airways] had just started their

Peter Anderson

A view from a marshals' post by Peter Anderson, who started marshalling at Brands Hatch in 1959 and was assigned to Post 4, on the infield at the bottom of Paddock Hill Bend

"I'd joined the BRSCC and spent the weekend on Post 4. That was a real education to marshalling, partly because the marshals were very knowledgeable, very friendly and very keen to be seen to do a good job.

"On Post 4, you met a regular crowd. It was usually the same observer in charge of the post, year in, year out. There was always a marshals' briefing on the post as well as a marshals' briefing in the paddock for everybody. Our observer would brief us before the meeting started, so that we were very clear what our duties were, what our actions would be in the event of an incident, and you stuck very rigidly to the code of being the best and doing the job properly. And certainly at Brands Hatch, which is where I did most of my marshalling, you would get a lot of compliments from drivers.

"Eventually Brands got the Grand Prix and it would frequently win the award for the best organised Grand Prix of the season, and I really think a lot of that was down to the way it was marshalled and the way the officials worked. Everybody just wanted to see a race meeting run to the highest standard and to the safest standard.

"For example, if you took a camera down to a marshals' post with you, you were told to take it back to the car. Taking pictures of incidents or your favourite driver was not on.

"First of all, you're a track marshal. In the event of an incident, you go to assist in whatever manner you can, and you clear up afterwards, brush the track, remove bits of debris, ensure the car is well clear of the track and the driver, if necessary, is being attended to properly.

"After a year or so as a track marshal, you usually go up to flag marshal, either yellow flag or blue flag, and even in the late fifties and early sixties there were marshals' training days. The chief marshals and sometimes even drivers would turn up to lend a hand. These were held at Brands and included demonstrations of the correct way to use fire extinguishers.

"The yellow flag and blue flag guys, in those days, worked very close together. You stood back-to-back, the blue flag guy looking at the oncoming traffic so he could see when it was needed, the yellow flag guy looking up the track so that his flag would be used in the event of an incident beyond the post. If there was anything dramatic going to happen around the post, and evasive action was needed, you would get an elbow in the back. You generally wouldn't turn round to see why you'd got the elbow – you would just dive for cover!

"I had a classic example of that in my first year as a flag marshal, when the original 500cc Formula 3 cars were racing with some very large fields. On the first lap, they came screaming round Paddock Bend and a young American guy was pushed onto the infield and came straight at the marshals' post, which in those days was a concrete bunker with straw bales in front of it. He hit the post virtually head-on. By the time he hit it, I'd had the elbow in the back and was lying on the ground with the rest of them. There was this enormous explosion and a cloud of straw dust everywhere. At the marshals' post further up the track, Post 5, they didn't see the car hit, they just saw the cloud of dust and straw and out of it, about six feet up, emerged the car. There was no sign of us marshals, because we were still on the ground. The car landed on two wheels on its side and tottered precariously. The driver

fell out and was seen scrambling around on the grass like a rabbit. When one of the course marshals got to him, he said: 'Don't move – my specs are on the ground here somewhere.' Fortunately for him, they were found intact and he was unhurt, but from Post 5 it had looked very, very dramatic – and very serious because all the marshals had disappeared.

"I never had a fatality to deal with – a few nasty bruises and broken limbs, but no fatalities. There were a couple of accidents I can remember at the top of Paddock, where people went off under braking, but most of the bumps and bangs were at the bottom of the corner and on the climb up towards Druids.

"We had cars up on the banks quite often, because the banking was not that high, and there was a token piece of wire strung along the top. We had this concrete bunker with straw bales in front of it and that was it. None of the marshals' posts had huts of any size or shape in those days, so you had no protection of any sort from the elements, nowhere to put your bag of food and change of clothing, no cover at all.

"In the late fifties early sixties, you brought what you were going to wear with you. There was no orange uniform supplied, that came quite a bit later. We had an armband and the two flag marshals for a while got a white coat, but that was it. It was up to the individual to come armed with the right gear for whatever the weather was.

"Although at an ordinary meeting you would have a lunch break and could get back to the car and change out of wet clothes, if it was something like the six-hour saloon car race you were on the post for, well, six hours. And at the two that I marshalled, it rained virtually from start to finish and we were soaked by the end of the day.

"In 1962, we arrived at Brands for the Boxing Day meeting and the circuit was covered in frost and ice, but they got rid of it by getting the marshals to get into their cars and drive round and round, and no one did any damage whatsoever. I thought it was a fairly hare-brained idea, but it cleared the circuit well enough for them to start qualifying."

The car parks and grandstands are full as Bruce McLaren in his McLaren M2B Serenissima leads a group of cars towards Druids during the 1966 British Grand Prix. The New Zealander eventually finished sixth with the first McLaren F1 car. Marshall's post No.4 can be seen on the infield. (LAT)

helicopter division and they had one Bell 47 helicopter – the one with a bubble cockpit and skeletal fuselage. I hired it with their chief pilot, Captain Jock Cameron, I think for £100, so that he could take me around and spot the traffic situations. We did that during the morning of the Grand Prix and there was no traffic problem."

The event was scheduled for Saturday 11 July, but started with a 'Miss Motor Racing' competition on the Wednesday before. The serious business of practice got under way the following day, when the *Evening News* awarded 100 bottles of champagne to Dan Gurney in his Brabham for the fastest lap of the session.

Thousands of people had camped overnight and they awoke to heavy rain and threatening skies on race morning. The rain had eased off by nine o'clock, when it was estimated that 30,000 people were already in the circuit.

"That first Grand Prix was heavily criticised by the purists," said Max Le Grand, "because John Webb provided a spectacle and had all sorts of things going on ancillary to the racing. He was looking after the punters."

Webb had certainly laid on a spectacle. A Dunlop Bridge spanned the main entrance road and the bands of the Royal Dragoons and the First Battalion Royal Scots Guards entertained the expectant crowd. A parade of Army vehicles and a demonstration of battle tactics with armoured cars and helicopters by military forces of Eastern Command all added to the atmosphere.

At 2.00pm, the F1 cars lined up on a dummy grid – the first time such a procedure was used – and then rolled forward to take up their places on the grid proper. Jim Clark's Lotus was on pole position, with Graham Hill's BRM and Dan Gurney's Brabham alongside. Clark stormed into the lead from Gurney and Ferrari's Lorenzo Bandini. Hill quickly moved up to third and, when Gurney slowed, he took second place. As the unfortunate American stopped in the pits, an over-enthusiastic fireman covered everything in foam, including the BBC's pit-lane commentator, John Bolster.

Hill continued to shadow Clark, but the Scot was at his best that day, driving one of the most exhausting races of his career. He held Hill at bay for the whole 80-lap race and established a new lap record of 1m38.8s, 96.56mph, and a race record speed of 94.14mph. At the finish, the gap between the two was just 2.8sec, with John Surtees third in another Ferrari.

An after-race concert was held from 6.30pm to 10.00pm, featuring Chris Barber's Jazz Band.

The following year, with no Grand Prix to run, John Webb instigated a season-opening non-championship Formula One race. "I created the Race of Champions to fill in the gap with the alternating Grand Prix, and it worked very well," he affirmed. The inaugural event, sponsored by the *Daily Mail* and run in two 40-lap heats, was a great success, with Mike Spence taking a surprise victory

in his Lotus 33 after team mate Jim Clark had crashed in the second heat.

During 1966, Paddock Hill Bend developed a reputation as a 'killer' but was defended by *Autosport* in its editorial of 12 August that year. "That notorious section of Brands Hatch, Paddock Bend, has recently been the subject of severe criticism," it said, "prompted by three fatalities this season and one near-fatal crash. While there is a tendency to blame the circuit owners for not providing sufficient 'run-off' area, *Autosport* feels that this is not a solution."

It went to say that it felt the answer lay instead with many of the cars and drivers permitted to race at the track. "It would appear that, far too often, inexperienced drivers manage to obtain competition licences and automatically believe that they are quite capable of controlling high-powered racing machines on circuits with which they may be completely unfamiliar." The magazine called for the RAC to ensure that all competition licence holders received elementary instruction from a racing school, such as Motor Racing Stables at Brands.

"There were very many fatalities in the fifties, sixties and early seventies," said Webb. "They were so frequent in my early days that you didn't go to funerals unless it was somebody you knew really well. When I started racing you didn't have a crash helmet, you didn't have seatbelts. It was just accepted. And then as the various safety movements kicked in, car construction improved and safety clothing came in.

BELOW *A classic shot of Minis going sideways at Paddock Hill bend in the sixties. (Michael Hewett)*

RIGHT *Extreme weather could often cause problems for competitors and delay proceedings, as happened in 1967. (LAT)*

RIGHT *The electronic scoreboard at Clearways remains blank amid the snowy conditions in 1967. (LAT)*

RIGHT *This lake at the bottom of Paddock Hill Bend caused the 25 June 1967 meeting to be cancelled. (LAT)*

"Very occasionally you would get the parent of someone trying to hold the circuit responsible, but it was all covered by RAC rules and indemnity clauses. Everybody understood it was a risk you took."

"Paddock was extremely dangerous for both bikes and cars," added Max Le Grand. "A lot of people were injured and some were killed there. Fleet Street got to know about this and there were often pictures in the Monday newspapers of people having dreadful accidents. A little later on, a chap called Bill Scragg, who was a freelance cameraman, used to photograph the most horrendous accidents which would then go out on BBC television news in the evening. So Brands Hatch, through one stretch of road, became notorious in the national media."

Peter Anderson, who marshalled at the circuit for many years, also remembered the hazards of Paddock Bend. "There were virtually no run-off areas in those days," he explained. "There was a car's length, maybe a car and a half's length on the outside of Paddock, and that was it. There was just a grass bank that people hit. It wasn't very safe at all. Speeds were relatively a lot slower than they are today, but you could still have a very nasty accident there.

"In the early sixties, it became the place where the photographers from the daily papers would always stand in the hope of a scoop, such as a car rolling. This all started because there was a photographer called Victor Blackman who worked for the *Daily Express* – a very nice guy, but always cashing in on the misfortunes of racing drivers. One Sunday, he got a series of photos of a Ford Anglia rolling down Paddock. This made the front page of the *Express* the next day and, from then on, all the other newspapers were represented at the bottom of Paddock.

"One time they were all down there at the start of a saloon car race, and on about the second or third lap, this guy lost control of his Mini. Instead of it going towards the outside of the circuit, it went to the inside, rolled down the track, collected Victor Blackman and broke his leg. So he was carted off on a stretcher, much to the undisguised joy of a lot of racing drivers who had been on the other end of his camera. From then on, photographers were kept a lot further back and treated corners like that with lot more respect."

The publicity angle of a crash, even a fatal one, was not lost on John Webb. "Brands Hatch seemed to be on television every other Sunday night," he said, "with a crash at Paddock Hill Bend."

"Webb was a hard-nosed business man," observed Le Grand. "Anything which would create an attraction for Brands, even if it were the ultimate sacrifice, he would say: 'That's going to be a big picture tomorrow.' If it was a death, it would be on the front page. He'd mourn the loss of a driver but he'd be the first with a pile of papers the next morning."

John Webb held an informal lunch before Christmas 1968 to announce to the press his plans for the season that would bring the decade to a close. Spectator attendances had continued to rise during the year at major Internationals but fall at the smaller club meetings. Even so, Webb felt it was necessary to run a large number of club events to cater for the ever-increasing numbers of competitors and clubs wanting to be involved in the sport.

In the coming season, Grovewood would continue to offer prize money rather than starting money for all races except F1 events and the BOAC 500 sportscar International. It had cost £70,000 to stage the British Grand Prix in 1968, of which £30,000 had been taken up by prize and starting money. The Guards cigarette brand was to continue to back all Group 4 and Group 6 sports car races at Grovewood circuits as well as sponsoring the Formula 5000 championship. All its support was in the form of prize money.

Agreement had also been reached on the televising of motor racing. ITV would have the television contract for Brands Hatch and cars would be allowed to carry eight pairs of advertising decals of a regulation size.

Admission charges at the circuit would go up from 7s 6d (37.5p) to 10s (50p) at club meetings and, due to overcrowding, the number of spectators allowed in the paddock at Brands was to be limited. Paddock passes would now cost 30s (£1.50) instead of £1.00.

BELOW *Graham Hill takes his Gold Leaf Lotus 49B around Kidney corner in the 1968 British Grand Prix on 20 July. Hill led the early part of the race before retiring. (LAT)*

1960

ATV (part of the ITV network) televised a karting gymkhana event for just over an hour on 31 January. It was the second event of its kind and was organised by the London Kart Club. A course, incorporating two 180deg bends and two straights with chicanes, was marked out by straw bales on the main straight. John Webb was one of the participants. A crowd of over 5000 watched the event, some of them without paying – they gained access by walking through the woods behind the circuit. The meeting was

BELOW *Graham Hill took part in a charity go-kart race between the British Racing Drivers' Club and the Lord's Taverners at the circuit in July 1960. (Michael Hewett)*

spoiled, according to *Motoring News*, by "a gang of hooligans on the remainder of the circuit in a Ford Zephyr, which they proceeded to drive round in a reckless fashion".

Racing on the original Club circuit continued as usual, starting on 18 April when David Piper's Lotus 15 won the first sports car race of the year from Alan Rees's Lola.

A light-hearted meeting took place in July, jointly organised by the BRDC, the BRSCC and the Lord's Taverners, with the proceeds going to the National Playing Fields Association. It featured a kart race between members of the Lord's Taverners

and the BRDC which, according to reports, turned into a 'no holds barred' contest. The first heat was won by Bruce McLaren from comedian Eric Sykes. The second went to Graham Hill from Innes Ireland, and the third was won by Jack Brabham, ahead of David Piper. The final was quite chaotic, with Eric Sykes overturning his kart but carrying on, and no one was quite sure who had won.

■ All 50 laps of the non-championship Silver City Trophy F1 race on Monday 1 August, the first big car event on the new Grand Prix circuit, were led by Jack Brabham's Cooper T53 Climax, which won at 92.86mph. The World Champion was challenged until just before halfway by pole man Jim Clark's Lotus 18, which then broke its gearbox. Graham Hill (BRM P48) inherited second place ahead of Bruce McLaren in the other works Cooper and Phil Hill (Ferrari 246 Dino). During their duel, Brabham and Clark established the lap record with 1m40.6s, 94.82mph. Clark won the Formula Junior race for Team Lotus, while the sports car and saloon events were both won by Roy Salvadori, driving John Coombs's Cooper and then his 3.8 Jaguar. The GT race fell to Jack Sears with Equipe Endeavour's Aston Martin DB4GT.

ABOVE *Phil Hill exits Kidney Corner in his Ferrari D246 at the Silver City Trophy F1 race in August 1960. (Phipps/Sutton)*

■ In order to help spectators better to appreciate the racing, especially those coming for the first time, Brands Hatch published an illustrated booklet about the basics of racing. Written by David Phipps and produced by John Webb Publicity Ltd, it contained a table of lap speeds, a circuit diagram, illustrations, brief descriptions of 31 competition cars and the biographies of 93 drivers. It was priced at 2s 6d (12.5p).

■ The 'Kentish 100' F2 International on 27 August was the second major car event on the extended circuit, and this time victory went to Jim Clark by just over 0.4sec from Dan Gurney in a similar Lotus 18 Climax. Jo Bonnier and Graham Hill finished third and fourth in Porsches. Stirling Moss wrapped up an excellent GT race in a Ferrari 250GT, with Jack Sears second in an Aston Martin DB4 ahead of Mike Parkes (Lotus Elite).

■ On Boxing Day, Jim Clark won again on the Club circuit, this time with a Formula Junior Lotus.

1961

■ The Silver City Trophy race on 3 June was held for the new 1.5-litre F1 cars and included entries from all the top British drivers and teams. John Surtees, having won three consecutive 500cc World Championships on bikes, had turned to car racing and led the first third of the race in his Cooper T55. He was passed by the Lotus 21 of Jim Clark, and then hit the bank at Stirling's Bend. Stirling Moss in a Lotus 18/21 pressured Clark for more than 20 laps and eventually took the win. Tony Brooks drove the third-placed BRM P57.

■ The Guards International Trophy on 7 August was for the superseded 'Intercontinental' 2.5-litre F1 cars. The gearbox of pole man Stirling Moss's Cooper T53 failed after 23 laps and, after recovering from a poor start, World Champion Jack Brabham won from Jim Clark (Lotus 18). Graham Hill (BRM P57)

finished third with Bruce McLaren on his gearbox in the other works Cooper. Moss won the GT race with his Berlinetta Ferrari, defeating the new E-Type Jaguars of Bruce McLaren and Roy Salvadori.

■ On the Club circuit, the new stars were the Mini racers, which attracted more women into motor racing. One of the most successful was Christabel Carlisle, a regular winner.

■ Graham Hill, who also took the role of Father Christmas, won the feature race on Boxing Day in a 3-litre Ferrari 250TR.

BELOW *The Christmas Trophy race on Boxing Day 1961 and eventual winner Graham Hill, driving Scuderia Serenissima's Ferrari Testa Rossa, prepares to lap a 2-litre Maserati A6GCS. (LAT)*

1962

■ On Easter Monday, 23 April, the first 80mph lap of the Club circuit was set by John Fenning, driving Ron Harris's Formula Junior Lotus 20, at 55.6sec, 80.29mph. Two weeks later, this new record was broken by Bryan Berrow-Johnson in another Lotus 20 with a lap in 54.8sec, 81.46mph.

■ The Grovewood Trophy for sports cars on 27 May was won by Jimmy Blumer in a 2-litre Cooper Monaco, from the 1100cc Lotus 23 of Mike Beckwith. Roy Salvadori set a lap record for four-poster beds, taking a motorised example round in 6m 5s, with a snoring Innes Ireland as his passenger.

■ On Bank Holiday Monday, 6 August, Mike Parkes won the Peco Trophy GT event in a Ferrari 250GTO. He then took a Jaguar 3.8 to victory in the saloon car race and finally, at the wheel of a 2.5-litre Ferrari 246SP, won a soaking wet Guards Trophy for sports cars.

■ The longest race to be held at Brands Hatch to date, the *Motor* Six-Hours for saloon cars, was run on 1 October. The winners were Mike Parkes and Jimmy Blumer in a Jaguar 3.8.

■ Denny Hulme won the Formula Junior race on Boxing Day in a Brabham BT6 and set a new outright lap record of 54.4sec, 82.06mph.

ABOVE *Mk2 Jaguars storm Paddock Hill Bend. Dicing for the lead of the The Motor 6 Hours in October 1962, Mike Salmon in John Coombs's white 3.8 and Mike Parkes in Equipe Endeavour's similar car attempt to lap Parkes's team mate, Roy Pierpoint, who has been in the pits to replace a damaged road wheel. Parkes won the race with Jimmy Blumer, after Salmon and Peter Sutcliffe had been halted by a broken wheelbearing. (Phipps/Sutton)*

LEFT *John Surtees (74) in a Maranello Concessionaires Ferrari 250GTO leads team mate and eventual winner Mike Parkes (73) and the rest of the field up towards Druids on the first lap of the Peco Trophy race for Grand Touring cars on 6 August 1962. (Michael Hewett)*

1963

■ Severe weather, combined with an outbreak of foot and mouth disease, caused British competitors to miss the Monte Carlo Rally. Instead, a pioneering rallycross-type event was held in front of television cameras on 9 February, with rally cars racing round the slush-covered car parks. Raymond Baxter of the BBC and the London Motor Club had arranged this event at extremely short notice. The event was won by Timo Makinen's works Austin-Healey 3000.

■ The second *Motor* Six-Hours saloon car race was held on 6 July in poor weather conditions. Mike Salmon/Peter Sutcliffe were initially declared the winners in their Jaguar 3.8, but were disqualified at post-race scrutineering the following day. The laurels went instead to Roy Salvadori/Denny Hulme, also in a 3.8 Jaguar.

■ The Guards Trophy for sports cars on Bank Holiday Monday, 5 August, was won by Roger Penske in his Cooper-based Zerex Special, a wrecked Formula One Cooper-Climax rebuilt as a sports-racer. The Cooper Monaco of Roy Salvadori finished second and Jack Sears (Ferrari 250GTO) won the GT class. In the supporting saloon car race, Jim Clark's Ford Galaxie beat the Jaguar 3.8 of Graham Hill.

■ To mark the final season of the Formula Junior class, an Anglo-European Trophy meeting was held on 14 September, but few continental entries arrived. Peter Arundell in a Lotus beat the Brabham of Denny Hulme. Newly crowned World Champion Jim Clark demonstrated his F1 Lotus 25 during the event.

RIGHT *When severe weather and an outbreak of foot and mouth disease caused British competitors to miss the Monte Carlo Rally, a pioneer rallycross-type event, with rally cars racing round the slush-covered car parks, was held in front of television cameras on 9 February 1963. (LAT)*

1964

■ After only two of the six races scheduled at the 15 March meeting, commentator Anthony Marsh had to announce that the meeting was being abandoned due to snow, which was falling heavily.

■ During private practice on 2 June, Graham Hill lapped his BRM P261 in 1m 39.4s, 95.98mph, the fastest-ever time yet on the long circuit.

■ The two Alan Mann Racing Lotus Cortinas of Sir John Whitmore/Peter Proctor and Henry Taylor/Peter Harper dominated the third and last *Motor* Six-Hours saloon car race on 6 June. The pair beat the more fancied Mercedes-Benz 300Se cars of Eugen Böhringer/Herbert Linge and Hans Herrmann/Peter Lang, which finished third and fourth.

■ On 11 July, Jim Clark won the first British Grand Prix to be held at Brands Hatch from pole position in his Lotus 25, with Graham Hill less than 3sec behind in his BRM P261 after a dramatic, race-long battle. John Surtees was third for Ferrari and his team mate, Lorenzo Bandini, fifth behind Jack Brabham in his own, Coventry

BELOW The action begins on British Grand Prix day in July 1964. The Willment team's Lotus Cortinas, driven by defending British Saloon Car Champion Jack Sears (from pole position, at left) and Sir John Whitmore, flank the works Team Lotus entry, with Jackie Stewart aboard. Stewart just has the edge here, but Whitmore won the race with Sears second and JYS third. (Phipps/Sutton)

Climax powered car. Sir John Whitmore, Jack Sears and Jackie Stewart finished 1-2-3 in the supporting saloon car race in Lotus Cortinas, while Sears beat Stewart's Jaguar E-Type to win the GT race with an AC Cobra. Hugh Dibley defeated Denny Hulme in the sports car race, both driving Brabham BT8s.

■ The Guards International Trophy Race on Bank Holiday Monday, 3 August, attracted the finest-ever entry of mighty, big-engined sports-racing cars. The expected threat from the American cars of AJ Foyt (Scarab-Chevrolet), Walt Hangsen (Lotus-Oldsmobile) and Augie Pabst (Lola-Chevrolet) never really materialised, though. Bruce McLaren in a Cooper-Oldsmobile qualified at the front of the 30-car grid, with Denny Hulme's Brabham BT8 and Graham Hill's Ferrari 330P alongside. McLaren went on to take the victory, ahead of Hulme.

■ The supporting F2 event was won by Jim Clark's Lotus 32. Clark, along with Graham Hill, Jack Brabham and others, had returned from the previous day's German Grand Prix to take part in the race.

■ The six-race Boxing Day meeting had to be cancelled due to snow and icy conditions. The event was rescheduled for 31 January the following year.

RIGHT Jim Clark (Lotus 25), Graham Hill (BRM P261) and Dan Gurney (Brabham BT7) lead at the start of the 1964 British Grand Prix while, in the background, Frank Gardner (Brabham BT10) crashes on the startline. (LAT)

1965

■ More than 30,000 spectators turned out for the rescheduled Boxing Day meeting on 31 January on a cold but dry winter's day. The event was so successful that John Webb announced plans to hold a similar meeting in 1966, to be called the Racing Car Show Trophy meeting. Alan Rees won the main race of the day, the Lombank Trophy for single-seaters, with the Willment team's F2 Lola.

■ The 7 March meeting was cancelled due to poor weather. The treacherous conditions caught out BRSCC secretary Nick Syrett, who fell and broke his leg at the circuit.

■ The first Race of Champions on 14 March was run in two 40-lap heats. Jim Clark easily won the first heat, but crashed his Lotus 33 in the second while leading from Dan Gurney's Brabham BT11. Then Gurney's engine failed, leaving Mike Spence in another Lotus as the winner of the £1000 prize money. Clark drove the first 100mph lap at the circuit with a time of 1m35.4s, 100.0mph. He also won 100 bottles of champagne for the fastest lap in first practice.

■ Jim Clark also took part in the Group 2 saloon car race which was held between the two heats of the main event. His Lotus Cortina lost a wheel while leading and the race was won by Roy Pierpoint in a Ford Mustang.

■ Rain and snow blighted the Easter Monday meeting on 19 April but 30,000 people still turned out and were rewarded with quality racing in a seven-event programme.

■ John Rhodes/Warwick Banks took their MGB, entered by Don Moore, to victory in the Guards 1000-mile sportscar event over the weekend of 22–23 May. The contest was run over two days in two 500-mile heats, making it the longest race to be held in Britain since the war. No one actually completed the full 1000 miles: the successful MGB won the first heat but finished fourth the next day, and was 10 miles short of the target. Mike Garton/Paul Hughes (Austin-Healey Sprite) were classified second on aggregate ahead of Jackie Oliver/Chris Craft (Jaguar E-Type).

■ Young Brabham drivers Piers Courage and Charlie Crichton-Stuart jointly set a new lap record for the Club circuit at 54.0sec,

RIGHT Graham Hill took his Lotus 35 BRM to fourth place in the British Eagle Trophy Formula 2 race, which supported the Guards International Trophy on 30 August 1965. (Michael Hewett)

82.67mph, during the F3 Challenge race on 6 June. They finished first and third respectively, split by Roy Pike in another Brabham.

■ A new outright lap record for the Club circuit, at 52.6sec, 84.87mph, was set by Denny Hulme in Sid Taylor's Brabham BT8 sports-racing car during a Formule Libre race at the London MC club meeting on 20 June.

■ All proceeds from the St John Trophy meeting on 8 August were donated to the St John Ambulance Brigade. A huge crowd attended the event, during which five new class lap records were set and three others equalled.

■ The 'big bangers' were back on Bank Holiday Monday, 30 August, for the Guards International Trophy, with the most powerful array of sports cars ever seen on a British track. Run in two 30-lap, 80-mile heats, the event was dominated by John Surtees in a 6-litre Lola T70 Chevrolet, with which he set a new sports car lap record of 1m36.0s, 99.37mph – only 0.6sec off Jim Clark's F1 record. The day was a real scorcher and the main A20 outside the circuit was at a standstill as between 60,000 and 70,000 spectators headed for Brands. Surtees led the first heat easily and won from Bruce McLaren (McLaren-Elva) and Jackie Stewart (Lola T70). The order was the same at the end of the second heat.

■ In the supporting Ilford Film Trophy race for saloon cars, South Bank was permanently shrouded in tyre smoke as Minis were thrown sideways round the corners and the works Lotus Cortinas were continually on three wheels. Jack Brabham won in a Ford Mustang and was presented with his trophy by Miss World. Chris Barber's Jazz Band entertained the crowd in the evening and the traffic jams did not ease until well after dark.

■ In brilliant sunshine on Boxing Day, in front of a large crowd, Piers Courage won the F3 event in a Lotus 41, from Chris Irwin in a Brabham.

BELOW *The first lap of the Guards 1000 mile event on 22–23 May 1965. The contest was run over two days in two 500-mile heats, making it the longest race to be held in Britain since the Second World War. (LAT)*

1966

■ In the *Autosport* Cup race for special GT cars on 6 March, John Miles had to pit at the end of the opening lap to have a loose engine cover removed from his Lotus Elan. He then drove the race of his life to take victory from Bernard Unett in a Sunbeam Tiger.

■ The Chequered Flag team took the chequered flag in the Ilford Films 500 on 8 May, its 7-litre Shelby American Cobra, driven by David Piper/Bob Bondurant, finishing seven laps ahead of its nearest rival on a rain-soaked circuit.

■ The *Autosport* correspondent reported that "motor racing and pop music do not mix" after the F3 race at the Radio London meeting on 19 June had to be delayed for 20 minutes while police and officials chased "adolescent schoolgirls who had run onto the circuit". The fans were in pursuit of pop stars such as the Walker Brothers and Radio London disc jockey Ed Stewart who were attending the event.

■ Brands Hatch staged its second British Grand Prix on Saturday 16 July after £25,000 worth of improvements had been carried out at the circuit in preparation. These included seven temporary grandstands, a new press box, the widening of the pit area and connecting roads, a 300-speaker PA system, 100 covered paddock bays and the acquisition of 100 extra acres of land for car parking.

BELOW Jack Brabham is interviewed by commentator Anthony Marsh after winning the 1966 British Grand Prix. (Phipps/Sutton)

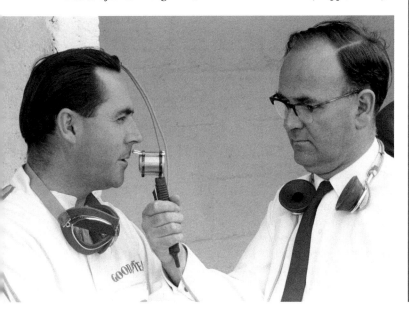

ABOVE South Bank is packed with spectators as Jack Brabham, in his 3-litre Brabham BT19 Repco, leads the first lap of the 1966 British Grand Prix on 16 July 1966. (LAT)

■ Jack Brabham and Denny Hulme took their 3-litre V8 Brabham-Repcos to a 1-2 finish in the British Grand Prix, the only cars to complete the full 80-lap distance. Brabham set the lap record for the new 3-litre F1 at 1m37.0s, 98.35mph – slower than Jim Clark's 1.5-litre record because of a wet track in the opening stages. Graham Hill finished third with his 2-litre BRM P261, and Clark fourth in a 2-litre Lotus 33 Climax ahead of the next best 3-litre car, Jochen Rindt's Cooper T81 Maserati V12. Brabham and his winning car set off on a lap of honour to the accompaniment of 'Waltzing Matilda'.

■ Hugh Dibley's Lola T70 beat the McLarens of Skip Scott and Chris Amon to win the Group 7 race at the Grand Prix meeting, while Roy Pierpoint's Ford Falcon won the saloon car race from Jackie Oliver (Mustang) and Sir Gawaine Baillie (Falcon). Off-track entertainment included the Red Arrows and a jet-propelled 'flying man'.

■ The Guards International Trophy race for Group 7 sports cars on Bank Holiday Monday, 29 August, was run as usual in two parts. The weather played havoc with the second heat, which had to be stopped after a cloudburst, but 30,000 people watched John Surtees again take victory in his Lola T70, shadowed by Chris Amon in a McLaren. Surtees won the first heat from Amon and Graham Hill's Lola-Chevrolet but the second heat was stopped after only eight laps, with cars flying off the wet track. After a long delay, it was restarted over a reduced distance of 20 laps, the preceding laps being declared null and void. Surtees won again with Amon, never more than a few lengths behind, in second place and Hill again third. It was the last appearance of the 'big bangers' at the circuit because FIA Group 7 was dropped as an International category at the end of the year.

■ Jim Clark won the supporting saloon car race in his Lotus Cortina, defeating Jackie Oliver's Ford Mustang, while Piers Courage's Lotus 41 triumphed in a very wet F3 race.

■ Chris Irwin and Piers Courage won the European F3 Challenge for Britain on the Grand Prix circuit on 2 October, despite the best efforts of Jean-Pierre Beltoise, who led the early stages in his Matra. Eight countries sent teams – Belgium, Britain, France, Germany, Italy, Portugal, Sweden and Switzerland. The British team comprised Irwin and Peter Gethin in Brabhams and Courage in a Lotus. Jacky Ickx (Matra) won the first heat for Belgium and Beltoise the second for France. In the final, however, Irwin triumphed with Courage second. Britain won the team challenge from Germany and Sweden.

■ The Motor Show 200 meeting on 30 October provided the swansong for the 1-litre Formula 2 cars, as the last race was run to the formula. Jochen Rindt in a Brabham-Cosworth beat the Brabham-Honda of Jack Brabham by a fifth of a second after the pair had battled wheel-to-wheel for all 40 laps of the final. Jim Clark's Lotus finished third ahead of the Matras of Jacky Ickx, Jean-Pierre Beltoise and Jo Schlesser. Jackie Oliver's Mustang won the two-part supporting race, in which John Fitzpatrick won his class in a Broadspeed Ford Anglia, securing the 1966 British Saloon Car Championship.

1967

■ The new season kicked off with the Racing Car Show Trophy meeting on 22 January. The F3 event was won by Derek Bell in a Brabham BT21 but the final race, for saloon cars over 1000cc, was marred by a number of serious accidents.

■ Grovewood Securities published its annual report at the end of January. The profit from motor racing before tax and interest was £129,810, compared with £83,022 the previous year. Its total investment in motor racing circuits and equipment was £950,599. During the year, one million people

BELOW Dan Gurney raced his Eagle T1G Weslake to victory at the 1967 Race of Champions on 12 March, winning both heats but nearly being pipped on the line by the Ferrari of Lorenzo Bandini. (Michael Hewett)

had visited Brands Hatch, Mallory Park, Oulton Park and Snetterton, and £40,000 had been spent on additions and improvements.

■ Over 45,000 people saw Dan Gurney win a thrilling Race of Champions on 12 March. Gurney, driving his own V12 Eagle-Weslake, won 100 bottles of champagne in the first practice session, which ended under heavy snow. Race day was bright and, despite a cold wind, there were long traffic jams leading to the circuit. From pole position, Gurney won both 10-lap preliminary heats but was almost pipped on the line in the 40-lap final by Lorenzo Bandini in a Ferrari 312, only 0.4sec separating them at the flag. During the last lap, commentators Anthony Marsh, Peter Scott-Russell and James Tilling shouted themselves hoarse with excitement. Jo Siffert was third in a

Cooper T81 Maserati. Frank Gardner's Alan Mann Racing Ford Falcon beat Graham Hill's works Lotus Cortina in the saloon car event.

■ The Easter weekend was a busy one at the track, with Stock Car Racing on a short oval on the Clearways infield on 26 March, Easter Sunday, and the *Evening News* race meeting on Easter Monday.

■ Torrential rain all morning created a lake at the bottom of Paddock Hill Bend, causing the BRSCC meeting on 25 June to be cancelled.

■ The first-ever Formula Ford race was held on 2 July and won by novice driver Ray Allen in a Lotus 51, beating Malcolm Payne's Lotus 31.

■ Japanese driver Tetsu Ikuzawa scored a hat-trick of wins on 9 July. He won the F3 and Formule Libre races in his Motor Racing Stables prepared Brabham BT21, and the 1150cc class of the sports car race in a semi-works Honda S800.

■ Mike Spence/Phil Hill gave Chaparral its first-ever victory against stiff opposition from Ferrari and Porsche in the BOAC 500 on 30 July, the final round of the FIA International Championship of Makes. The Group 7 sports cars of the Guards Trophy had gone, but in their place was a mouth-watering array of Group 6 cars including the 7-litre Chaparral 2F Chevrolet with its huge rear wing, similarly engined Lola T70 Mk3s, Ferrari 330s and 275LMs, Porsche 910s and 906s, Alfa Romeo Tipo 33s, Ford GT40s and Lotus 47s. Despite a gloomy weather forecast, a crowd of around 30,000 turned out to see Spence and Hill take their victory. Ferrari secured the championship as Chris Amon/Jackie Stewart were second in a 330P4, ahead of Jo Siffert/Bruce McLaren in a Porsche 910. Although the event was named the BOAC '500', it was actually six hours in duration, and the winners completed a total of 559.15 miles.

■ Jochen Rindt won the Guards International Trophy F2 race in his Brabham BT23 on Bank Holiday Monday, 28 August, ahead of Jackie Stewart in a Matra MS7. Five of the drivers – Rindt, Stewart, Jack Brabham, Graham Hill and Chris Irwin – had competed in the Canadian Grand Prix near Toronto the day before. The Mosport Park race had finished at midnight UK time, and they had flown back overnight, arriving just in time for morning practice. Rindt won the first heat from Stewart, while Hill, in a Lotus 48, took the second heat ahead of team mate Jackie Oliver. Rindt won the final from Stewart and Jo Schlesser (Matra MS5).

■ The Guards Motor Show 200 meeting on 29 October featured the final round of the British Saloon Car Championship and the Lombank Trophy F3 race, which featured 60 cars. Frank Gardner clinched the saloon title in his Ford Falcon, winning by over a lap from the Ford Mustang of Jackie Oliver. The final of the F3 event was stopped early in torrential rain after Peter Deal's Brabham BT18 ran over a marshal, breaking his leg, and an ambulance

ABOVE *The 1967 BOAC 500 six-hour sportscar race was won by Mike Spence and Phil Hill in the high-winged Chaparral 2F Chevrolet. (LAT)*

collided with Mike Knight's BT21. Mike Beckwith's Chequered Flag DAF was declared the winner over Henri Pescarolo's Matra MS5.

■ At the Boxing Day meeting on 26 December, John Miles broke the Club circuit outright lap record in his F3 Lotus 41C, leaving it at 51.8sec, 86.18mph.

1968

■ In January, the Brands operating company, Motor Circuit Developments, announced reduced admission prices at big meetings, apart from the Race of Champions, the BOAC 500 and the Grand Prix. In most cases, admission would be 15s (75p) instead of £1. MCD said this was possible because the starting money that had been paid was being replaced by prize money.

BELOW No wonder John Surtees looks a little nervous – the rear wing support of his Honda RA301 has collapsed during the 1968 British Grand Prix. Despite this handicap, Surtees managed to finish in fifth place. (Michael Hewett)

■ A crowd of 40,000 meant long queues for the Race of Champions on 17 March. Held eight weeks before the first Grand Prix in Europe, it provided the opportunity for F1 teams to try out new cars. Ferrari sent three but it was the new McLaren M7A of Bruce McLaren which led from start to finish. It was the first single-seater race that the New Zealander had won at the track since 1958. Pedro Rodriguez was second in a V12 BRM P139, having made a poor start and carved his way through the field. Denny Hulme was third in the other McLaren-DFV. Brian Muir's Falcon beat Vic Elford's Porsche 911 and Frank Gardner's Escort in the saloon event.

■ In his column in *Autosport* the following week, Bruce McLaren reported that it had been thrilling to keep full throttle over the brow climbing out of South Bank as the car almost left the ground there. "It was accelerating at such a rate that it was nearly lifting me out of the cockpit," he wrote. "The weight transfer, particularly with our car with a lot on the rear, nearly had the front wheels off the ground. We were going over at about 150mph and reaching 160mph in the dip."

■ For the second running of the BOAC 500, the event was moved from July to 7 April, becoming the third round of the International Championship for Makes for the Group 6 and Group 4 cars. The race was run under the cloud of Jim Clark's fatal F2 accident that same afternoon at Hockenheim, news of

ABOVE Jo Siffert takes the flag to win the 1968 British Grand Prix on 20 July with Rob Walker's Lotus 49B. (LAT)

which filtered through the crowd by word of mouth. The event heralded the debut of the turbine powered Howmet TX, which would have won its team £1000 if it had just completed the event. Alas, its throttle stuck open 10 minutes after the start and the car buried itself in the bank at Druids. Another brand new car making its first appearance was the Ford 3L, which impressed in the early stages but was retired after two hours. Jacky Ickx/Brian Redman came home the winners in their JW Gulf team Ford GT40, just 22sec ahead of the Porsche 907 of Lodovico Scarfiotti/Gerhard Mitter after six hours of racing.

■ The Spring Bank Holiday meeting on 2 June, organised by the BRSCC and the Mini Se7en Club, featured a Mini Festival, with all drivers of BMC Minis admitted free. Tim Schenken won the main F3 race in a Sports Motors Chevron, while other entertainment included Terry Lightfoot's jazz band and the Red Arrows.

■ At the 7 July BRSCC meeting, racing policeman John Gott, who was the chief constable of Northamptonshire and a vice-chairman of the RAC Competitions Committee, had his Mini Cooper S road car stolen from the paddock while he was racing.

■ Jo Siffert was a popular winner of the British Grand Prix on Saturday 20 July in Rob Walker's privately entered Lotus 49B. It was Siffert's first Grand Prix victory but the race had been

dominated for 20 laps by Graham Hill's works Gold Leaf Team Lotus entry, until a driveshaft broke. Transmission failure ended a fine drive by his new team mate, Jackie Oliver, who had replaced Jim Clark. Chris Amon brought his Ferrari home a close second, far ahead of team mate Jacky Ickx.

■ Despite arguments earlier in the year over the level of advertising on racing cars, ITV covered the Grand Prix with five separate transmissions from the circuit, which was covered by 12 camera positions. The schedule comprised broadcasts from 2.35pm until 2.40pm, 2.50pm until 3.20pm (covering the start at 3.00pm), 3.30pm until 3.40pm, 3.45pm until 4.00pm, and 4.55pm until 5.05pm. The interruptions were to cover horse racing. The race was also covered by BBC Radio 3.

■ The F3 race at the Grand Prix was won by John Miles (works Lotus 41X) and the saloon car race by Frank Gardner (Alan Mann Escort).

■ Despite having held a Grand Prix the previous day, the circuit was used by the Jaguar Drivers' Club on Sunday 21 July for a seven-race meeting. Tony Lanfranchi took an easy victory in the Formule Libre race in an F3 Brabham BT21.

■ In August, the new Formula 5000 category was announced by John Webb. This was open to single-seater racing cars with mass-produced pushrod engines of up to 5000cc. An eight-round championship for the cars would be run in 1969.

ABOVE *Chris Amon finds a passenger awaits as he prepares to leave the pits in his Ferrari 312 during the 1968 British Grand Prix meeting. (sutton-images.com)*

■ Frank Gardner took a Lola T70 Chevrolet to an easy win in the 50-lap Guards International Trophy race for Group 4 cars on Bank Holiday Monday, 2 September, ahead of Ulf Norinder's similar car. Peter Gethin was third in a Chevron-BMW and won his heat and the final of the supporting F3 event, also in a Chevron.

■ The only club meeting of the year to be held on the full circuit was the BRSCC-run event on 29 September. Tim Schenken won the F3 championship round in his Chevron B9 from the works Lotus 41X of John Miles.

■ Frank Gardner in Alan Mann's Ford Escort set a new outright saloon car record for the long circuit of 1m46.6s, 89.49mph, on his way to victory in the Guards Motor Show 200 on 20 October. David Hobbs took his Ford Falcon to second place, ahead of the Porsche 911 of Toine Hezemans. Tim Schenken's Sports Motors Chevron won the F3 support race from Tony Lanfranchi's Merlyn.

■ The Boxing Day meeting was held a day later than usual, on 27 December and Tony Lanfranchi was the victor in the F3 event in his aerofoiled Merlyn Mk14A.

RIGHT *Colin Youle's Mini Cooper S gets a tow back to the paddock in September 1969. (Gerald Swan)*

1969

■ Tony Lanfranchi raced a F5000 Lola T142 in the Formule Libre event on 19 January and set a new Club circuit record of 49.2s, 90.73mph – the first official 90mph lap.

■ Indianapolis-style qualifying was used for the Race of Champions on 16 March with each car completing four laps – one out-lap, two flying laps and one in-lap. The race was won with ease by Jackie Stewart in Ken Tyrrell's DFV powered Matra MS80. Stewart led from start to finish and was never seriously challenged, setting a new race record along the way of 108.65mph. Graham Hill was second in a Lotus 49B and Denny Hulme third in a McLaren M7A. Jochen Rindt in the other Lotus set a new lap record of 1m29.8s, 109.91mph. The Falcons of Roy Pierpoint and Brian Muir dominated the two saloon car races.

BELOW *A bunch of Formula 3 cars, led by Jean-Pierre Jaussaud's Tecno, rounds Druids in a cloud of cement dust on 1 September 1969. (Gerald Swan)*

■ Two days after the first-ever Formula 5000 event at Oulton Park, the cars lined up at Brands for the Guards Championship race at the Easter Monday meeting on 7 April. The race developed into a battle between three Chevrolet V8 powered cars, Peter Gethin's Church Farm Racing McLaren M10A, David Hobbs's works Surtees TS5 and motorcycle World Champion Mike Hailwood's works-backed Lola T142. Unfortunately both Hobbs and Hailwood retired, leaving Gethin an easy winner. A huge crowd turned out in glorious weather and Thames Television (part of the ITV network) showed the start and the closing stages of the race.

■ The BOAC 500 long-distance sports car race on 13 April, the first European round of the 1969 International Championship of Makes, was a walkover for Porsche, with Jo Siffert/Brian Redman heading a trio of 908/2s. The sole Ferrari 312P of Chris Amon/Pedro Rodriguez was fourth. The winners covered over 600 miles during the six hours of the race.

■ Peter Gethin's McLaren took him to his third consecutive Guards F5000 win on the Club circuit on 11 May, winning both 50-lap heats, fighting off the attentions of Frank Gardner and Keith Holland, both in Lola T142s.

■ Hubert Hahne/Dieter Quester won the Guards International 6 Hours in a works turbocharged BMW 2002Ti on 22 June. The race was the British round of the European Touring Car Championship, and this was the first time it had been held at the circuit since 1963. John Fitzpatrick/Trevor Taylor were second in a 1300cc Broadspeed Ford Escort, just 7sec behind the winner and having only been passed in the closing stages. The two-hour race the previous day for smaller cars was won by the Mini Cooper S of Rob Mason from Ed Swart's Fiat-Abarth.

■ At the Sutton & Cheam Motor Club event on 3 August, Emerson Fittipaldi finished runner-up in only his second-ever F3 race, having initially led in his Lotus 59. The race was won by Bev Bond (Brabham BT28).

■ Two weeks later, on 17 August, Emerson Fittipaldi scored his second F3 victory (having won at Mallory Park the week before), setting a new Club circuit lap record of 50.0s, 89.28mph, jointly with Roy Pike's Lotus 59. Pike was second, ahead of James Hunt in a Brabham BT28.

■ Formula 3 was back on Bank Holiday Monday, 1 September, and this time Reine Wisell in a works Chevron B15 was victorious in the Guards Trophy race. Tim Schenken's Brabham BT28 finished virtually alongside Wisell at the flag, the two being credited with the same race time. John Miles in a Lotus Europa 62 won the supporting Lombank Trophy race for Group 4 and Group 6 cars, while Dennis Leech won the British Saloon Car Championship round in his Ford Falcon.

■ At the BARC meeting on 7 September, James Hunt, in an F3 Brabham BT21, emerged victorious from a wheel-to-wheel dice with Peter Deal's BT18 in the Formule Libre event.

■ The final round of the Guards F5000 championship was held on 28 September. Going into the race, Peter Gethin (Church Farm McLaren M10A) just headed the points table from Trevor Taylor (Team Elite Surtees TS5), and the two battled hard in the first heat until they collided with a backmarker and were eliminated, leaving Mike Hailwood to win in Jackie Epstein's Lola T142. Only nine cars were on the grid for the second heat. Hailwood won again but Gethin still clinched the inaugural F5000 title.

■ Reine Wisell in his works Chevron B15 scored a narrow victory in the F3 final at the Motor Show 200 on 18 October, ahead of Mo Nunn's Lotus 59. The drive of the race came from Howden Ganley in a Chevron B15, who worked his way up from 22nd to fifth, driving the first 100mph F3 lap on the way. In the British Saloon Car encounter, Frank Gardner's Ford Escort beat the Ford Falcon of Dennis Leech.

ABOVE *Barrie Williams leads another Mini Cooper and an Escort round Druids in September 1969. (Gerald Swan)*

■ Emerson Fittipaldi in his Lotus 59 clinched the Lombank F3 Championship at the Sevenoaks & District Motor Club's meeting on 8 November.

1970s

A MAJOR INTERNATIONAL CIRCUIT

Anyone who visited Brands Hatch on Sunday 12 April 1970 will have seen a pale blue car piercing its way through teeming rain, slithering, sliding, dancing as if on ice. Water streamed off the car and was kicked up in mountainous plumes from its rear tyres, while the windscreen wipers fought a losing battle. It seemed inconceivable that it could complete the race without mishap, yet the scene was repeated lap after lap.

The race was the BOAC 1000, Britain's round of the International Championship of Makes, and the weather was foul. The blue car in question, with its distinctive orange stripe running from nose to tail, was the No.10 Gulf Porsche 917K of the John Wyer Automotive team. The driver was the Mexican, Pedro Rodriguez, and that day he put on one of the greatest displays of wet-weather driving ever seen.

Sports car racing was enjoying something of a golden age at this time. These were the days when Grand Prix drivers regularly raced in endurance events as well as Formula One races, and so spectators were able to relish the likes of Jacky Ickx, Denny Hulme, Jack Brabham, Jo Siffert, Chris Amon and Piers Courage battling against each other in Porsches, Ferraris, Alfa Romeos and Matras.

John Wyer Automotive, which that year ran the works Porsche team, had entered two 917s, one to be driven by Rodriguez and Leo Kinnunen, and the other by Siffert and Brian Redman. The Porsche Salzburg team had Hulme alongside Vic Elford, and Hans Hermann with Dickie Attwood, also in 917s.

Ferrari team leader Ickx was partnered by Jackie Oliver, and Amon was sharing his similar 512S with the diminutive Italian, Arturo Merzario. Scuderia Filipinetti was running a privately entered 512S for Herbert Müller and David Hobbs. Matra had brought two of its V12 engined Spyders for Brabham and Jean-Pierre Beltoise, and Johnny Servoz-Gavin and Henri Pescarolo. From Alfa Romeo the

RIGHT *James Hunt in his McLaren M23 heads towards victory in the controversial 1976 British Grand Prix. He would later be disqualified, handing victory to Niki Lauda's Ferrari. (Phipps/Sutton)*

Autodelta team fielded a single car for Courage and Andrea de Adamich.

Ickx was on pole, and alongside him on the 3-2-3 grid was his team mate, Amon, together with Elford in the Porsche Salzburg entered 917. Back in the middle of the third row was Rodriguez in the pale blue and orange JW Gulf car.

When the flag fell at midday, Ickx led off the line but the white 917 of Elford slithered past and was still ahead by the time the cars splashed their way back into sight at the end of the first lap. At the back of the field, a Lola T70 spun in the treacherous conditions and wiped itself out along the Top Straight.

On the second lap, Ickx regained the lead from Elford and a while later Rodriguez, who had been rapidly making up places, was called in for a dressing down from the BRSCC's clerk of the course, Nick Syrett – not only for overtaking under a waved yellow flag while the debris on the Top Straight was being cleared up, but also for narrowly missing Syrett himself as he did so.

After his stop-go penalty, Rodriguez put his head down and drove as though he were oblivious to the conditions. Around the same time, the second Wyer Porsche of Siffert pitted with a puncture.

Rodriguez now produced an astonishing display of wet-weather driving. Ickx, so often regarded as the 'regenmeister', was in the lead but he pitted with windscreen wiper problems – the last thing he needed on this day. Elford now led from Amon in the second Ferrari, and then came Rodriguez. Pedro passed Amon under braking for Paddock and then, coming out of Clearways, pulled alongside Elford and into a lead he was never to relinquish.

Brian Redman still marvels at the display put on by Rodriguez that day. "After he was black-flagged for overtaking under the yellow, he came in the pits to be told off and then went storming out," he said. "From then on he produced one of the best races of his career, or anybody else's, sliding the 917 at 120mph, and went on to win the race."

The Elford Porsche held second place but fell further back from the leader as the race progressed, while the Ferraris paid frequent visits to the pits with problems such as wet electrics, as Jackie Oliver, who was co-driving Ickx's 512S, recalled. "I remember the wipers packing up," he said, "but even without that, the Ferrari was no match for the Porsche that day, not with Pedro driving."

Rodriguez stayed at the wheel for the maximum three and a half hours permitted before handing over to Kinnunen. By this time, the rain had stopped but the track was still far from dry.

"That was a fantastic race," recalled Peter Anderson, who was a pit-lane marshal at the event. "In those days the pits were separated from the Top

Straight by wooden sleepers, which were probably four and a half feet high, and in the pouring rain, with Rodriguez coming out of Clearways on full opposite lock, pedal to the metal, it was really quite frightening. I wasn't the only one to comment that, in the event of a collision, a car could come over into the pits."

After a short spell at the wheel, Kinnunen, totally outclassed on this day by his co-driver, handed the 917 back to Rodriguez for the remainder of the race. Ickx was making up time by this stage, working his way through the field. Redman went off at Westfield and was delayed while the bodywork on the second Gulf Porsche was repaired. "We were lying in second place," he explained, "and I guess I was probably holding up Chris Amon in the factory Ferrari because I suddenly felt a tap from behind. I was sent spinning and hit the bank fairly hard."

It did not help Amon's cause for long, because the two works Ferraris started to suffer fuel-feed problems, but the No.10 Porsche just kept going. At a quarter to seven in the evening, Rodriguez took the chequered flag, five laps ahead of the Elford/Hulme car with Attwood/Hermann third. Ickx/Oliver finished a distant eighth, 22 laps behind the winner.

"Pedro was just phenomenal in the rain," added Oliver. "A very brave little driver, with super car control. He would just go through the puddles and the streams of water that were running across the circuit. The conditions that day were very, very dangerous, but he was just a master."

One report of the race described it as a "virtuoso display of wet-weather driving that has rarely been matched". A slight figure, Rodriguez looked almost mischievous at the prizegiving, with an impish grin on his face. It was obvious that he had thoroughly enjoyed himself.

The lead driver in the second Gulf Porsche 917 that day had been Jo Siffert, the popular Swiss who had scored his first Grand Prix victory at the circuit in 1968, driving Rob Walker's Lotus 49B. Siffert and Rodriguez were great friends but also great rivals, nicknaming each other 'Crazy Swiss' and the 'Mexican Bandit' respectively. Rodriguez lost his life in July 1971 at the Norisring in Germany and, a few months later during a non-championship Formula One race at Brands Hatch, so did Siffert. The accident not only highlighted the need for greater safety measures at the circuit, but also the contemporary attitude towards incidents of this kind.

The Formula One Victory Race was held on 24 October 1971 to celebrate Jackie Stewart's success

BELOW *One of the most memorable races ever to take place at the circuit was the 1970 BOAC 1000 Kms, won in appalling conditions by the Gulf Porsche 917K of Pedro Rodriguez and Leo Kinnunen. During the race, Rodriguez put on one of the most brilliant displays of wet-weather driving ever seen and the pair eventually finished five laps ahead of the rest of the field, after six and three-quarter hours of racing. (LAT)*

in winning the World Championship for a second time. Siffert was driving a BRM P160 when he crashed heavily at Hawthorn Bend on lap 15. He came under the bridge on the preceding straight and snaked left and right, before veering left again, demolishing a 100-yard marker board and bouncing off the bank. The car travelled partially over marshal's Post 14 and hit the bank again, bursting into flames.

Max Le Grand was standing at the scene when the accident occurred. "I was behind the marshals' post," he said. "When I saw him lose control, I was almost ready to leap out of the way, but he ended up upside down in front of the marshals' post. I heard that man's cries of agony and for help. This is where I admire the marshals. They did what they could with what little equipment they had.

"It was a very unusual scene because, when the other cars came round on the next lap, they stopped because the race was red-flagged. And you had this sight as they appeared under the bridge of them pulling up, and stopping while the marshals were trying to get Siffert's car extinguished and rescue him. It was bizarre, because they were all sitting in their cars. I wondered why no one tried to get out to help. I asked Jackie Stewart afterwards and he said he knew it was too late. It was a blazing inferno."

In November, the inquest into Siffert's death was held at the Coroner's Court in Tonbridge. The court heard that a flag marshal at Post 14, Geoffrey Barnes, had tried to get through to race control on the telephone, but could not make himself heard. The fire marshal at the post, Barry Foot, reported that three of the fire extinguishers had not operated correctly. Siffert had died from asphyxia, his only injury being a broken left leg. According to Anthony Marsh, who was track manager at the time, the extinguishers had been tested by the manufacturers on 21 October. When questioned, Grahame White, the clerk of the course for the BARC, the organising club, agreed that firefighting methods could be improved, but thought it would be too costly and impractical to implement.

The eight-man jury recorded a verdict of accidental death but with a rider suggesting "better supervision of safety and fire precautions".

John Webb referred to the accident during Motor Circuit Development's annual press conference at the end of the year to announce plans for the following season. "MCD have kept a dignified silence on the wild and uninformed comments made by people who should know better," he said. "For the last 22 years, Brands Hatch has been the busiest circuit in the world. Cars and motorcycles have completed half a million laps since 1961 when

Grovewood took the circuit over. But until October 1971, not one Grand Prix driver had been killed."

Webb added that the fire extinguishers at the accident had actually been in perfect working order and all but one had been totally emptied. Only one small extinguisher, which had been incorrectly loaded and would not have made any difference, had not worked.

Over the winter, a lot of safety improvements were made to the track, with wooden railway sleepers, six feet high, installed around most of the lap, separated from the track by flat, but what now would be considered narrow, run-off areas. A single strip of steel Armco barrier ran along the bottom of the sleepers to act as a cushion. Hawthorn Bend now had a wide run-off area. A number of earth banks, including the one on the inside of Pilgrim's Rise, were removed and the dip between Pilgrim's Rise and Hawthorn was partially filled in. The sleepers on the inside of the track finished just after Westfield and a large area alongside Dingle Dell and Dingle Dell Corner was now out of bounds to spectators. The sleepers continued at Stirling's but were so high it was difficult to see over them. *Autosport* commented that Brands had become a poorer spectator circuit as a result of these changes.

Nevertheless, a good crowd turned out for the annual Race of Champions on 19 March 1972. The admission price for this non-championship F1 meeting was just 50p. F5000 cars had their own race on the Saturday and then joined the F1 cars for the main event on the Sunday, when the programme started early, at noon. The support races were for

LEFT *A black day at Brands. The non-championship Formula One Victory Race on 24 October 1971, intended to be a celebration of Jackie Stewart's second World Championship, has been brought to a premature halt by a crash at Hawthorn Bend which has claimed the life of BRM driver Jo Siffert. (Michael Hewett)*

BELOW *The burned out wreckage of Siffert's BRM P160. (Michael Hewett)*

Emerson Fittipaldi

"Brands Hatch was a good circuit for me throughout my career. I raced Formula Ford there, I won the British F3 championship there, and I won in F1 there. I loved being at the track. The

Emerson Fittipaldi made his grand prix debut at Brands Hatch in a Gold Leaf Lotus 49C Ford at the 1970 British Grand Prix on 18 July. (LAT)

British fans have always been so good to me – racing in Britain is still like racing at my second home and I love that feeling. I won the 1972 British Grand Prix in the John Player Special Lotus there and I think that was the turning point of the championship for me. After that, I won in Austria and Italy, but Brands Hatch was what started it. It was such a challenging place to drive, but a real thrill to do well there."

the British Saloon Car Championship, the Shell British Formula 3 Championship and the BOC Formula Ford Championship.

In late 1973, the world suffered a fuel crisis. The introduction of petrol coupons and severe cutbacks on the use of petrol throughout Europe and America made the outlook for motor sport very bleak.

MCD announced that, as from 19 November, all race organisers were being asked voluntarily to reduce the lengths of their races by 20 per cent. "The management hope that their prompt action will create an alternative to measures which will imperil the livelihood of thousands of workers now employed in performance car production and motor sport generally," read the statement. "Grovewood aim to prevent consequent weakening of Britain's multi-million pound racing car export effort which would be brought about by restriction of testing and development under racing conditions."

Ironically, the weather at the first winter club meeting held at Brands after this initiative came into force was so bad that the organisers, the Romford Enthusiasts' Car Club, had to give competitors three warm-up laps instead of the usual one, thereby cancelling out the fuel-saving benefit of any reduced race length.

The annual Boxing Day meeting, due to be televised on the BBC, was cancelled on the grounds that it was felt by the RAC, against the wishes of Brands Hatch, that it would be wrong to be seen to run televised motor racing. Other British sporting events, however, went ahead as usual.

Despite the uncertain future that motor sport seemed to be facing, a 10-point plan of improvements was announced in November for a £50,000 facelift to the circuit. The proposals included an additional 550-seat grandstand opposite the pits and next to the Grovewood Suite; 1600 terraced aluminium bench-type spectator seats to be built on the existing terrace between Paddock Hill and the main grandstand; the internal road linking the tunnel and the pits to be widened to allow two-way traffic; the pit road to be widened to 25 feet; the existing pit buildings to be lengthened and brought up to latest standards; a wider road to be built behind the pits to allow two-way traffic; safety work to be extended to include the stretch between Westfield and Stirling's and for this to be reopened up to the public; spectator earth banks at Paddock and Clearways to be pressure-seeded with grass; new toilets; and exclusive use of the existing paddock area for the F1 teams and trade vehicles at the following year's Grand Prix.

It led to one wag writing in to *Autosport* to ask if they were reseeding the banks at Brands to stop them receding.

The work meant that the circuit was shut throughout January and the first half of February 1974, but the work was completed in time for the Race of Champions in March. About 41,000 people turned out for the event, which was held in pouring rain, but it was chaotic conditions in the paddock that came under fire in the *Autosport* editorial the following week. The magazine claimed that there seemed to be poor policing of the area and little organisation as regards allocation of bays.

It has to be remembered that the old paddock at Brands Hatch was on a steep slope, that it comprised rows of corrugated iron and scaffolding shelters, and that it was a difficult area in which to work even at a normal race meeting, let alone a

ABOVE *No motorhomes in those days. A converted bus provides the transport for this Formula 3 GRD 373 in the paddock for the Motor Show 200 meeting in October 1973. (Author)*

Grand Prix. In addition, the cars had to be taken through the narrow tunnel underneath Paddock Hill Bend to gain access to the pits and track. The circuit had its hands tied, though, because a full resiting of the paddock complex could not be undertaken until work began on the new M20 London–Dover motorway, which was not expected until the autumn of 1974.

Car parking arrangements were also criticised, *Autosport* claiming that: "There were plenty of officious car parking marshals on arrival at the circuit, but when it came to getting out, with cars stuck in the mud all over the place, there wasn't anyone to be seen."

To resolve the problem before the Grand Prix, Webb decided that the whole of the existing paddock would be used for the F1 teams, while the rest of the competitors would use the level car park area on the other side of the service road, opposite the rear of the clubhouse. All but one row of the existing shelters was removed for the event.

The Grand Prix in July caused controversy on track (see later) but Webb came under fire from spectators as well. Correspondence in *Autosport* complained about the lack of access in the paddock to some of the F1 teams, the lack of sufficient toilets and water standpipes in the campsite, and the cost of a can of lager at the catering outlets.

In a letter to the magazine the following week, Webb addressed the points that had been made. "So far as the camping site is concerned, we have explained before that Brands Hatch is situated in the green belt and is subject to rigorous planning restrictions which broadly confine our activities to motor racing and do not permit the official operation of a campsite. However, to reduce the risk of nuisance by campers to local residents and to keep the roadside verges free, we are able to make two outside fields available free of charge but are not permitted to install related permanent facilities. For this reason, intending campers approaching us for permission to use these fields are always told that they must be self-contained in terms of toilet equipment and water supplies. In this connection, it is worth mentioning that for the first Grand Prix in 1964 we willingly allowed campers to make use of lavatories and water supplies within the circuit, but unfortunately this gesture was rewarded by every single lavatory and wash basin in the paddock being smashed deliberately on the night before practice; hence we discontinued the facility."

He went on: "With regard to the paddock, it was the original joint intention of the Formula One Constructors [Association] and ourselves that visitors would be able to see almost all of the cars, but a situation arose during the week of the

BELOW *Second-place finisher Niki Lauda puts a move on third-place finisher Emerson Fittipaldi during the rain-soaked Race of Champions in 1974. (Phipps/Sutton)*

meeting whereby the Tyrrell team received more than one extremist threat to destroy Scheckter's car by fire, and not unnaturally the police were called in for their advice and this naturally included removing the Tyrrell equipe as far away from the public as possible and also restricting the area of public access."

As an aside, it is interesting to record that Webb's notes show that prize and starting money for the Grand Prix cost £77,000 in 1974 – and £150,000 in 1976.

In September 1975, Grovewood chairman John Danny appointed John Webb as the managing director of the individual circuit companies, Brands Hatch, Mallory Park and Snetterton, and as the vice-chairman of Cheshire Car Circuit Ltd (Oulton Park). Chris Lowe relinquished the position of general manager of the circuit companies, which he had held since 1966, becoming the MD of Aerosigns, a Grovewood subsidiary company, but remained on the MCD board and as the director of motorcycle racing at the track.

Lowe was succeeded as the general manager by Jackie Epstein, who assumed responsibility for operational capability, planning, construction and maintenance. At the same time, Angela Webb joined the boards of the four circuit companies with

responsibility for spectator amenities, customer services, catering and celebrity races.

Already an enthusiastic spectator, the future Mrs Webb had joined the staff of Brands in March 1972 as John's P.A. "During the interview, I declared openly that my shorthand and typing speeds were lousy, and I nearly got fired after only two weeks for my honesty," she said. "My first unauthorised decision was to call in a local vet and put down the circuit's ailing guard dog. My second was to marry the boss in 1973.

"When I became a director, I was in charge of developing and organising the utilisation of weekday track hires and any other area of land that could be used to earn money," she explained. "This would include hiring the circuit to Pinewood Studios for the making of *Silver Dream Racer*, horse shows in one of our car parks, police dog trials in the centre of the Grand Prix circuit, the massive annual 'Festival of Lanterns' for the Caravan Club of Great Britain & Ireland – when we made the Guinness Book of Records for doing the conga with over 8000 people – quite apart from car launches, car manufacturers' fleet-buying days, TV adverts and F1 test days.

"In addition, I was in charge of all hospitality suite and marquee hiring, circuit catering and selling trade sites on race days. We initially had contract

BELOW *The slope of the Brands Hatch paddock can be clearly seen in this photograph of Jack Brabham's Brabham BT33, taken during the 1970 Race of Champions meeting. (Swan)*

caterers but at some stage, using our own circuit secretarial staff, I started doing our own VIP catering. This then developed to a point where the spectator and hospitality suite catering was in-house at all four circuits."

At the time of the new appointments, John Webb said: "My brief is to make Brands Hatch one of the finest circuits in Europe. I have a small and compact team which I feel is just right." His confidence in his team was to be justified over the next few months.

"The construction of the M20 motorway took away some of our land and resulted in the relocation and modification of the paddock in 1976," explained Webb. "The FIA also wanted vastly improved pits and a lot more safety work. So that was a big spend year. Fortunately Jackie Epstein, who was our track manager at the time, formed a very good friendship with the directors and management of McAlpine, who were building the motorway, and so that bill was very much reduced because we got a lot of things done on the QT. Kenneth McAlpine was the original sponsor of the Connaught Grand Prix team, so I knew him as well, but Jackie formed a much better liaison with the people doing the job on site."

Epstein was a fully qualified engineer with a vast amount of racing experience as well, having competed in sports cars, non-championship Formula One with a BRM and some Formula 2 in the early sixties. He later turned to team management, running Paul Hawkins in sports cars and Mike Hailwood in Formula 5000, and ran the Speed International and ShellSport Luxembourg F5000 teams, as well as looking after the Brands Hatch fleet of ShellSport Mexicos. He had not been in his new role for long before he had a major construction project on his hands.

"In late 1975, soon after I took over as track manager, I had a deputation from Bernie Ecclestone and Ken Tyrrell," explained Epstein. "We had a long meeting and Bernie said: 'Before the Race of Champions, I want this, this and this done, and before the Grand Prix – if you're going to keep the Grand Prix – I want double this, this and this.' One of the things he wanted was much more space behind the pits to park transporters. He wanted them backing on to the pits, so I suggested that, if we had to back them up to the pits, why didn't we arrange it so that the pits were higher and when the teams dropped their tailgates, they could roll the cars straight off the trucks and into the pit garages, rather than drop them onto the ground and have to lift it up again. They thought it was a good idea, and that's what we did.

"To achieve all this, we needed a lot more space behind the pits, which we didn't have. So that meant moving the track, and it was all becoming a major construction project. This was in the winter of 1975. I explained to John Webb that we were threatened with not having a Grand Prix if we didn't do the work and he said: 'Give me the costs, and I'll go to the finance people.'"

Despite having already extended the existing pits two years before, Webb did not blanche at the prospect of a complete rebuild. "The extra pits we had to build in 1974 were pretty simplistic and needed because of the sharp increase in Formula One entries," he said. "Widening the pit road was also long overdue. We have to remember that, prior to the 1.5-litre F1, the number of rounds in the World Championship could be counted on one or one and a half hands. After this we soon got into the teens – mainly because so many new circuits with 'modern' facilities had been built throughout the sixties and early seventies. This made many circuits, including Brands, Silverstone and Monza, pretty archaic, so the full revamp in 1976 was essential. Car widths, speeds and safety expectations had all increased in the early seventies."

The result was a £300,000 project to realign the track at Paddock Hill Bend and South Bank, and to build a complete new pits complex with a dedicated F1 paddock behind it. Epstein knew that he wouldn't be able to get planning consent for a project of this scale within the available time, so took the decision to press ahead without it. "In fact, it wasn't too bad, because there were certain things we could do," he said. "For instance, estate roads were not bound by planning consent and the track could be regarded as an estate road.

"For the first time in my life, the weather in 1976 was on my side. We had to build a whole new pits structure, a new control tower and a new pit-lane, and we had to fill the valley where the old paddock was. The old paddock was very steep and everything used to roll away downhill.

"Eventually the whatsit hit the fan and I was notified that the planning committee in its entirety wanted to see me in my office at 10 in the morning. I alerted John Webb and David Isaac, the financial director, and I also alerted the kitchen to lay on a really good lunch in the boardroom, which we might or might not use. The committee stood on top of the banking at the north side of the circuit and said: "What's going on here?" We had six full-size JCBs roaring backwards and forwards. We'd put in a plant crossing with traffic lights on Scratcher's Lane behind the circuit, because these JCBs weren't taxed. And by this time we'd half-filled the valley, we'd ripped up the old track, we were starting to do the ground works for the new track, and the place was a hive of activity.

Jackie Stewart

"I never liked it. It was bumpy, it was undulating, it was constantly corkscrewing a car. I hardly ever drove a car at Brands Hatch that felt good. I didn't find it satisfying. The reality for me was that it didn't take the same type of driving skill – it was a graunchy driver with a graunchy performance that would have to be graunchy to take on the track. Nothing wrong with that, and I won a few races there, but I never really enjoyed it. A couple of corners might have been quite good but it wasn't somewhere I ever felt comfortable."

Rear wheels spin as the 1971 European Formula One season gets under way with the non-championship Race of Champions on 21 March. Eventual winner Clay Regazzoni in his Ferrari 312B2 is already edging ahead of Jackie Stewart's Tyrrell 001 and Denny Hulme's McLaren M19. (Michael Hewett)

"So I told them I was moving an estate road, for which I didn't require consent, and that I was filling in a valley that had been a source of aggravation to everybody. I then got a message from John Webb asking if they would care to take a spot of lunch. So we had lunch in the boardroom and afterwards they said that, by Monday morning, they wanted an official planning application on their desk, which I got the architect to do, and it went through. With much muttering and mumbling, they signed off the planning consent. And I got my new track, new pits and new control tower."

What Epstein had failed to tell the planning people was where the spoil had come from for filling in the valley where the old paddock had been. "The quantity surveyor for McAlpine miscalculated how much spoil they were going to get from putting the M20 through Brands," he explained. "We were about the only local landowners who hadn't objected to the motorway, because we had car parks that were utterly unusable if it rained, due to the slope. So when we were approached by what was then the Department of the Environment, we said yes, we would encourage them to build the motorway through Brands. Which they did, and I got various things out of them, including 10 ducts laid under the motorway, sealed off at each end, which nobody knows are there.

"We had planned to build a service station either side of the motorway because we owned the land both sides, and all the electrical cables would have gone through these. We never did go ahead but the ducts are there to this day."

By the end of February 1976, work was progressing well on the track alterations. Fine weather enabled the new Paddock Bend and Bottom Straight to be surfaced in time for the Race of Champions and new names for sections of the track were brought into use for the first time. "I set a policy of renaming them after racing drivers," explained Webb, "except for the Derek Minter Straight, after a motorbike star."

The changes involved the Top Straight being renamed the Brabham Straight and Paddock Hill Bend moved towards the pits, making it tighter and forcing cars to turn in earlier. The old track was left in place as a run-off area. The run up to Druids became Hailwood Hill and the spectator bank around the hairpin was moved back to provide run-off space. Bottom Bend was renamed Graham Hill Bend and here the track changed again: what had been Bottom Straight, but was now called Cooper Straight, was moved back into South Bank all the way to Kidney Corner, which now became Surtees. The long sweep of Clearways was renamed as three corners, McLaren, Clearways and Clark Curve. On

BELOW The 1976 British Grand Prix, and major revisions have been made to the track, as can be seen in this aerial view. Paddock Hill Bend has been tightened but the old track left in place as a run-off area. In the background, the M20 motorway is under construction. (LAT)

the long circuit, the bridge over the track on the exit of Surtees was removed so that a run-off area could be created, and the Portobello Straight between Hawthorn and Westfield was renamed, as mentioned, after Derek Minter.

The relocation of the old Bottom Straight into South Bank freed up the much-needed area behind the pits for a large, flat Formula One paddock. The pit road was doubled in width and 37 new pit garages were constructed, with running water, electricity and doors both front and rear, along with a new control tower and changing room block. The F1 transporters would access the new complex from a widened ambulance gate at the top of Paddock Bend and, during the course of a meeting, the whole circus would be completely self-contained in this area.

All the work was completed in time for the John Player British Grand Prix on 18 July. This was the first year that a Grand Prix had been run on a Sunday in this country, as John Webb explained: "When I first came into contact with motor racing in the early 1950s, it was the law of the land that you could not charge for admission to sporting events on a Sunday. Before my arrival, Brands had apparently been advised that, providing they didn't charge for admission to the basic perimeter of a property, they could organise a special activity

within its inner confines in a 'special enclosure', to which a charge could legally be applied providing the word 'admission' was not used. Different areas treated this contention on an individual local basis but, so far as Kent was concerned, we were never challenged. Thus Brands always operated on Sundays but Silverstone, for example, could not.

"In those days," he continued, "public affairs were subject, much more than now, to church influence. When we negotiated for the Grand Prix in 1962, the RAC observed that the event would have to take place on a Saturday, as the Queen, who was their patron, was also the head of the Church of England and could not be compromised. Apparently, sometime in the seventies the RAC got the nod from the Palace that a Sunday Grand Prix would not cause a problem. By this time, other sports were also involved in cautious expansion to Sundays."

The 1976 Grand Prix was the one that sticks in everyone's mind. James Hunt was battling for the World Championship with Niki Lauda. It was a hot, dry summer and the weather was glorious for the 77,000 crowd that turned out, most of them hoping for a home victory. Hunt and Lauda lined up on the front of the grid but, as they headed towards Paddock for the first time, the Austrian's team mate, Clay Regazzoni, edged ahead of Hunt to take second place. In his enthusiasm, though, he tried to go

BELOW The new Formula One paddock behind the pits was used for the first time for the 1976 John Player British Grand Prix. Around 50,000 tons of chalk and soil were brought in from the nearby M20 motorway site to level the area. (LAT)

inside Lauda's car as they entered the corner and the pair touched. Lauda snapped sideways but managed to hold the slide. Regazzoni spun backwards across the path of the chasing pack.

"It was Clay at his best," said Hunt at the time. "He just didn't appear to brake at all and then he assaulted Niki. For a brief moment I thought I had the pleasure of watching the two Ferrari drivers take each other off the road – and then I realised I was in their accident as well."

Almost everyone managed to avoid the errant Ferrari but poor Hunt had nowhere to go. He nearly scraped around the outside of it but their rear wheels touched, tipping the McLaren into the air. It hung lazily up on two wheels for what seemed an age and then came back down with a thump. Hunt carried on slowly but could tell something was broken.

"I set off again but it was immediately obvious that the steering was damaged," he wrote in his book, *Against All Odds*. "The front suspension was damaged, too, and it was leaping about but still just driveable. I was motoring through the Druids loop when I saw the 'race stopped' flags, the crossed yellow and oil flags, and I gave a whoop of delight."

With chaos at the first corner, cars seemingly everywhere, the senior safety observer had made an instant decision to stop the race. In retrospect, it may have been hasty since, when the dust cleared, it could be seen that the track was not blocked and that most cars had got through unscathed. In many

people's eyes, however, there was sufficient debris in the form of large stones, chalk, dust and pieces of glassfibre to justify the decision. The red flag flew at the start-finish line and now the arguments began.

Brian Jones was enjoying his first Grand Prix as a commentator and remembers the occasion well. "I was despatched to the commentary box at Westfield," he said, "because, although I'd been commentating for a while by then, John Webb didn't think I'd had enough experience to do the main box, so he brought Anthony Marsh back for the weekend. I was fortunate because I had alongside me Keith Douglas, who was a respected commentator himself but that weekend was an RAC observer for the meeting. The one thing I wanted to do at my first Grand Prix, as they came through Hawthorn into Westfield and down into Dingle Dell for the first time, was to call them through and get them all right.

"I think my enthusiasm got the better of me, though. Shortly after the race started and all hell broke loose at Paddock Hill Bend, some of the field came through and I was busy calling them. I was vaguely aware in the background of Anthony Marsh trying to interrupt and I thought: 'No, you bugger, this is my call, my shout.' What he was saying was: 'Brian, the race has been stopped!' So eventually I had to give way.

"What unfolded then was that James, who'd been involved, was able to continue and nipped into the

BELOW *Battle of the titans: James Hunt (McLaren M23) and Niki Lauda (Ferrari 312T2) line up on the grid for the start of the 1976 John Player British Grand Prix. The author is somewhere in the crowd on the startline terrace in the background. (Michael Hewett)*

pits through the slip road on Cooper Straight, and the legality of this was questioned. Anthony was aware that something was going on and this was a delay over whether Hunt was going to be allowed to restart. I decided to rev this up. I said: 'Yes, of course he's got to be allowed to restart.' Keith got out the rulebook and kept feeding me lines as to why he should be allowed to start, rather than why he shouldn't be.

"And Anthony kept saying: 'I don't think we should speculate, we should wait until the officials have made their judgements.' Of course, he was absolutely right. There was only one reference to commentators in the rulebook, and it said: 'Commentators are not officials of the meeting and they should be careful not to contradict or call into question decisions made by the officials of the meeting.'

"Well, I didn't know that and, anyway, they hadn't made a decision at this stage, so we were winding it up. We had no idea about the fuss and kerfuffle and furore that was developing on the Club circuit where the vast majority of spectators were. And we didn't realise that we were actually fuelling the fire of what I can only describe as a popular revolt. I think it was the first time that we saw spectator power in British motor sport."

What was happening back on the start-finish line was an argument over who should be allowed to restart the race. The cars of Hunt, Regazzoni and Jacques Laffite had all been damaged and their spares wheeled into position. But because it was deemed to be a restarted race, rather than a completely new one, spare cars were not allowed. The rule book also stated that no driver should be allowed to take the restart if he had not completed the red flag lap and Hunt, on realising the race had been stopped but not being aware of this rule, had pulled into the back of the pits instead.

When the crowd was informed of this, there was a roar of disapproval, followed by slow hand-clapping. Then beer cans began to be thrown onto the track. John Webb recalled: "The police were badgering Angela in particular and saying: 'You're going to have a riot on your hands, so how are you going to deal with it?'"

Poor Jackie Epstein was right in the firing line. "All the team managers were shouting at each other," he said. "The crowd were throwing bottles and John Webb was on the phone to me saying: 'Sort this out. I don't care what you do, but sort it out.' He was blowing his gasket at me, I was blowing mine at Teddy Mayer of McLaren and Daniele Audetto of Ferrari. They repaired the McLaren on the tarmac in front of the pits, because the whole thing was delayed. But the real drama was that Audetto had put the damaged Ferrari in the pit garage, locked the door and wouldn't let anybody in. Well, I suspected what they were doing was moving the chassis plate from the damaged car to a

BELOW *Clay Regazzoni's Ferrari 312T2 continues to spin, after making contact with James Hunt's McLaren M23 at the start of the 1976 British Grand Prix. (Phipps/Sutton)*

RIGHT *After a first-corner clash with his team mate, Niki Lauda, Clay Regazzoni brings his damaged Ferrari 312T2 into the pits for repair in the 1976 British Grand Prix. Arguments raged about which cars would be allowed to continue while the Ferrari mechanics carried out 'repairs' behind closed garage doors. Ultimately it was established that they switched chassis plates and wheeled out the spare car.* (Michael Hewett)

BELOW *Hunt and Lauda line up on the grid ready for the re-start of the 1976 British Grand Prix.* (Phipps/Sutton)

spare car. You were allowed to repair a car but you weren't allowed to replace it. I was deeply suspicious, as was Teddy Mayer, and that's why there was such a holdup because we were trying to get this sorted out. Everyone was shouting and bawling in the control tower. In the end, Ferrari produced the allegedly repaired car from out of the garage and the whole thing started off. I think they swapped cars but I didn't have the authority to demand they opened the garage."

In fact, Ferrari was indeed using a spare car for Regazzoni, who would eventually have been disqualified had he finished the race.

While all the arguments raged, the McLaren mechanics had worked feverishly to repair Hunt's original car, which was now wheeled back onto the grid. The only question remaining was whether he should be allowed to take the restart, because he had not completed the red flag lap. Eventually it was decided that, as he had still been mobile at the time the red flag was shown, he should be allowed to restart, and the legality of it all could be sorted out later.

After a delay of 50 minutes, Lauda led away again with Hunt behind him. By halfway, the McLaren was closing in on the Ferrari. On lap 45, Hunt dived

ABOVE *Formula 3 cars
line up behind the pits
in June 1976, in
readiness for their heat.
(Author)*

inside his rival at Druids to take the lead. Once more, the crowd made its feelings known.

"I loved racing at Brands Hatch," said Hunt later. 'A real driver's circuit. And it's special because, being a natural amphitheatre, it's very intimate – the crowd are very close to you. And when I arrived at Clearways in the lead, the place just went mad. But you can feel the presence of the crowd, sense the emotion and the movement all the time, even though you are not necessarily looking at them. It's there, and you respond to it."

Respond he did and, at the end of 76 laps, Hunt took the chequered flag to a tumultuous reception, raising both arms aloft in triumph. Over two months later, in September, he was disqualified from the results and the win was handed to Lauda. But right then, nothing else mattered.

By the mid-seventies, Brands Hatch was hosting some form of racing virtually every weekend and was justly dubbed the busiest motor racing circuit in the world.

Webb had succeeded in bringing motor sport to an entirely new and younger audience. In May 1974, a normal BRSCC championship meeting was transformed into something quite different, with sponsorship from and participation by BBC Radio 1. As *Autosport* pointed out, an otherwise run-of-the-mill club meeting, which might only draw 1000 spectators, pulled in 20,000 to see the same races injected with entertainment from radio and pop personalities. Noel Edmonds led the DJ team to victory over a *Top of the Pops* team in the 'Gallon of

Fun' event which rounded off the day and disc jockey Dave Lee-Travis broadcast his Sunday afternoon show live from the track.

"We were innovative, we didn't serve up the same thing," said Webb. "We took the view that, if we give 10,000 free tickets to Vauxhall to give to customers, they wouldn't have come otherwise. And they'd bring some people who wouldn't have free tickets, they'd buy grandstand seats, they'd buy programmes, they'd spend money on catering …"

In readiness for the Grand Prix in 1978, double Armco barrier was installed to replace the sleepers all the way round the long circuit and from Paddock round Druids and to Cooper Straight. Wider run-off areas were made around the Grand Prix circuit and new earth spectator banks created. Toilets and buildings were also now connected to mains drainage.

To promote the race, Webb hired the Royal Albert Hall for £1200 and, on 13 July, staged a BBC televised 'Night of the Stars'. Shirley Bassey topped the bill while other stars included Chris Barber's Jazz Band, Patrick Moore, Lena Zavoroni, Bruce Forsyth, Brotherhood of Man and many of the Formula One drivers. James Hunt played a trumpet solo. "This was all made possible by the BBC chief, Bill Cotton, who enjoyed competing in our Ford Mexico celebrity races and whose father, Bill Cotton Sr, had finished fourth in a shared ERA in the 1949 British Grand Prix at Silverstone," explained Webb.

Two days after the Albert Hall spectacular, on the Thursday before the Grand Prix, Webb also staged a 'meet the F1 drivers' press reception in the

Jody Scheckter

"They altered Paddock Bend over the years and there was one stage, maybe it was the way the car was set up, when you could just throw it into the air, sideways, and just go down the hill. But after that they changed it and you couldn't do that so easily. Maybe the tyres changed. But throwing it up nearly square in the air, then going down the hill like that, it was fantastic. The race I remember best was a non-championship

Jody Scheckter won the 1974 British Grand Prix at Brands Hatch on 20 July in his Tyrrell 007 Ford. (LAT)

F1 race [1976 Race of Champions] and I was one and a half seconds a lap quicker than anybody in the Tyrrell, quite early on. And on the second lap I went into the bend at the back and it just went straight on. In those days, the tyres took a long time to warm up. I think I'd slid the back all the time and heated up the rears, so they stuck and the fronts didn't do anything. I just went straight. My other memory of the place is changing gear ratios in 1971 when I first came over and then, 35 years later, changing the same gear ratios for my son in his Formula Ford in the same place."

banqueting room of the House of Commons. This was made possible because of contacts gained through the annual House of Commons *versus* House of Lords Escort Mexico charity race. Margaret Thatcher, who was at that time leader of the opposition, was one of the MPs who attended. An hour later, official scrutineering took place alongside the Thames next to the Festival Hall and was open to the public free of charge, much to the delight and curiosity of office workers on their way home.

With so much pre-event publicity, it is little wonder that a record crowd of 84,000 turned up on race day. The event also marked the opening of the new Kentagon, which was made available for members of the BRSCC, BARC and BRDC. This £140,000, hexagonal function suite, which was to be available throughout the week as well as during race weekends, was built to replace the old clubhouse and served as a club, bar and conference centre as well as a venue for prizegiving after race meetings.

The Kentagon was opened to the public for the first time later in the year, during the Indycar event – one of Webb's more ambitious, but sadly less successful ventures.

"Angela and I were at Mid-Ohio, watching an F5000 race, and we ran into Dick King, the president of USAC [United States Auto Club]," explained Webb. "It was a throw-away line – would they be interested in coming? And he said he'd take it back to his people and see if they'd take a gamble. I didn't get a

direct answer so I went back to America, saw King again, and fixed it all up. We promoted it under the banner 'The IndyCars Are Coming'. It never crossed our minds that it wouldn't be other than a great success. To amortise the expense, I hired Silverstone as well and ran it over two consecutive weekends. We took all the risks and hired it – I think we paid £10,000 for it. I'd just assumed that the British public had heard of Indianapolis and that they'd know what this was about."

Unfortunately, despite being described by *Autosport* as "the most important British motor racing promotion for many years", the events failed to draw the crowds. "This was an infamous promotion of John's," recalled Brian Jones. "He was always a great one for pursuing ideas and he had the idea that it would be great for the British public to have the opportunity to see the great stars of American racing – AJ Foyt, Gordon Johncock, Danny Ongais, Tom Sneva, Johnny Rutherford, the Unser brothers, Bobby and Al, Rick Mears. The great British public largely said: 'Who?' So instead of getting huge numbers of people, it was a bit of a disaster."

"We flew the Indycars over and ran them at both circuits," said Jackie Epstein. "I had to liaise with the RAC and all the marshals and stewards, because the cars ran on methanol and nobody knew anything about methanol in England. You can't use cement to mop it up if it splits the tank. You have to use something called diatomacious earth [a soft, chalk-

ABOVE *Mario Andretti and Ronnie Peterson, in JPS Lotus 79s, lead away at the start of the 1978 John Player British Grand Prix on 16 July. Although the black-and-gold cars dominated for much of the season, they were out of luck at Brands and both retired early on. (LAT)*

like sedimentary rock that crumbles into a fine powder]. I found out about this when the Indycar people came over early to sort out arrangements and said: 'You can't use cement, you've got to use diatomacious earth because that won't harm the engines and cement will.' And they told me that cement didn't mop up methanol very well, either.

"I'd never heard of this diatomacious earth but I had a chance conversation with an old friend who had a business building swimming pools, and he said: 'We use that in our swimming pool filters. I know all about it. How much do you want?' We took about half a ton of the stuff. We had to train all the marshals how to use it. They also had to learn that, if a car caught fire, the chances were they wouldn't see the flames, because methanol burns clear."

The first race was scheduled for Saturday 30 September at Silverstone, but it rained. The American cars did not run on wet track surfaces and the race had to be postponed until the following day. Consequently the following weekend's event, which was due to be held on the Brands Hatch long circuit, was switched at the last minute to the Club

circuit. The reasoning was that, if it rained, there would be a greater chance of drying out the shorter track more quickly. Fortunately, the weather was fine throughout the weekend and the thin crowd thrilled to the sound of the whistling turbos and the scream of the engines. Danny Ongais, driving a Parnelli VPJ6B, was timed through the speed trap on Brabham Straight at 173mph, but Rick Mears won the race with a Penske PC6.

"We needed 25,000 a day at Silverstone and Brands and we only got about 15,000," said Webb. "We lost £250,000 on the venture, which was about what we'd made on the Grand Prix a few weeks before. To put Grovewood in its context, I didn't get my wrists slapped. John Danny's attitude was: 'Tough luck, but don't do it again.'"

"That was one of the secrets of John Danny," said Brian Jones. "He controlled the company, there was no doubt about that, but he gave John Webb a leash. He did allow JW the room to go with an idea if he thought it was good enough. And a lot of his ideas came off magnificently and were developed and were huge successes, but he had one or two notable failures and this was one of them."

BELOW Hawaiian driver Danny Ongais was the star when USAC's Indycars visited the circuit on 7 October 1978. Driving a Parnelli VPJ6B, Ongais was leading by over a lap when he retired, leaving the win to Rick Mears in a Penske PC6. Ongais shattered the short circuit lap record, leaving it at 41.40s, 104.66mph, and was timed through the speed trap here on Brabham Straight at 173mph. (LAT)

1970

■ Jack Brabham looked all set for victory in the Race of Champions on 22 March until, with just three laps to go, his Brabham BT33 was hampered by ignition problems, leaving Jackie Stewart to win in Ken Tyrrell's new March 701. Brabham limped in fourth behind Jochen Rindt's Lotus 49C and Denny Hulme's McLaren M14A. The two saloon car races produced victories for Frank Gardner's new Boss Mustang and Chris Craft's Broadspeed Escort, Gardner winning on aggregate.

■ Peter Gethin won the Easter Monday Guards F5000 event in his McLaren M10B on 30 March, and repeated his triumph at the 3 May meeting.

■ The BOAC 1000 on 12 April produced one of the greatest drives ever seen at the circuit. Pedro Rodriguez slid his JW Gulf Porsche 917K around a streaming wet Grand Prix circuit to win by five laps, partnered by Leo Kinnunen. Vic Elford/Denny Hulme and Richard Attwood/Hans Hermann finished second and third with more 917s, ahead of the Porsche 908 of Gijs van Lennep/Hans Laine and the best Ferrari 512S, driven by Chris Amon/Arturo Merzario.

RIGHT *Bruce McLaren stands alongside his McLaren M14A in the sloping paddock at the 1970 Race of Champions meeting, watched by an interested crowd. (Gerald Swan)*

BELOW *Jack Brabham rounds Druids corner in his Brabham BT33 during practise for the 1970 Race of Champions. Notice how photographers were allowed to stand on the infield, right next to the track, with no protection whatsoever. (Gerald Swan)*

■ Superb weather greeted the crowds at FordSport Day on 24 May. Jackie Stewart demonstrated his March F1 car and a race for stars such as Stewart, Graham Hill, Piers Courage and John Surtees in identical Ford Capris, eventually won by Courage, was described in *Autosport* as "heart-stopping from beginning to end". As well as the on-track action, spectators were treated to rides around the circuit, a cinema showing racing films, and Chris Barber's Jazz Band.

■ Jack Brabham's bad luck at the circuit continued in the British Grand Prix on 18 July. This time he was just two corners away from taking the chequered flag when his Brabham BT33 ran out of fuel, and Jochen Rindt swept past to victory in the Lotus 72. In post-race scrutineering, Rindt's rear wing was initially judged to be too high but eventually the win was allowed to stand. Behind Brabham, Denny Hulme (McLaren M14D) and Clay Regazzoni (Ferrari 312B) were the only other drivers to complete the race distance.

■ At the Bank Holiday meeting on 31 August, Gerry Birrell won the F3 encounter in a Brabham BT28.

■ At the Guards Motor Show 200 meeting on 18 October, Tony Trimmer, who lived just a mile down the road at West Kingsdown, won the last-ever 1-litre F3 race in his Brabham BT28, thereby securing the Shell F3 championship title.

■ The Boxing Day meeting was cancelled because the circuit was under several inches of snow.

ABOVE *Jochen Rindt and Jack Brabham battle for the lead of the 1970 British Grand Prix. Here Rindt's Gold Leaf Lotus 72 leads the Brabham BT33, but the Australian eventually got past – only to run out of petrol on the final lap, allowing the Austrian to take the win. (Michael Hewett)*

BELOW *Pedro Rodriguez steers his Gulf Porsche 917K through the gloom during the 1970 BOAC 1000 race, in front of a life-size cut-out of a BOAC Boeing 747. (Phipps/Sutton)*

1971

■ Vern Schuppan won the first-ever Formula Atlantic race on 7 March driving a Palliser WDB3, and went on to become the first Yellow Pages Formula Atlantic champion.

■ Clay Regazzoni was a popular winner of the Race of Champions on 21 March in his Ferrari 312B2, beating the Tyrrell 001 of Jackie Stewart and John Surtees's Surtees TS9. The race marked the first appearance of a gas turbine F1 car, the Pratt & Whitney engined Lotus 56B, in the hands of Emerson Fittipaldi, who failed to finish due to a suspension failure. The saloon car races were won by John Fitzpatrick's Broadspeed Escort and Brian Muir's Chevrolet Camaro, and the former won on aggregate when Muir was slowed by a puncture. Colin Vandervell (Brabham BT35) and Bev Bond (Ensign) finished the F3 race side-by-side, and Vandervell got the verdict.

RIGHT *James Hunt in his March 713 turns into South Bank ahead of Bev Bond's Ensign and the Brabham BT35 of eventual winner Colin Vandervell during the Formula 3 race on 20 March 1971. Note the high bank on the outside of the corner. (Gerald Swan)*

BELOW *Andrea de Adamich (pictured) and Henri Pescarolo won the 1971 BOAC 1000 Kms on 4 April with their Alfa Romeo T33/3. It was the marque's first major victory for 20 years. (Phipps/Sutton)*

■ The Autodelta Alfa Romeo T33/3 of Andrea de Adamich/Henri Pescarolo scored the marque's first major win for 20 years in the BOAC 1000 on 4 April, beating the works Ferrari 312P of Jacky Ickx/Clay Regazzoni, which had been delayed after a collision with a backmarker. Jo Siffert/Derek Bell were third with a JW Gulf Porsche 917K. Bev Bond delivered Ensign's maiden victory in the F3 race.

■ Brian Redman in Sid Taylor's McLaren M18 won the Easter Monday F5000 race on 12 April from Frank Gardner in a Lola T192. He repeated the feat at the 26 September meeting with Gardner, who had by then been crowned as the Rothmans European Champion, again in second place.

■ At the summer Bank Holiday meeting on 30 August, Ronnie Peterson won the F2 Guards Trophy in his works March 712M, 15sec ahead of the duelling Brabham BT36s of Graham Hill and Carlos Reutemann. The support races fell to John Miles (Chevron B19) and John Fitzpatrick (Ford Escort RS1600).

■ Tragedy struck the non-championship Formula One Victory Race on 24 October when Jo Siffert was killed in his BRM P160. His team mate, Peter Gethin, was declared the winner of the shortened event over Emerson Fittipaldi (Lotus 72).

DUNLOP
CASTROL
AVON TYRES AVON
FERODO
DAILY EXPRESS
Motor
Oil
AVON TYRES
LUCAS
AVON
CASTROL
CASTROL
PROHIBITED AREA

1972

■ Emerson Fittipaldi gave notice of the season ahead by winning the Race of Champions on 19 March from pole position in his JPS Lotus 72, from Mike Hailwood (Surtees TS9B), Denny Hulme (McLaren M19A) and Peter Gethin (BRM P160). In the previous day's F5000 encounter, Brian Redman

BELOW *Jacky Ickx and Mario Andretti dominated the 1972 BOAC 1000 on 16 April in their Ferrari 312PB. (Phipps/Sutton)*

BOTTOM *Emerson Fittipaldi scored his third victory of the 1972 season on his way to his first World Championship in the John Player British Grand Prix on 15 July, appropriately enough driving a John Player Special Lotus 72D. Here he leads the Ferrari 312B2 of Jacky Ickx. (LAT)*

had taken the laurels in a McLaren M10B. Tom Pryce's Royale RP11 won the F3 event and Frank Gardner's Chevrolet Camaro the saloon race.

■ Two weeks later, the F5000 brigade was back on Easter Monday, 3 April, and this time Graham McRae took the spoils with a flag-to-flag victory in his Leda L27/GM1. Redman had to settle for second place.

■ Ferrari dominated the BOAC 1000 sports car event on 16 April, with Jacky Ickx/Mario Andretti leading home team mates Ronnie Peterson/Tim Schenken in their 312PBs, and the Alfa Romeo T33TTs of Peter Revson/Rolf Stommelen and Vic Elford/Andrea de Adamich.

■ Regulations for the Rothman's 50,000 race were published in April. Billed as the richest motor race in Europe, it was to have a prize fund of £50,000. The race would run over 118 laps of the Grand Prix circuit (312 miles) with a first prize of £20,000. One hundred entries would be accepted, the fastest 30 going into the race. A consolation race would be run for non-qualifiers. The race would be open to all racing cars of unlimited engine swept volume, using pump or turbine fuel.

■ The pits and paddock facilities at the John Player British Grand Prix on 15 July were criticised by the Grand Prix Drivers Association, as was the state of the track at Druids, where holes appeared in the surface due to the heat. At a meeting on the Thursday before the event, the GPDA requested that 20 yards of kerbing was placed at the exit of Kidney Corner, and the work was carried out that night.

■ The Grand Prix was a three-car fight between Emerson Fittipaldi's JPS Lotus 72, the Tyrrell 003 of Jackie Stewart and Jacky Ickx's Ferrari 312B2. Ickx led initially but his V12 lost pressure on lap 49, leaving Fittipaldi and Stewart to battle it out. The Brazilian eventually emerged as the winner, with Peter Revson (McLaren M19A) third. Graham McRae's McRae-Chevrolet won the F5000 race from the back of the grid, and the other support races fell to Roger Williamson's F3 GRD 372 and Frank Gardner's big Camaro.

■ A 'Tour de Hatch' bicycle race was held before the main event, contested mainly by F3 drivers over a single lap of the Club circuit. The winner was Ray Mallock, ahead of James Hunt and Jochen Mass.

■ The much-publicised Rothmans 50,000 on 28 August failed to live up to expectations. It had been billed as Europe's richest motor race and was open to any type of racing car. Entries had been expected from Formula One, Formula 2, Can-Am, sports car and Indycar teams for the 500-kilometre race, which would require refuelling stops. However, the CSI, the governing body of motor sport, had wanted to introduce pitstops to F1 in 1973 but this had been opposed by the Grand Prix teams, who were then hardly in a position to compete in a long-distance race which would require fuel stops. They either had to modify their cars by adding larger fuel cells or not turn up, and the majority chose the latter course. Safety in the pits at Brands was also called into question and the expected entry was depleted due to clashing rounds of the USAC and Can-Am championships in America. In the end, Emerson Fittipaldi took his JPS Lotus 72D to a third victory at the circuit that year, ahead of the McLaren M19A of Brian Redman.

■ One of the sideshow events at the Rothmans 50,000 was a tractor race, contested among others by Emerson Fittipaldi, Tim Schenken, Jody Scheckter, Henri Pescarolo and the winner, Carlos Reutemann.

■ Alan Rollinson was the comfortable winner of the F5000 round on 24 September with Alan McKechnie's Lola T300.

ABOVE *A Yardley McLaren merchandising booth at the 1972 British Grand Prix, selling T-Shirts for £1! (Phipps/Sutton)*

■ Rikki von Opel in his Ensign was crowned as the Lombard North Central F3 champion on 15 October by winning after Andy Sutcliffe, whose works GRD had led the title chase all year, was eliminated in a first-lap clash.

■ A poor crowd of only 15,000 turned up to watch the John Player Victory Meeting on 22 October – the fourth F1 race at Brands that year (including the Rothmans 50,000). Intended as a celebration of the World Championships recently clinched by Emerson Fittipaldi and John Player Team Lotus, the race was ironically and unexpectedly won by Jean-Pierre Beltoise with a Marlboro BRM P180. Fittipaldi's engine broke and Surtees TS9B drivers Carlos Pace and Andrea de Adamich were second and third. Brian Redman's Chevron B24 pipped Graham McRae's McRae to win the F5000 race. The French Martini team beat the British F3 regulars with Jacques Coulon, and Frank Gardner's Camaro won the saloon race. John Webb conceded that he thought there would have to be a reduction in the number of expensive meetings "because the spectators can't afford to pay for them". The admission charge for the meeting had been £1.50 (£1.25 in advance). A covered grandstand seat cost £2.00 extra while an uncovered seat was £1.50 more. Paddock transfers were also another £1.50.

1973

Pre-event publicity through the *Daily Mail*, which was sponsoring the event, and also on Radio Luxembourg, ensured that a 45,000-strong crowd turned out for the Race of Champions on 18 March. *Autosport* reported that people were being turned away at the gate because the event was a sell-out. Peter Gethin won the previous day's F5000 event in his Chevron B24 and emerged the surprise winner of the main race on Sunday as well. Second place in the incident-packed event went to Denny Hulme in a McLaren M23, ahead of F1 debutant James Hunt in a Surtees TS9B. Yet again, Frank Gardner's Camaro won the saloon race.

In May, Noel Edmonds completed his lunchtime show on Radio One and headed for the circuit to take part in a Radio DJ *versus* Record Company race. The DJs included Dave Lee Travis, John Peel and Emperor Rosko. Edmonds won by 5sec in atrocious conditions and announced that he wanted to do more racing. True to his word, he returned in September and won another Radio One DJ race in the ShellSport Mexicos.

A new overhead starter's gantry, sponsored by Lucas, was used for the first time for the FordSport Day on 27 May.

Tony Brise scored a popular home win for his *Kent Messenger* sponsored team in his March 733 in round nine of the John Player International F3 championship on 29 July. Italian F3 driver, 31-year-old Lella Lombardi won the supporting ShellSport Mexico race on her first visit to the circuit.

BELOW *Tony Brise pilots his March 733 on his way to victory in the John Player International F3 Championship race on 29 July 1973. (Phipps/Sutton)*

On 12 August, the Radio Luxembourg Day featured a host of personalities from the music world including Slade, Olivia Newton-John, Suzi Quatro, Keith Emerson, Greg Lake and Carl Palmer, along with Luxembourg DJs Tony Prince and Paul Burnett. More than 11,000 people turned up for the Sutton & Cheam Motor Club organised event. Dennis Priddle demonstrated the ShellSport Luxembourg dragster and nearly had an accident on the top straight.

At the Rothmans F5000 event on Bank Holiday Monday, 27 August, Peter Gethin led from pole but retired after 58 of 65 laps, handing victory to Teddy Pilette in the VDS team's similar Chevron B24.

Brian Henton's works Ensign LNF3/73 scored a convincing win in the F3 championship finale on 30 September, on a cold and blustery day, ahead of Tony Brise's March 733.

Lotus F1 star Ronnie Peterson presented the trophy to Tony Brise, the winner of the final round of the John Player F3 championship, at the annual Motor Show 200 meeting over 20–21 October. By taking the win, Brise also snatched the title from GRD driver Alan Jones. In Sunday's F5000 series finale, Guy Edwards in his Barclays Lola T330 chose the right tyres for the cold conditions to win over 45 laps of the Grand Prix circuit. Among the runners was BRM F1 driver Clay Regazzoni, also in a Lola T330. Despite retiring with a blown engine, Teddy Pilette secured the drivers' championship. The ShellSport Luxembourg team of Tom Belso, Clive Santo and Gijs van Lennep, which was run from Brands Hatch by Jackie Epstein, won the entrants' title.

1974

■ The European Formula One season kicked off with the Race of Champions on 17 March with a very strong entry. McLaren sent three cars, Brabham, Ferrari and Shadow two, and Lotus, Surtees, Lola, BRM, Ensign, Lyncar and Hesketh one each. James Hunt won pole position on the debut of the Hesketh 308, but crashed out of the race. Jacky Ickx, driving the singleton JPS Lotus 72, stunned the spectators with a masterly overtaking move around the outside of Paddock on a streaming wet track, to take the lead from Niki Lauda's Ferrari 312B3 six laps from the end. Peter Gethin had an easy F5000 victory with the VDS team's brand new Chevron B28.

■ The F5000 brigade were back as usual on Easter Monday, 15 April, when Bob Evans in his Lola T332 held off Brian Redman's similar car to take victory. In those days the cars ran at Oulton Park on Good Friday and then headed south for the Brands encounter on the Monday.

■ A record crowd of 93,000 over three days, with 68,000 on race day itself, saw a record entry of 36 cars for the John Player British Grand Prix over 18–20 July. The RAC came in for strong criticism over its handling of the event, however. Niki Lauda's Ferrari, which had dominated the race, developed a slow puncture. The Austrian tried to hang on but, with two laps to go and the tyre almost off the rim, he headed for the pits. A quick tyre change later and he was off, only to find that the exit from the pits was blocked by a course car. He was classified ninth as Jody Scheckter took the flag in his Tyrrell 007 ahead of Emerson Fittipaldi's McLaren M23. Lauda was later awarded fifth place on appeal. Stuart Graham's Chevrolet Camaro Z28 won the Group 1 saloon race and Alan Jones the Atlantic event with Harry Stiller's March 74B.

■ Heavy rain caused the tunnel under the circuit at Paddock to be flooded at the Rothmans F5000 event on Bank Holiday Monday, 26 August. The 60-lap main race was stopped due to torrential rain after 20 laps and restarted 20 minutes later. Bob Evans had been leading easily in his Lola T332 up until that point but, at the restart, Tony Dean got away best and took the win with his Chevron B24.

■ After a year away, the World Championship of Makes sports cars returned to the circuit for the British Airways 1000 on 29 September. The former sponsor of the event, BOAC, had by now merged with BEA and become British Airways, and hence the change in title. The event did not live up to the reputation of its predecessors, because the dominant Matra-Simcas swept to a crushing victory. Jean-Pierre Jarier/Jean-Pierre Beltoise led home team mates Henri Pescarolo/Gérard Larrousse in their MS670Cs. The event was not an economic success, either, because only 7000 paying spectators turned up. Tony Brise dominated the Atlantic race with his works Modus.

■ In the final F5000 race of 1974 on 20 October, Vern Schuppan took the laurels in his Chevron B24/28, while Bob Evans clinched the championship, despite retiring his Lola T332 on the fourth lap.

■ The annual Boxing Day meeting was sponsored by Warner Brothers to promote their film, *Freebie and the Bean*. David Purley brought his F2 Chevron along and won the *What's Up Doc* Formule Libre race.

BELOW *Ronnie Scott leads the opening lap of the 1974 British Grand Prix Ford Escort celebrity support race. (Phipps/Sutton)*

1975

■ The former British women's alpine skiing captain, Divina Galica, embarked on a motor sport career with backing from Southern Organs and ShellSport, in a deal arranged by John Webb. Galica was to drive a Ford Escort in the special saloon and super-saloon car championships.

■ The Club circuit was resurfaced early in the year.

■ Welshman Tom Pryce was a popular winner of the Race of Champions on 16 March in his Shadow DN5, after early leader Jody Scheckter's DFV engine blew in his Tyrrell 007. John Watson made it a British 1-2 with a Surtees TS16, ahead of JPS Lotus 72E drivers Ronnie Peterson and Jacky Ickx. Ian Ashley's Lola T330 was unstoppable in the F5000 event, and Tony Brise's Modus in the Atlantic race. The weather was bitterly cold with snow flurries during the day.

BELOW *Tom Pryce in the UOP Shadow DN5, on his way to victory in the 1975 Race of Champions on 16 March. (Author)*

■ After years of F5000 domination by the 5-litre Chevrolet engine, the new 3.4-litre Ford V6 powered David Purley to victory in his Chevron B30 at the Easter Monday meeting on 31 March.

■ Many 500cc racing cars returned to the circuit on 20 April at the Silver Jubilee Car Race meeting, to mark the circuit's 25th anniversary. The main event of the day was for Formula Atlantic cars and Tony Brise took his fourth win in a row in the category with the works Modus M1.

■ Alan Jones was a popular winner of the Bank Holiday F5000 race on 25 August in the RAM team's V6 March 75A, ahead of Tony Brise and Guy Edwards in Lola T332s. Jones also set a new outright lap record for the short circuit of 43.7s, 102.15mph. The saloon car races were won by Vince Woodman's Camaro and Andy Rouse's Triumph Dolomite Sprint. The meeting had to be switched from the Grand Prix circuit at the last minute because the track was breaking up.

■ It was announced that, in 1976, Formula 5000 would be replaced by a new series for all single-seaters powered by engines up to 5 litres, but would still be called the ShellSport 5000 championship. The idea was popular with everyone except existing F5000 drivers, it seemed.

ABOVE *Peter Gethin in his VDS Lola T400 won the last-ever Formula 5000 event to take place in Britain on 19 October 1975. Gethin had also been the victor in the first-ever F5000 race in 1969. (Author)*

■ In October, the British motor racing community was shocked to learn that Sidney 'Jim' Miller of Southern Organs, and his partner John Bellord, had been listed as missing persons. Southern Organs and its offshoot companies had been major sponsors of many national racing championships and individual drivers. The case was reported as involving the Fraud Squad and Interpol.

■ The last-ever Formula 5000 event in Britain took place at the Motor Show 200 meeting on 19 October. Just like the first one, six years before, it was dominated by Peter Gethin, this time driving a Lola T400. His VDS team mate, Teddy Pilette, clinched the drivers' title. In the RAC British Touring Car Championship event, Stuart Graham took the laurels in his Chevrolet Camaro Z28, but it was Andy Rouse who secured the overall crown in the Triumph Dolomite Sprint.

■ The traditional Boxing Day meeting was run on 27 December and renamed the Christmas Car Races.

1976

■ The second-ever rallycross at Brands (the first having been in 1963) took place on 25 January. The course used the normal starting grid, then turned right onto the grass halfway round Paddock, running down the hill parallel to Pilgrim's Rise, turning right onto the grass behind the marshals' post at Bottom Bend. It then ran across the camber of the hill towards the start, turning left onto the track at Bottom Bend and along the circuit and into Clearways, where it cut across the grass, joining the circuit again at the exit of the corner. A layer of overnight snow did not deter a healthy crowd turning up for the event, which was won by John Taylor with a Ford Escort RS1800.

BELOW *Second-place finisher Alan Jones (Surtees TS19) leads winner James Hunt (McLaren M23) in the 1976 Race of Champions. (Phipps/Sutton)*

■ The Race of Champions on 13–14 March boasted two cars from Lotus and singleton entries from Ferrari, Tyrrell, Brabham, March, McLaren, Shadow, Surtees, Williams, Ensign, Hesketh and Penske, plus private entrants RAM Racing with two Brabhams and Scuderia Everest with last year's Ferrari. It was the first race on the revised track layout. Controversy surrounded the

event as the BBC decided at the last minute not to televise it – due to the "unacceptable" level of advertising on the cars. It was felt, however, that it was the Durex contraceptive sponsored Surtees of Alan Jones that had brought the problem to a head. The race was a cracker, with Jones leading for nearly half the time. Jody Scheckter (Tyrrell 007) forgot he was on cold tyres and threw away second place at Dingle Dell on the second lap. Jones held off a charging James Hunt until the McLaren M23C driver squeezed past and went on to win by 18sec. Jacky Ickx was third with a Williams FW05. The Ford Capris of Gordon Spice and Chris Craft were first and second in the saloon car race.

■ Future World Champion Alan Jones took his Lola T332 to a flag-to-flag victory and set a new lap record of 42.6s, 101.70mph, along the way at the Easter Monday ShellSport 5000 meeting on 19 April. On 30 June, though, it was David Purley's turn to take the honours in his Chevron B30, after a close battle with the March 751 of Damien Magee.

BELOW *A Modsports race gets under way in June 1976.* (Author)

ABOVE *James Hunt shakes hands with Niki Lauda on the podium after the 1976 British Grand Prix. (LAT)*

■ James Hunt won a dramatic British Grand Prix in his Marlboro McLaren M23 after the race had been stopped due to a first-corner pile-up. Hunt had been one of those involved and there was initial uncertainty as to whether he would be able to take the restart, much to the anger of a 77,000-strong crowd. Hunt did start, and beat Niki Lauda's Ferrari 312T2 into second place, but he was disqualified from the results two months later. The main support races were won by Bruno Giacomelli's works March-Toyota and Vince Woodman's Ford Capri.

■ Despite a good entry which included seven F1 cars, nine F5000s, 19 F2s and 11 Formula Atlantics, nearly all of which turned up, only a small crowd turned out to see David Purley's V6 Chevron B30 take victory in the ShellSport 5000 Bank Holiday Monday event on 30 August, ahead of Bob Evans's V8 McLaren M25 and Eddie Cheever in Ron Dennis's Project 4 Ralt RT1 F2 car. Divina Galica won the ShellSport Ladies' Escort race from pole position.

■ The penultimate round of the ShellSport 5000 championship at the Motor Show 200 meeting on 24 October resulted in a win for Keith Holland in Len Gibbs's Lola T400.

■ John Webb decided to stage an extra ShellSport 5000 round during the Formula Ford Festival on 7 November and turn the meeting into a tribute to Britain's new World Champion, James Hunt. David Purley, who had already secured the ShellSport title, won in the rain in his Lec Chevron B30, while Derek Daly was the winner of the Festival in a Hawke DL17. Hunt demonstrated his new McLaren M26 for an 11,000 crowd and Niki Lauda was also there to sign autographs.

RIGHT *In 1976, the old Formula 5000 gave way to the ShellSport 5000 series, open to all single-seaters up to 5-litres except Formula Ford. The field makes a spectacular sight through the trees on August Bank Holiday Monday as it exits Paddock Hill Bend. (Author)*

1977

■ Despite the absence of the Grand Prix, the circuit crammed in 72 days of racing and qualifying. A season ticket for Brands Hatch cost just £15 and provided admission for 37 race meetings.

■ A faulty ignition switch robbed Mario Andretti of victory in the Marlboro *Daily Mail* Race of Champions on 20 March. James Hunt trailed the JPS Lotus 78 all race in his McLaren M23 but had not been able to pass the American. A fine drive by pole man John Watson in his Alfa Romeo V12 engined Brabham BT45B, which was delayed by a puncture, recovered third place behind

Jody Scheckter (Wolf WR1). Colin Vandervell's Capri won the saloon race.

■ Val Musetti in a March 751 won the ShellSport International race on Easter Monday, 11 April, ahead of Bruce Allison's Chevron B37.

BELOW *Mario Andretti (JPS Lotus 78), James Hunt (McLaren M23), John Watson (Brabham BT45B), Jody Scheckter (Wolf WR1) and Ronnie Peterson (Tyrrell P34) lead the field around Druids at the start of the 1977 Race of Champions on 20 March. (Author)*

ABOVE *Stephen South sits on the grid in his March 763 during the BP F3 meeting on 29 May 1977. (Author)*

■ The BRSCC moved its offices from Chiswick to Brands Hatch in May, taking over the former offices of John Webb and MCD.

■ The new paddock was completed with the planting of over 1000 trees in 'garden' areas between the hard-standing. The paddock now featured a ring road with two intersections running between the hard-standing areas. *Autosport* reported that the garden areas were intended to provide shade and to be used for picnics, but that competitors were parking on them and draining their excess oil into them.

■ Stephen South won the BP F3 championship final in his March 763 on 29 May, from Derek Daly's Chevron B38. Despite a full entry and fine weather, the crowd was disappointingly small.

■ Brands Hatch Racing was launched at the end of May, with the intention of providing members of the public with the opportunity to train and race at the circuit. It was emphasised that this was not just another racing school or a revamped Motor Racing Stables, but would allow the man-in-the-street to do anything from drive his own car around to receiving race tuition, and right up to the chance of driving an F1 car. The expert team of instructors included Tony Lanfranchi, Gerry Marshall, Barrie Williams, Ian Taylor, Mike Wilds and Tony Dron. A fleet of 27 cars was available, including ShellSport Escorts, Elden FF1600s and a Lola T490 Sports 2000.

■ World Champion James Hunt was honoured at a special meeting on 26 June, which included an extra round of the ShellSport International Championship for the James Hunt Trophy. Hunt signed autographs and presented the trophy to Tony Trimmer who was victorious in his Surtees TS19.

■ Australian driver Brian McGuire and fire marshal John Thorpe were killed during practice for the ShellSport Group 8 race on

ABOVE *Jacky Ickx (Martini Porsche 935-77) and Hans Stuck (BMW 320) lead the pack around a streaming wet Druids Bend on the first lap of the FIA World Championship of Makes endurance race on 25 September 1977. (Author)*

Bank Holiday Monday, 29 August. McGuire's car crashed at Stirling's Bend, turning upside down and striking three fire marshals who were standing on the bank at the exit of the corner. The race was won by Emilio de Villota in a McLaren M23. Tony Trimmer was robbed of victory by a deflating tyre on his Surtees TS19.

■ During his season-long battle for the BP championship with Derek Warwick, Derek Daly won the F3 race on 11 September with Derek MacMahon's Chevron B38. Warwick's Ralt RT1 finished third behind Eje Elgh's Chevron.

■ The Martini Porsche 935-77 of Jacky Ickx/Jochen Mass dominated a very wet FIA World Championship of Makes endurance race on 25 September. The race, for Group 5 cars, was stopped after an hour and a quarter due to the conditions. After an hour's delay, it was restarted without the only car able of challenging the latest works Porsche, a works turbocharged BMW 320 driven by Hans Stuck/Ronnie Peterson, which the former had buried in the catchfencing. Privately entered Porsche 935s filled the next four places.

■ The Motor Show 200 meeting on 16 October featured the last-ever ShellSport Group 8 race, won in style by Guy Edwards in his March 751 from the 1977 champion, Tony Trimmer in a Surtees TS19.

■ The Brazilian driver, Chico Serra, driving a Van Diemen, was the winner of the Formula Ford Festival on 6 November.

1978

■ The opening round of the European Touring Car Championship on 12 March provided a win for the BMW CSL of Tom Walkinshaw/Umberto Grano. Walkinshaw had closed inexorably in on team mates Carlo Facetti/Martino Finotto over the last few laps of the race and finally took the lead just two laps from the end.

■ At the Aurora F1 event on Easter Monday, 27 March, Guy Edwards's March 751 led Tony Trimmer's McLaren M23 for much of the race until the pair tangled at Druids. Edwards spun down to fourth place while Trimmer raced on to win.

■ Derek Warwick won the F3 encounter on 16 April in his Ralt RT1, ahead of Nelson Piquet's similar machine. On 11 June, it was Piquet's turn to win, ahead of Warwick.

■ Carlos Reutemann, driving a Ferrari 312T3, emerged the surprise winner of the British Grand Prix on 16 July, after the much-fancied JPS Lotus 79s of Mario Andretti and Ronnie Peterson had both retired. Niki Lauda looked the winner in his Alfa Romeo powered Brabham BT46 but, on the 60th lap, he was baulked as he went to lap the McLaren of Bruno Giacomelli at Clearways, and Reutemann was through. John Watson in the

BELOW *Guy Edwards in his March 751 spins at Druids after tangling with the McLaren M23 of Tony Trimmer during their battle for the lead of the Aurora F1 event on Easter Monday, 27 March 1978. (Author)*

BELOW *Niki Lauda's Brabham BT46 Alfa seemed on its way to victory in the 1978 British Grand Prix on 16 July. However, as he came up to lap Bruno Giacomelli in the third McLaren M26 at Clearways, he was momentarily baulked, despite the Italian apparently waving him through (as seen in the photograph). This allowed Carlos Reutemann to haul his Ferrari 312T3 upalongside the Brabham and take the lead into Paddock Bend. (Michael Hewett)*

other Brabham and Patrick Depailler (Tyrrell 008) were the only other men to run the full distance. The BP F3 championship race had 35 starters and was stopped after a big first-corner shunt. After the restart, Nelson Piquet spun his Ralt RT1 and could not catch winner Chico Serra's March 783 and the Ralts of Derek Warwick and Andrea de Cesaris. Jeff Allam's Capri won the saloon car race and, in a hectic Escort Celebrity race, Frank Williams defeated Stirling Moss and Jackie Oliver.

■ Tony Trimmer again took victory with his McLaren M23 in the Aurora F1 race on Bank Holiday Monday, 28 August, clinching the title. It was Brian Muir's turn to win the British Saloon Car event with his Ford Capri.

■ A disappointingly small crowd turned out on 7 October to see the USAC Indycar race. Danny Ongais was leading in his Parnelli VPJ6B by over a lap when his clutch broke, leaving Rick Mears and Tom Sneva to bring home a 1-2 for Roger Penske's team. Ongais shattered the short circuit lap record, leaving it at 41.40s, 104.66mph. The Club circuit was subsequently renamed the Indy circuit to commemorate the visit of the American cars to the track.

■ On the last lap of the last round of the Vandervell F3 series, which supported the Indycars, Derek Warwick's Ralt RT1 caused the March 783s of Chico Serra and Brett Riley to collide. Warwick's win cemented his title.

■ Everything came right for Irishman Michael Roe at the Formula Ford Festival on 5 November. Fourth at the end of the first lap in the final, the works Van Diemen driver took the lead as others fell off at Paddock Hill Bend and won the race, with just 0.9sec covering the first four cars.

BELOW *A US racing legend visited Brands Hatch for the 1978 USAC Indycar race on 7 October – AJ Foyt drove his Coyote-Foyt 78 to fourth place. (LAT)*

1979

■ Originally scheduled for 18 March, the Race of Champions had to be postponed due to heavy snow. MCD and the organising club, the BRSCC, had to make hundreds of telephone calls the Thursday before to notify all the F1 teams, officials, marshals and supporting race competitors of the postponement. They were not in time to stop the Ferrari team, which had already set off from Italy, from arriving.

■ The race was rescheduled for Easter Sunday, 15 April, and only seven FOCA entries were received. To make up the numbers, the F1 cars were included from the Aurora AFX championship, a round of which had been due to take place on the Monday. It meant a tough schedule for the Aurora teams, which were also running at Oulton Park on Good Friday. The F2 and Atlantic runners from the series were given their own separate race. On an unseasonably warm day, Niki Lauda's Brabham BT48 led the main event but was soon in the pits for new tyres. Mario Andretti's Lotus 79 took over but faded to finish third behind the Ferrari 312T3 of Gilles Villeneuve and Nelson Piquet's Brabham. Rupert Keegan's Arrows A1 was leading the Aurora F1 class but blew its DFV five laps from the end, handing it to Guy Edwards (Fittipaldi F5A). Divina Galica finished second in the F2/Atlantic race behind Norman Dickson, both in F2 March 792s.

BELOW *Motoring journalist Sue Baker presents Mario Andretti with champagne for securing pole position for the 1979 Race of Champions. (Phipps/Sutton)*

■ The FIA European Touring Car teams returned to the track on 29 April, with Raymond van Hove, Jean Xhenceval and Pierre Dieudonné taking victory in their Luigi team BMW CSL. From pole position, Carlo Facetti/Martino Finotto led for a long while with their similar, Jolly Club entry, but Facetti crashed on oil at Clearways.

■ World Championship sportscars returned to Brands for the Rivet Supply 6 Hours endurance race on 5 August. The four-year-old Porsche 908/4 Group 6 sports-prototytpe of Reinhold Joest/Volkert Merl dominated the event, overcoming a terrific drive by Klaus Ludwig in the Kremer team's second-placed Porsche 935 K3 Group 5 car.

■ In the Aurora AFX F1 meeting on Bank Holiday Monday, 27 August, Ricardo Zunino's Arrows A1B took the lead from Guy Edwards's Fittipaldi F5A at Paddock on the first lap and Zunino never looked back, taking an effortless win.

■ Donald Macleod won the Formula Ford Festival for a second time on 4 November, having first been victorious in 1973. This time he was driving a Sark, a car he had manufactured himself, and steered it to victory in appalling conditions.

■ In order to deter corner cutting by competitors, heavily ribbed rumble strip kerbing was installed on the inside of Druids Hill Bend at the end of the year.

RIGHT *Gilles Villeneuve demonstrates his typically spectacular driving style on the way to winning the 1979 Race of Champions on 15 April in his Ferrari 312T3. (LAT)*

1980s

A TIME OF CHANGE

A piece of motor racing history was made in 1980 when Desiré Wilson became the first woman to win a Formula One race, taking a Wolf WR4 to victory in the Aurora championship round at Brands Hatch on Easter Monday, 7 April.

John Webb had always seen the publicity benefit of running female racing drivers and had encouraged and helped a few along the way. "The first was Lella Lombardi," he remembered. "We saw her in the Formula 3 race at the Monaco Grand Prix. We'd just started running celebrity races in Ford Mexicos and Angela invited Lella to come over and drive in one. She did and she won it. Jackie Epstein was then running a Formula 5000 team and I said to him: 'This girl's quite good, at the end of the season give her a run in the 5000.' She did 52 laps round the full circuit, quicker than anybody else had done, and she came in and said she thought a tyre was going down. Jackie realised she wasn't just a quick driver, she had sensitivity.

"There was also Divina Galica, and Ann Moore – although that wasn't so successful. But Desiré was incredible. When she became the first woman to win a Formula One race, that was a particularly satisfying moment, and one of my favourite memories." In recognition of this remarkable feat, Webb named the grandstand at the end of the main straight for her.

Wilson had come to the UK in 1978 from South Africa with her husband, Alan, at Webb's invitation to drive in one of the ladies' Escort races. Desiré had come to his attention having won the South African 'Driver to Europe' award the previous year and had spent 12 months living and racing in the Netherlands. It was to prove a fortuitous meeting.

"We flew back to England, we had no money, one-way tickets, no work permits, nothing," explained Alan Wilson. "We just went on the off-chance. We met John and he told Des he would see what he could do to help her, but there were no promises or anything like that. Then he asked me

RIGHT *A capacity crowd saw Nigel Mansell take a dramatic win in the final Grand Prix to be held at Brands Hatch in July 1986.*
(sutton-images.com)

about my background. I'd come from the Ford Motor Company, and John asked if I would like to come and work at the track and get it ready for the British Grand Prix in July. This was Easter weekend, March 1978. I started but we had no work permits. So I was working as an illegal immigrant, basically.

"It was going to be a temporary job," Wilson continued, "just helping getting the track ready. John had lost his previous track manager after Jackie Epstein, who left in late 1976, and only had a track foreman. The place was looking pretty decrepit and John hated that. He was a stickler for things looking good.

"There had been bad feeling between the labour force and the previous track manager, and the place was fairly run-down. I got on top of the job fairly quickly. I went in and the labour force would sit around while I negotiated with the shop foreman. He was a really good guy and played a huge role behind the scenes in resolving union problems, getting Brands operating well.

"It took me about two months to get the track workers on my side. When they wouldn't work, I went out on the track and put stakes in myself, and when they saw what I was doing, they said: 'He's OK,' and came and worked with me. We had a labour team of 14. By the time of the Grand Prix, we had a really good team and had redone the track. I

BELOW *John Webb poses with three of his female protegées. Left to right: Juliette Slaughter, Divina Galica and Desiré Wilson. (John Webb Collection)*

had a standard policy – I put a can of white paint in each of the trucks and said: 'If anything's standing still, paint it white.' And by Grand Prix day we had the place absolutely pristine.

"So then John wanted me working full-time, so he went and pulled strings with various politicians and Members of Parliament, all of whom he knew through the annual Lords *versus* Commons race. There was a very good reason for holding that event, because it gave Brands and John tremendous access to decision makers in government. He's not stupid.

"John Webb was the best motor racing promoter the world has ever seen. I've seen some of the best, and none of them ever came close to him.

"So he was able to get them to call the Home Office and suddenly Des and I became legal. Then he made me track manager and at the end of the year he made me track manager of all four tracks. A year later, I was on the full board of directors of MCD and my role was construction, development, safety and all operations. At that stage, four of us ran the company: John was in overall charge, Angela handled all marketing and hospitality, David Isaacs was the finance officer and I was the director of operations. Those titles evolved, as John never gave titles, but the four of us, along with Juliette Slaughter who looked after the media, ran the circuit at that time."

After the 1978 Grand Prix, Alan Wilson's next task was to bring the track into line with the latest safety requirements. Thinking on safety had evolved over the years. Earth banks, lined with old railway sleepers, had once been the norm, but now providing run-off areas and catchfencing to slow down errant cars was the thinking. Wilson puts the change in requirements down to the change in design of the cars.

"Jackie Stewart was the first person really to bring safety to race tracks," he said. "They had barriers right on the edge of the track in those days, and no run-off areas, because the cars he raced broke apart so easily it was better to hit the wall and stop – to have one impact rather than have the car bouncing across a run-off area, rolling and disintegrating, because they just weren't so strong.

"But as the cars got stronger and motorcycles got faster, that situation killed bike racers, because they were running straight into barriers. So the next phase was to move the barriers back as far as we could, and that was my responsibility.

"I worked particularly with Robert Langford and Derek Ongaro from the RAC, who were the FIA safety inspectors for Grands Prix," he continued. "They would go round the world and come back and say: 'Alan, we've seen this in Australia, or wherever,' and I'd run a test on it at Brands or Oulton or Mallory or Snetterton.

"We actually developed tyre walls. There'd been tyre walls before, particularly in America, but they were just tyres thrown up against the bank. We were the first people to strap tyres together and put a fence in front of them. There was one day when I arranged at Mallory to have three different types of construction of tyre walls put up on the outside of the 'S'. And we went and stood on top of the bank during a Formula Ford race and watched the cars hit the tyre wall, and decided which construction worked best. It was testing by reality!"

One of the problems Wilson faced was accommodating the different safety requirements of car racers and bike riders.

"We put catchfencing up at Brands before the 1978 Grand Prix," he said. "Catchfencing was incredibly effective at reducing damage and injury – except that a motorcyclist could hit the upright, or a car could break the post and a post would swing around attached to the fence. At Silverstone, Kenny Gray from South Africa was critically injured and never raced again through an upright hitting him on the head, and there was a rider killed at Zandvoort.

"What we did was go to the ACU, who then ran bike races, and tell them what we were doing. I worked closely with Steve Potter, who was then one of the top short-circuit riders. He was instrumental in making the motorcycle people happy with what we were doing. Sadly, he was killed at Oulton when he fell on his head. That was a real tragedy because he was quietly, behind the scenes, very important in mixing the bike safety with car safety."

Another difficulty for Wilson was getting the right balance between providing a suitable run-off area at a corner, by moving earth banks back, but still making the circuit spectator-friendly. "The secret is to push the barriers away in a head-on situation and put the spectators on the sides looking at the cars cross in front of them, not coming at them," he explained. "John took a leading role in giving me the budget I needed. We did work at Paddock and Clearways and put up all the spectator banks around that area, and we did Westfield. These are all things that five years later were out of date. The big thing at Brands was that all the guardrail posts were rotten. We had a programme where every morning the crew went out changing guardrail posts. Nobody knew it was happening. We went round the whole track putting in debris fencing and spectator fencing, and we built the new medical centre."

The £50,000 medical centre was built on the edge of the Clearways loop and was completed in time for the 1980 British Grand Prix in July.

BELOW *A feature of the 1980 Grand Prix season was the Procar championship, which supported eight Grands Prix. It featured the top five drivers from the first practice session for the Grand Prix, along with the series regulars, all in identical BMW M1s. Here Didier Pironi (25) gets very sideways at Druids as Wolfgang Schütz, Sigi Müller and the rest of the field follow. (Author)*

"We'd had a phone call the previous December from Bernie Ecclestone, telling us we had to have a new medical centre," explained Wilson. "And he told us to speak to Sid Watkins about it. I knew that we wouldn't get formal planning permission in time to have it ready for the Grand Prix in July, so I spoke to David Isaacs and we decided to build it as a temporary unit, rather than a permanent one. So I went to Wales and found a modular company which would build the medical centre for us. They designed it there, built it, shipped it in and erected it in time for the Grand Prix. So we had a medical centre in six months that would probably have taken two years of obtaining permanent planning consent plus a hell of a lot of money to build.

"We opened it for the first time at the motorcycle club race meeting the weekend before. Then, during a Saturday practice session on the Grand Prix weekend, Peter Mann, who had entered an ERA in the Historic race, went end-over-end at Clearways. They pulled him out, got him into the medical centre, opened him up, removed his spleen and saved his life.

"At the same time, we built the first of the two hospitality units, the one nearer Paddock, which became the Brabham Centre. John gave me a budget of £150,000 to build it and he got it funded by renting out all the units for three years. So it was fully paid for before we even built it. It came in at £155,000 and John gave me hell for being £5000 over budget."

The Grand Prix was very much a three-day affair, admission on practice days priced at £2.50 for adults and £1.00 for children. A paddock pass was just £2.00. On race day, tickets cost £7.50 (£6.50 if booked in advance) and £2.20 for children, and a paddock transfer £5.40. The grandstands had long been sold out. There was plenty of entertainment packed into the weekend. Spectators could take coach rides around the circuit on race morning from 06.30 to 09.00 and the programme included a BMW Procar race on the Saturday, in which some of the Grand Prix drivers took part, a Formula 3 race on the Sunday morning, a Lords *versus* Commons race, an Historic race, and a round of the British Saloon Car Championship to round things off. The two practice and qualifying days drew a record crowd of 30,000, while 90,000 people attended on race day.

What not many people realise is the degree of cooperation that existed between Brands Hatch and Silverstone at the time, particularly regarding the organisation of the British racing calendar.

"There was a short period when I was being groomed ultimately to take over from John," said Alan Wilson. "He was looking longterm to retire and I would be the guy to run it. So he used to take me to the RAC meetings where schedules were authorised and the politics and strategy of British racing was planned, theoretically by the RAC because they headed it. In reality, John would go for lunch with Jimmy Brown and Sidney Offord, and they would sit around the table and thrash it out. I had the privilege to be a fly on the wall. I just kept my mouth shut and listened.

"Between them, they would plan the full operation of British club racing. They would agree: 'You guys run this race, we'll run that.' We would sit there and they would strategise everything and then the RAC would rubber-stamp it and take the credit for it. At that time, *Autosport* and *Motoring News* were always saying how much Jimmy hated John, and they never talked to Sid, and there was always competition between them. And they played along with this, but in fact they were on the telephone, not daily, but on a regular basis. They ran British club racing, which is why it was so good at that time. They were brilliant, those three, and when they all left it just disintegrated into a morass of different championships and one-make series and everything that's wrong with it at the moment. You could absolutely put a time line on that – when the three of them ceded control of British racing, it went downhill."

"What usually happened was that I would do the first calendar," said Webb. "Normally the others hadn't even started to think about it. They had little option but to adopt my vision of what they should be doing. Without wishing to sound big-headed, I think I was always the leader when it came to the calendar, certainly. My relationship with Jimmy Brown at Silverstone was excellent. Certain other people on the BRDC board always took the attitude that Brands shouldn't really be there – 'We're Silverstone, so we're British motor racing.' But Jimmy and I were commercial people, we got on very well.

"I would meet with Jimmy and Sidney Offord of the BARC," Webb continued. "I would do the initial schedule because I was more of a motor racing man than they were. Unlike me, they didn't watch every race, every weekend, and form opinions from it. So I didn't find it difficult for Jimmy to take a lead from me. He was protective of his key dates – if I'd scheduled something that clashed with the *Daily Express* Trophy Race at Silverstone, he would pick up on that and tell me to get off it. But so long as it seemed logical to him, and I'd taken his particular circumstances into account, that was fine. I would even allocate some rounds of their championships for them."

Johnny Herbert

"The Brands I knew in the early eighties, when I did Formula Ford, was great. The Grand Prix circuit was damn good, especially the old Dingle Dell and the old Westfield. Then they changed it in about 1987 and now there's the Dingle Dell we have today, which I don't like. The old Dingle Dell was a wonderful, wonderful corner.

"The Formula Ford Festival of 1985 is one of my outstanding memories. The first lap out of the pits in qualifying, on a slightly damp track, I was looking up to Druids thinking: 'In 20 minutes, that'll be much drier.' The next minute, I was clambering out of the car in the catchfencing. It was not the most positive start to the weekend. Having to qualify with the pre-74s, getting on the back of the first heat with a 10sec penalty, moving through towards the front as the rounds went by, and then being on the front row for the final – that was all fantastic in itself. But then to get just the perfect start and then win the race itself, well, it was very, very important for my career. It was the first time anybody had won from the back in a Formula Ford Festival. I know a couple of people have done it since but that was, wow, fantastic.

"When I looked at it, I reckoned there were probably only half a dozen of us who could win it: I think the others were Jonathan Bancroft, Damon Hill, Mark Blundell, Bertrand Gachot and Paulo Picasci. That meant I could probably get to the back end of that lot by the final, because I'd be able to beat everybody else. So that was my way of looking at it.

"The Formula 3000 race in 1988 was something else. It was all very good in qualifying and I was on pole. Martin Donnelly, my new team mate, was second on the grid. I made a good start and had about a 10–12sec lead when they red-flagged the race because Gregor Foitek took off Roberto Moreno.

Unfortunately, on the restart I parked differently on the grid – why, I really don't know, but the pole at Brands was always a pain because it was in a dip. So I parked it up thinking that, by the time I got moving, it would come down, but in fact it just sort of carried on going that way. And the wheels were spinning and I lost out and I think I was third.

"But I knew it was an aggregate race anyway, so it didn't matter so much because of the 12 seconds in hand. Foitek sort of banged wheels with me at Druids and then, as we went onto the Grand Prix circuit, I saw he had a slight run on me. But I knew that, if I went to the middle of the track, slightly left, then he wouldn't be able to pass me. But he tried to do it on the grass, on the left-hand side just before we came to the bridge, and he just clipped my rear wheel. That just turned me left which was where, unfortunately, the bridge was. The Armco didn't go straight down the hill, it actually went round the bridge. If it had been flat I would have just glanced it and ricocheted, but I hit it head-on. The impact basically broke off most of the front of the car, but I think I took most of my damage when I spun across the track and then hit the barrier head-on the other side, because my legs were just hanging out at the front. The second impact gave them a good old smack.

"So that was the negative side of it, but it never put me off, because it was a fabulous track and that's part of racing. It was a shame, but it could have been worse. At least I was still able to have a career afterwards. It wasn't what I wanted, it wasn't the same as before, but I was still able to do it."

1985 Formula Ford Festival winner Johnny Herbert leads the field in his Quest FF85 during the final on 27 October. (sutton-images.com)

Brands Hatch fixture booklet was out before the Racing Car Show each January."

A footnote to the relationship between Webb and Brown was provided by Brian Jones. "When Jimmy Brown was retiring as the general manager of Silverstone," Jones said, "he was invited down to Rochester and John arranged to put him in a Spitfire, which he'd flown in the war, and he flew over Brands Hatch. That was a gesture by a man who had huge respect and regard for his leading competitor. They had had some incredible fights over the years, but I think it says a great deal about both the relationship and the style of people in those days."

Not only the way the racing calendar was put together was different in those days. The very content and organisation of a race meeting has also changed. In the late sixties and early seventies, John Symes was a member of the Sevenoaks & District Motor Club, which ran two meetings a year at Brands Hatch. He started marshalling at the meetings and steadily increased his involvement, moving up in the organisational side until becoming secretary and clerk of the course.

"At that time, a lot of the smaller clubs were also running race meetings, people like West Essex, Maidstone & Mid-Kent and Rochester Motor Club," he explained. "Motor racing then was still about 'trophy' races, it wasn't centred on championships the way it is now. A typical meeting at Brands might have a round of the Townsend Thoresen Formula Ford championship and a round of some other series, but all the other races would be stand-alone events for a trophy. Whereas now, they tend to be all championship races. So in those days, the smaller clubs could put on race meetings at Brands quite successfully.

"It was cost-effective for a club to hire the circuit and we did a fairly reasonable job. I eventually became chairman of Sevenoaks club, which meant I had the job of negotiating the rent with John Webb. One year I was negotiating with him for the hire for our race meeting in November, and he'd hiked the hire fee, so I was arguing with him. I threw in the comment: 'Think of all the gate money you get.' He answered: 'The gate money isn't even worth collecting – it's so worthless, you can have it.' So I agreed. We shook hands on it and we ran our meeting. At that time, for a winter 'clubbie', a typical crowd would be around 700–800, and each would pay about £1.50. Neither of us could ever work out why, but at that particular meeting we had a crowd of 2300 people. I walked in the Kentagon at the end of the meeting and John was in his usual place at the bar, and he said: 'You've done alright today, Symesy –

In fact, it is fair to say that Webb was guiding, if not actually running, the whole of British motor sport at the time. "Not by intent," he said. "I was allowed to. I think one of the key factors was that I did watch every race. I'd keep a lap chart of everything. I can't remember individual races now, I can't tell you who won what, but I would come away from a meeting with a definite opinion about a particular class of racing or if a particular driver was cheating. That really got up my nose more than anything else. Cheating drivers – using their tactics on the track or using a part of the circuit that wasn't the track consistently to gain an advantage."

Doug Jennings, who was the competitions secretary of the Brands Hatch Racing Club from 1987, also remembered the meetings to set the calendar. "They would get together before Christmas in C20, John Webb's hospitality suite at Brands Hatch, and the entire motor racing calendar for all the circuits would be dovetailed together," he said. "My equivalents at Thruxton and Silverstone and I would be having a coffee in the Kentagon and, by lunchtime, this sheaf of paper would arrive. We'd go into C20 and, if we didn't come out with the motor racing calendar for all our circuits by the end of the afternoon, we'd get some earache. We'd already have the International dates, because they'd have been sorted already. We'd just build the rest round them. One of JW's targets was that the

you've made more money than me. Well done – but you won't do it next year!' But there was never any argument, because we'd done the deal and that's what happened, end of story. You will never, ever find anyone who will say anything other than, if you did a deal with John, you'd done the deal and that was it. Absolutely cast-iron. A man of honour."

By the mid-eighties, however, as far as car racing was concerned, it was almost exclusively the BRSCC (British Racing & Sports Car Club) and the BARC (British Automobile Racing Club) which were the organising bodies. Webb was not convinced they were doing a good enough job, particularly the BRSCC which, by that time, was based at the circuit. He decided to do something about it and set up his own organising club.

"In the case of the BRSCC, it was because of continued diminution of ability compared to where they used to be in the seventies," he explained. "By the eighties, they weren't as good. They began to get more and more committee-bound, which is a fault of motoring clubs. To run motor sport efficiently, you've got to be a dictator. You need somebody to be in charge. I was lucky there – I was always in charge."

The man Webb chose to run the club for him was John Symes, who took up the story: "At that time, the BARC wasn't doing terribly well, and the BRSCC wasn't doing much better. John, in common with one or two other people, felt there was a distinct possibility that one or other of them could go under or, alternatively, that they would amalgamate. That would basically give him a choice of 'x' or 'x', and already he only had a choice of 'x' or 'y'. So his logic behind setting up the club was that he felt it would do two things. First, it gave him an insurance policy so that if one of them went under or they amalgamated, then he would have an alternative, his own race organisation. And second, he felt that, by setting up his own club, it would encourage the BRSCC and the BARC to get their backsides into gear and raise their game. Which it did.

"The original deal was that he provided all the admin support and so on, and I put a team together. Fortunately, because I was already running race meetings at Brands, albeit only two a year, I'd already got the basics there. So all I did was surround myself with friends and we started off just running four meetings a year."

One of the people who joined Symes at the new Brands Hatch Racing Club was Doug Jennings. "I started as the competitions manager in September 1987," he explained. "It was my job to put all the event timetables together. I'd submit them to John Webb, who'd throw them back! I produced all the documentation and paperwork for the

championships. John Symes fed me the technical information because he was the operations director then. So I did all the paperwork, all the dates, and liaised with John Nicol, who was in charge of the BRSCC.

"People thought it would be a 'them and us' situation, but John Nicol and I had a good relationship. We bridged it and, instead of working against one another, we worked off one another. It was good and the standards of both clubs went up. I was the clerk of the course for most of the events."

At any race meeting, the clerk of the course is the person with whom the buck ultimately stops. "He's the guvnor on the day," explained Jennings. "He has total responsibility. The only person with greater authority than the clerk of the course at a race meeting is the MSA [Motor Sports Association] steward in respect to safety. The clerk of the course gets involved early on, sorting out what the race content is, what races you've got on the programme, what the timetable is, what officials he wants – timekeepers, scrutineers, and so on. He makes sure they're all around, and checks that all the awards and furniture and other facilities and services are being looked after by the secretary of the meeting.

"In the case of a commercial operation like the Brands Hatch Racing Club, it's a team of people, but in a club it will be a lot of volunteers. The clerk of the course should be the first there, to make sure everything starts on time. You're then responsible for making sure everything runs smoothly, that everybody's reasonably happy, looking after the interest of everybody – spectators as well, even though you're not responsible for anything the other side of the fence. You make sure the ambulances and doctors are there and get various signatures from officials to say they are there. Everybody signs on, you get reports, you open the track, you inspect the track. For the rest of the day, it's like being on the bridge of a destroyer. I relied on the people with me, the team, to do what they were meant to be doing. Others, if there was an incident out on the track, they'd be out the door, down the stairs and off. I didn't do that. I waited to see if anybody wanted me out there."

The Brands Hatch Racing Club ran four club meetings a year through 1986 and 1987, before moving into larger, International events. In July 1988, it supported the BRSCC in the organisation of the 1000-kilometre sports car race and then, in August, the arrangement was reciprocated, the BHRC being the organising body for the International Formula 3000 meeting and the BRSCC supporting it. Jennings was the clerk of the course

Anthony Reid

"My career started in 1976 and I spent a lot of time at Brands Hatch. At one time I even used to rent a garage, No.18. The rental was something like £5 a week and you got free testing two or possibly three times a week. There were a lot of racing nomads who based themselves in the pit-lane in caravans or buses, or actually in the garages. Brands turned a blind eye to it. It was extra revenue for the circuit, renting out the garages when there was no motorcycle Grand Prix there or the British Grand Prix.

"So there was a real little community. You'd go to the old clubhouse for a drink in the evening, or up to the Kentagon when they built that. John Webb would be there, and Brian Jones, Tony Lanfranchi and Gerry Marshall. There were a lot of London boys who came down. I remember seeing Roy James (the getaway driver for the Great Train Robbery) and gentlemen in Escorts you wouldn't want to have an argument with.

"So there was a tremendous atmosphere, especially for an impressionable young kid like myself, starting racing. When I crashed my Formula Ford PRS and damaged a corner, I just went to the garage next door and asked my friend, who had a Crosslé, if I could borrow his suspension. The PRS and the

Anthony Reid finished second in the Formula Ford 2000 World Cup race at the Formula Ford Festival on 4 November 1984, driving an Argo JM14. (LAT)

Crosslé had the same chassis, so I borrowed his suspension, did a race and then handed it back afterwards.

"I lived in the garage on and off because, coming from Glasgow, I found accommodation pretty expensive in the south-east of England, even in the 1970s, so it was a way of saving money and spending more on the car. It was for a three-month period and good fun.

"There's nothing quite like the Brands Hatch Indy circuit anywhere else in the world. For such a short circuit, it has many different elements. There are some technical, very ballsy, challenging corners, and a mix of other corners which are brilliant for teaching a driver how to race in the early stages of his career. The big boys' track was the Grand Prix circuit, before it was adulterated. Hawthorn hasn't really changed but Westfield was an awesome corner. The old Dingle Dell was marvellous and it's been spoiled, but many of the features are still retained.

"There was a race I did in FF2000 against drivers like Julian Bailey, Martin Donnelly, Damon Hill and Dave Coyne. I can't remember where I qualified but I was fighting for the lead and I tried to overtake Julian and he chopped my wing off, so I didn't have very much front downforce and I dropped back to fourth. Then I sort of relearned to drive the car the way it was handling. I caught up with Donnelly, passed him on the outside of Druids, and a few laps later passed Julian on the inside of Clearways. I won the race with a car that wasn't handling properly."

for the support races while Symes, who by now was the full-time operations director at the circuit, clerked the F3000 event with Nicol of the BRSCC acting as his deputy.

"John Nicol and I got on fine but we had a totally different style of clerking at race meetings," explained Symes. "Neither was right, neither was wrong. My style was that I stayed in Race Control and never moved. I made the decisions and everyone else did all the running around. John was very much more hands-on, so that if something happened on the track, he would jump in the course car and go round. The only time I ever did that was when Johnny Herbert crashed in 1988 and the stewards said they wanted me to take them around because I was the clerk. Other than that, once I was in Race Control I was there for the duration of the meeting. The only thing I always did, when the flag dropped for the last race of the day, was to jump in the course car and as the marshals were coming off the posts, I would drive round, window open, and say: 'Thanks, guys, look forward to seeing you next time.' Just to show appreciation. And I would stand in the Kentagon afterwards and buy a few beers. My whole philosophy was to try and make sure that it didn't matter whether it was spectator, competitor or marshal, that they all enjoyed their day at Brands, and I worked on the basis that if they did that, they'd probably come back again."

This fitted in well with John Webb's reasoning about looking after the public and ensuring they had a good day. Even the structure and timetable of a race meeting was carefully thought out and controlled, and there was a set formula to follow.

"JW maintained that you didn't start too early," explained Doug Jennings. "Let the spectators have their lunch and then come to the circuit, that was his philosophy. The first event would be a little, quick clubbie opener – the MG or Jaguar car club perhaps. In front of the feature race, you would run a fairly mundane one that you weren't going to have any trouble with – a club Formula Ford race perhaps, where they're all responsible for their own cars, so they aren't going to cause a lot of carnage and stop you starting the main event on time. The main race would be the third race. If that was for single-seaters, the next one would be a saloon race, or something radically different. The next race had to be a good-quality event with a good entry that wasn't the same as the previous two, so it might be Sports 2000. Preferably the last race would be for something like Mini Sevens or Mini Miglias – great fun with lots of overtaking, and lights in case it got dark.

"With the full International meetings, we were told what the timetable would be and would have to work round it. But again, if it was a Formula 3000 meeting, say, you wouldn't fill it up with single-seaters for the support races, you'd have touring cars. I learned all that from John Webb."

While John Symes was responsible for sorting out the car race calendar and meetings, the bike racing at that time was run by Peter de Ritter. "Peter and I worked together, no problem at all," explained Symes. "Actually getting the bike side and the car side together was quite difficult. People tend to be ingrained as either a bike person or a car person. At one stage, we did run some combined bike and car meetings, where there were four or five car races and eight or 10 bike races. We ran them for a couple of years, one or two a year, but they weren't the greatest success. Some people just pitched in and thought: 'I'm here to enjoy myself and this is a bit different, isn't it?' But others adopted the attitude that they were there for the cars, or for the bikes. So some spectators wouldn't come for half a day's bike racing when they could pay the same money and see a full day's bike racing.

"And it was quite difficult to get the marshals working together. What we did was to have a car observer who ran each post for the car side, and a 'corner commander' (as they're called in the bike racing world) to run the post for the bike activity. All the minions were common. It was slightly uneasy and it didn't actually work that well.

"But one of the things I learned from John Webb, and I can remember him telling me, was: 'The only way you'll find out is to try.' That was always his philosophy. You'll find people around who'll have a little chuckle at John's expense, because not all of his ideas worked, but quite a lot of his ideas did work. But he was never frightened to try."

As well as not being afraid to try new ideas, one of John Webb's greatest abilities was to make things happen. This was never more apparent than in 1983, when he and his team organised an extra Grand Prix at very short notice.

Brands Hatch had already been awarded the prestigious Formula One Constructors Association award for the best organised Grand Prix of 1982, and had also won the 'Prix Orange' from the International Racing Press Association for the best media facilities at any Grand Prix that year. But now the team was about to surpass itself.

It was Silverstone's turn to run the British Grand Prix in the odd-numbered years, which were relatively lean for Brands Hatch. But even before news came through that the proposed 1983 New York Grand Prix had been cancelled, Webb was lobbying hard to run a Grand Prix of Europe. When the go-ahead for the 25 September date was given, there were just 10 weeks in which to organise it.

"We were always looking for opportunities," said Webb. "There were a couple of Grands Prix cancelled in 1983 and 1985. I liked to think ahead all the time and look for opportunities. So I could see the cancellations coming. I just kept my mouth shut, and chased Bernie [Ecclestone] at the earliest opportunity: 'You're in trouble? Here's a deal.'

"I sussed the 1983 one was going to happen when I was in Monaco. I had a quiet word with the top guy at the RAC. I asked him whether he would back me if I followed it through, and I got a 'yes'. A few weeks later, the Canadian Grand Prix was held in early June. I jumped on a Concorde, saw Bernie and got it sorted."

Webb makes it sound so easy, but many of us would have trouble planning a family holiday in that sort of timescale. Robin Bradford was the press officer at Brands at that time and well remembered the weeks leading up to the race.

"It was one of the most exciting periods of my working existence," he said. "We got confirmation in June and we had 10 weeks to stage the Grand Prix. We knew how to do it but nevertheless it took some doing and everybody had one aim, which was to make this happen. We didn't have a big staff, but we created a Grand Prix and from the word 'go' things happened. We were mailing out press releases (we didn't have email in those days) and Webby would come down to the press office and ask: 'Anything I can do?' As far as he was concerned, his job was done. He had secured a Grand Prix in a non-Grand Prix year. He didn't have anything else to do. So he would come down, fold press releases, stuff them in envelopes, lick them and put them on the pile. It was frantic …"

The opportunity to host an extra race on the calendar presented itself again in 1985. The cancellation of the projected Rome Grand Prix, scheduled for 13 October, left the way clear for Brands Hatch to step in.

That May, it was announced that the circuit would host the European Grand Prix on 22 September. In June, at a reception at the House of Commons, it was revealed that Shell Oils would sponsor the event, together with the following year's British Grand Prix at the circuit. The sponsorship deal also included backing for the World Endurance Championship events at Brands for 1985 and 1986, which would have the title Shell Gemini 1000. It meant that the circuit would be staging a Grand Prix for the fourth consecutive year. "We've been working hard since February 1984 to gain this event," commented Webb at the time. "It didn't just fall out of the sky. We're

geared up and ready to go, unlike in 1983 when we had only 10 weeks notice but still enjoyed a great success."

The date for the Grand Prix was only a week away from the scheduled 1000-kilometre WEC meeting, and Webb used the opportunity to promote the events in tandem. Spectators booking in advance for the Grand Prix would receive a free £7.00 admission ticket for the Shell Gemini 1000, to be run on the previous Sunday, 15 September. The price of admission for the Grand Prix was £15.00, with covered grandstand seats at £30.00 and uncovered ones £20.00. *Autosport* reported that Webb, in committing to this £1,350,000 promotion, was hoping to attract as many spectators as had come to the previous year's British Grand Prix at the circuit, when the race had broken all records. However, things did not run smoothly.

In June, it was announced that the date had been put back a week to 29 September because the Belgian Grand Prix, postponed from earlier in the year, had to be accommodated in the overcrowded autumn schedule. Then, in July, the date was changed yet again, to 6 October. The changes occurred because the teams were facing the prospect of five Grands Prix in six weekends. Webb reprinted his publicity material yet again. "We're disappointed, of course, but we'll endeavour to do our best to run the event to our usual standard," he said. Refunds were offered to those spectators who could not attend the event on the revised date.

A knock-on effect of this date change was that some of the WEC teams announced in July that they would boycott the Brands Hatch and Fuji races, because they would now clash with Grands Prix. Thus they would be denied the services of F1 drivers, some of whom in those days ran in both championships. As a result, both the Group C events were rescheduled, the Brands fixture to 22 September, two weeks before the European Grand Prix.

The prospect didn't faze Webb one bit. "As I'd got all those grandstands hired and had to pay for them, it made sense to run the Grand Prix and the sportscar race back-to-back," he explained. "The grandstand companies don't take them down for several weeks anyway because, on the quiet, they like to store the steel. You normally didn't get a big crowd for the sportscar race, so I gave everybody who came to the Grand Prix a free ticket to it. But not a free stand seat or free paddock pass or programme. The effect of that on revenue made the 1000km race profitable, which it never used to be."

The Grand Prix itself was an outstanding success. All grandstand seats were sold out, so an extra 2000-seat stand was erected at South Bank to cope with the heavy demand. The event was a landmark, with

Nigel Mansell

"The biggest thing you always remember about Brands is the different levels in elevation. The whole circuit, certainly the Indy circuit, has this amphitheatre effect, so there's very good visibility for anybody who's watching.

"I always looked at it as a challenging circuit, never a frustrating one. The more challenging a circuit, the harder you have to work. I have very exciting memories from the early days, though not very good from 1977 when I broke my neck there. But then I came back from that to win the championship, so that was pretty special.

"It was very damp and wet off-line, and another guy who was slowing down in front didn't see me and helped me off the circuit – I think that's the nicest way I can describe it. It was very dangerous in those days because the barriers were very close to the track. But the biggest problem there was that we never had proper seats in the cars, and we never had proper headrests.

"I had my maiden Grand Prix win there in 1985. When Keke Rosberg and I had been testing there with the Williams guys several weeks before, Patrick Head made a couple of good suspension changes on the back of the car, and all of a sudden it was almost a second a lap quicker. We knew then that we would be competitive in the race. It was wonderful suddenly to have a car that was capable of winning, and at my home Grand Prix, as well. It was like Christmas.

"You have a greater sense of the crowd at Brands because, with the change of elevation, sometimes you're looking above them going into Paddock, then as you drop down you're looking at them, then as you come out of Paddock again you're lower than them and looking right at their feet.

"In 1986, at the first start, the driveshaft broke and there was a horrendous accident at the first corner. Because they stopped the race I jumped into the T-car, which was set up for Nelson Piquet. There was no time to change the pedals or anything. All they managed to do was put my seat in the car, and of course I went on to win the race, which was truly fantastic.

"I think I started to drive it the way I wanted to by about half distance, but there were a couple of things I just had to put up with. My driving style was different, but I just adapted and got the car going quick enough to give Nelson a hard time for probably two-thirds of the race. He probably only missed one gear in the whole race but, when he did it, it was enough and I was alongside.

"I think my special memory of Brands is going across the start-finish line at 200mph plus and approaching Paddock Hill Bend. You have to remember the safety aspects then, compared with what we have now. It really got your attention! You knew that, if you did anything wrong, it would be a huge shunt. Every time you went over the start-finish line, still accelerating, Paddock got your attention, but equally it was very satisfying."

Nigel Mansell on his way to victory in the last Grand Prix held at Brands Hatch in 1986. (sutton-images.com)

Martin Brundle

"My strongest memory of Brands would be going there in the sixties, when I was a kid, to watch the Grand Prix. I remember walking around and getting all the paraphernalia from the Yardley-BRM team, and Acker Bilk playing on the start-finish line at the end. Those are the first memories that come to mind.

"I drove several Grands Prix there, which I enjoyed. I think I scored points there and I won my first-ever circuit race there in a Formula Ford 2000. I also had a mega win for Jaguar in the 1000km race in 1988. It's one of the all-time great circuits."

Nigel Mansell scoring his first-ever Grand Prix victory and Alain Prost becoming the first Frenchman to secure the World Championship.

Rumours were circulating over the 1985 European Grand Prix weekend about the possible sale of Motor Circuit Developments, the operating company of Brands Hatch, after Eagle Star Holdings had been sold to British American Tobacco (BAT). Having absorbed Grovewood Securities, Eagle Star owned MCD and there were fears that it would have to accept a bid from an unnamed supermarket chain. Clearly this would have jeopardised the motor racing activities at the circuit.

John Webb supplied the background: "In 1972, Grovewood's major financial backers, Eagle Star, took over the whole of the company and from that point onwards Grovewood was a subsidiary of Eagle Star," he explained. "In about 1984, Allianz, the German insurance company, made a hostile takeover bid for Eagle Star, who had to look around in a hurry for what's called a 'white knight' – a friend who will take it over instead. They didn't want Eagle Star to go to Germany. The 'white knight' turned out to be British American Tobacco. BAT wanted Eagle Star but it came with a whole package of companies that included Grovewood, the Cambridge Theatre, a plastics company and an optical company. Within a couple of years, they'd looked at all the things they'd picked up in this massive takeover, and decided to get rid of everything except the financial services businesses.

"This rocked John Danny quite a bit. It had been his life up until then, and he was now 75 years of age. Angela had done a favour, without knowing it at the time, to the chairman of BAT, Patrick Sheahy, and so the door was open for me to write direct to him and ask if he would give me the time to raise a management buy-out. I got a favourable reply and that was when I went to John Foulston."

Foulston was a 38-year-old millionaire who raced in Historic and Thundersports championships and whose computer leasing company, Atlantic Computers, also sponsored Historic sports car championships.

"I was in fairly regular contact with him and he had the money," Webb continued. "The concept I took to him was that, at the end of the day, it wouldn't cost him any money because he and I could make about £30 million out of it by floating it as a public company, which he already had experience of with Atlantic Computers. That was the plot. He put up the money, and he took 80 per cent. Angela and I took 20 per cent and provided the concept."

Prior to this, though, Webb had tried to negotiate a three-way deal involving the principal of the Formula One group of companies, Bernie Ecclestone. He explained: "I went to Bernie and John Foulston, proposing that they would put up

the money, half each, and I would provide the management. They would get 40 per cent each and there would be 20 per cent for Angela and me. We had a meeting at Fairoaks airfield in Surrey and it was agreed in principle.

"Bernie later rang me and said: 'John, I've gone cold.' I replied: 'Don't tell me, tell John Foulston – you've made an arrangement with him.' So he did. According to Foulston, Bernie wanted him to lend him his share of the money, interest-free. Foulston said he would lend Bernie the money, but at bank rate. When Bernie insisted it should be interest-free, Foulston said: 'OK – I'll do it myself.'"

Eagle Star's original asking price for the circuits had been around £3.5 million. However, David Wickins of British Car Auctions then also became interested in buying the company and, as a result, the price rose. At the Thundersaloon meeting at Brands Hatch on 18 May 1986, it was announced

that John Foulston had bought Brands, Oulton Park and Snetterton in a £5.25 million deal.

Webb continued: "According to Foulston, Bernie threw all the toys out of the pram when the deal was announced, and took the Grand Prix away from Brands Hatch. Part of the secret negotiation was that the Grand Prix would take place every year at Brands Hatch."

This version of events is also recounted in Terry Lovell's book, *Bernie's Game* which, according to Webb, "has never been challenged". However Bernie Ecclestone disagreed that this is what happened.

"I don't know about Foulston lending me money interest-free," he said. "I really don't remember what happened with Foulston, but we just didn't get it right in the end. If we had, I would have done what I had wanted to do in the first place – build Brands into a premier circuit. It was partly whether John [Foulston] was prepared to ante-up where it had been needed to ante-up.

BELOW *Paddock Hill Bend, and the Brabham Centre hospitality building can be seen in the background as Nelson Piquet's Brabham BT52 BMW leads the field away at the start of the 1983 European Grand Prix on 25 September. The race had been organised at short notice by John Webb and his team after the cancellation of the proposed New York Grand Prix that year. (LAT)*

Jonathan Palmer

"It was a circuit I certainly loved racing on, because of its undulating character. Going down through Paddock is a phenomenal feeling in any car. Paddock is always one of those corners that you know you've never quite got the most out of. There's always a bit more to be had. It's so demanding. You can't see it, so it's a little bit scary.

"I used to love coming here, it was my local circuit. I used to come up here when my father was the chief medical officer for the BARC and he used to bring me to watch races here too.

Jonathan Palmer and Jan Lammers took their Canon Porsche 956 to a dominant victory in the 1984 British Aerospace 1000kms on 29 July. (LAT)

"My biggest success here was winning the 1000km race in 1984 with Jan Lammers in the Canon Porsche 956. We'd modified the car. As usual I was pretty determined and opinionated about what it would take to make the car quick, and I was the first person to get a front wing put on the front of a Porsche, on the nose, to try and stop the understeer. I badgered Keith Greene, who was running the car, into making a front wing and bolting it on. We hadn't run it before – we just arrived and went out. I remember going out for a few laps in practice, and I came in and said: 'Yeah, it's not bad, still some understeer, crank up the angle a bit more …' There was not much wind tunnel work in those days. We just screwed the thing on, came in, another two laps, put more angle on it, decided it was about right, and off we went. We got pole position and led the race from start to finish."

"I'd forgotten John Webb was involved as well," added Ecclestone. "He wanted us to fund it and let him have a fair chunk for free, even to the extent that, when it was developed, we would put all the money up and he would still have his share."

The deal with John Foulston ended speculation that Eagle Star would sell to a supermarket chain and secured a motor racing future for the three circuits for the foreseeable future. "I liked it so much I bought the company," Foulston joked. It was planned to form a new operating company, Brands Hatch Leisure Ltd, with the Webbs taking a 20 per cent shareholding, the remainder being owned by Foulston and his family. Sir Jack Brabham, Derek Bell and Sir Geoffrey Johnson-Smith MP, a long-time director of Brands Hatch Circuits Ltd, agreed to join the board as non-executive directors.

David Isaac, the long-serving financial director of MCD, and Peter Todd, the operations director at the time, would continue in their capacities and the full-time staff, which numbered 106, would not be affected. Major improvements were planned, including other leisure developments to interest the whole family on race days. With the circuit now served by the recently opened M25 motorway, it was reported that building a motel was also a possibility.

But the celebrations were short-lived. A few days later came the shock announcement that Silverstone had secured an exclusive deal with Bernie Ecclestone to host the British Grand Prix every year for the next five years, with another five-year option after that. Brands Hatch was out in the cold.

When asked in 2006 whether he had taken the Grand Prix away from Brands Hatch because he had been 'grumpy' over the failed deal with John Foulston, Ecclestone replied: "Again, I don't remember those details. It may well have been that, but I think in the end it wasn't that at all. It was that they weren't prepared to do what we wanted. That was the reason. I'm a lover of Brands Hatch, so the last thing I would do is just take a Formula One event away from them. Unless there was a very good reason."

It is ironic that the original plan had been to take the Grand Prix permanently to Brands Hatch, since John Webb had opposed a proposal earlier that year to stop individual countries alternating the venues for their Grands Prix (as happened in Britain with Brands and Silverstone). The matter had been brought up at a meeting of the Formula One Commission on 22–23 January and, as president and representative of the international circuit owners, Webb had argued against the proposal and had abstained from voting.

Another irony is that, years after the deal, Bernie Ecclestone and the British Racing Drivers' Club (BRDC), the owner of Silverstone, fell out. Ecclestone severely criticised the facilities at the Northamptonshire circuit. Asked in 2006 whether, in retrospect, he regretted giving Silverstone the exclusive deal, he replied: "Absolutely. One hundred per cent. One million per cent. If we could have kept the race at Brands, that would have been, for me, the best thing that ever happened."

Ecclestone's exclusive deal with Silverstone cast a doubt over the financial viability of Brands Hatch and the continuation of domestic racing there. Webb had always stated that any other form of racing in Britain could not survive without the profits made by both Brands Hatch and Silverstone. Even so, he seemed to take the news very stoically and adopted a different attitude towards the financial necessity for a Grand Prix.

"Angela couldn't understand how John Foulston and I took it so calmly," he said. "My attitude was – well, we're just going to have to work harder to make up that deficit. From that moment onwards, Brands Hatch was more commercially successful because a Grand Prix diverts the attention of your team at every level to an enormous extent. It's a drain. OK, you can make money on it, but I think the most we ever made on a Grand Prix was £700,000. In my last year at Brands, we made a profit, substantially more than for any earlier period in the history of the circuit, without a Grand Prix, really by applying our energies to necessity.

"I persisted for about 18 months in badgering Bernie to get the Grand Prix back, but I knew as a fact that the contract with Silverstone had already been signed, so they couldn't give it to us. Without a lawsuit, it couldn't happen."

Instead, Foulston and the Webbs went it alone, determined to make a success of Brands Hatch Leisure. "John was not terribly popular with some of his fellow drivers, or some of his fellow businessmen," said Webb. "He was a very ambitious man and he didn't like being argued with. He had the money with which to win and he was a very determined man. He was a good driver, and also a brilliant helicopter pilot.

"Through some uncanny circumstance, he and I always thought the same way and we could have a conversation almost without resorting to words. It was total understanding. You don't have to be bosom friends to get on well, as long as you have an understanding and trust each other. I was due to retire anyway, I think in 1992 according to my contract. So we worked out between us that, at that point, he would retire from his other business commitments and would become the chief executive of Brands Hatch, and I would succeed him as the chairman. So we'd both be involved, him at a more active level and me at a less active level. And that would have suited both of us very well."

But an event 16 months later ensured that this plan was never realised. On 29 September, 1987, Foulston was killed at Silverstone while testing his Historic racing Indycar, a 1970 McLaren.

Webb took the news philosophically. "When you're in the motor racing business as long as I've been, particularly in the fifties and sixties, you were losing friends every week," he said. "You just got used to it. I've been in aviation, too, so I've never been a person to react, not just to death but to any sort of bad news. Obviously I realised that Mary, John's widow, would inherit and that for some time she would be distraught and disorganised. I recommended that John Tompkins, who was John Foulston's number two at Atlantic Computers, and who was also on the Brands board as a non-executive director, should be made chairman. Mary agreed to that and I became chairman of all the individual companies. Within a matter of months, Mary and Tomkins were disagreeing, mainly on Atlantic Computers matters, so he was asked to go. I

proposed Mary as chairman and there were two years of relative peace, until the daughter began to grow up and wanted to play with the train set."

The daughter to whom Webb referred was 21-year-old Nicola Foulston, who had already been running an Historic racing team for her father, based at the circuit.

"Dad bought Brands in July 1986 as I was just finishing school," she explained. "I was about to do a bunk over to America. I had a job lined up. My parents wanted me to go to university and I wasn't remotely interested. So my father said: 'If you think you're so good at work, come and run my racing team.' So I did. I was really the MD. We had a team manager and he ran all the technical side and I managed the business. And I did that for two years, until my father died.

"What people find surprising," she continued, "is that I wasn't shocked, because my father had talked a lot about dying young. I don't think it was a premonition – he was a bit of a fatalist. He was doing a lot of dangerous things, he was flying helicopters and driving cars, and a lot of people he'd

BELOW *Nigel Mansell (Williams FW10B) challenges pole-position man Ayrton Senna (JPS Lotus 97T) into Paddock Hill Bend at the start of the 1985 European Grand Prix, which would provide Mansell with his first Grand Prix win. (Phipps/Sutton)*

known who learned to fly helicopters had died, and he assumed that would be the way he would go."

It's probably an understatement to say that Webb and the young Nicola Foulston did not hit it off. "John Webb and I didn't have a brilliant relationship when my father was alive," she said. "I was certainly a fairly outspoken kid who had views about motor racing from the inside. Most people who have raced, or have been part of race teams, all have fairly strong views on how motor racing should be run, and I was exactly the same. I was a young kid of a girl and I thought I knew everything. And as a youth, you're arrogant, and I had strong views about the way Webb operated the business."

If Foulston was unimpressed with the way Webb operated, the feeling was certainly mutual. "Her mother asked me if I would have her on the board and call her 'commercial director'," explained Webb. "I said: 'It's not going to work, Mary. But I'll go with it providing you sign an agreement with me to buy my shares if it doesn't work out.' Mary, who I've always found to be absolutely straight, did exactly that before Nicola was appointed.

"So in about October 1989, Nicola took up residence as our commercial director. Angela and I had a quick holiday and, while we were away, she did some things I regarded as major management interference. It got to a point, very quickly, where I asked for a meeting with Mary's financial and legal advisers and said: 'This isn't going to work. You must make up your minds what you're going to do. If she stays, I go.' Which is not something one says lightly.

"Mary had as her financial adviser an accountant named Nigel Eastaway who, with her, was one of Nicola's trustees. Angela and I got on very well with Nigel and we went to him in late November 1989 to explain our inability to work with Nicola. In turn, he called a meeting with us and Mary. They advised us that they had decided to take the option of replacing my service contract with a full compensation consultancy and to purchase my shares. Angela was left to decide for herself and she elected to follow the same route."

A statement issued by Brands Hatch Leisure read: "Coinciding with the 40th anniversary next Easter of Brands Hatch as a surfaced race circuit, John and Angela Webb are retiring to Spain. John Webb will then be in his 60th year. As a result the Webbs are relinquishing, from 28 February 1990, their day-to-day responsibilities as chief executive and deputy managing director of Brands Hatch Leisure plc. Following nearly 55 enjoyable years of joint service, and an anticipated record trading year in 1989, Mr and Mrs Webb are seeking a more relaxed life together in the future. They will continue, however,

to act as consultants to the group. As of 1 March 1990, Mrs Mary Foulston, chairman of the board, will assume the additional role of chief executive of Brands Hatch Leisure plc and Nicola Foulston, the commercial director, will become chief executive of Brands Hatch Circuits Ltd and its associated operating companies." At the time, Webb himself refused to comment.

He recalled: "I wasn't in the mood to fight. I was coming to the end of my contract and I didn't intend to stay as managing director or chief executive any longer. There was only another couple of years to run. I'd just bought a property in Spain, so we moved there.

"From that time onwards, Nicola methodically broke up what was probably the best team in British motor sport."

Nigel Mansell

A lap of the Brands Hatch Grand Prix circuit with Nigel Mansell, the last driver to win a Grand Prix on it

"It's one of most exhilarating rides in the world on one of the great old Grand Prix circuits. Starting a lap on the Brabham Straight, you cross the start-finish line and the first thing you think about is positioning the car and getting ready for a bump going into Paddock. The car goes light and you turn in, it's very skittish under braking. As you drop down Paddock Hill, it's very important to hold the car in balance and up towards Druids. There can be quite a lot of positive 'g' at the bottom of Paddock Hill.

"Druids is a great little corner – you could possibly have three different lines on entry, but the middle of corner is the same, hugging the apex and then powering it out. Down the hill to Graham Hill Bend, it's very important on entry and exit to carry as much speed as you can onto Cooper Straight. As you turn in for the entry into Surtees, the uphill left-hander, the steering goes light and you drift out as you enter the straight. It's flat-out into Pilgrim's Drop and very quick down Hawthorn Hill. Hawthorn Bend is a very quick corner, carrying a lot of speed, and then down the short straight towards Westfield.

"Again, it's a very quick corner that opens out, but a very dangerous corner too. Coming out of Westfield, dropping down into Dingle Dell, there have been a lot of changes over the years. Sheene Curve has been modified over the years, and is very quick and bumpy. Then there's a lot of camber entering Stirling's Bend which is a great little corner. You slingshot through it as quick as you can and then enter Clearways. You can enter very quick and then it tightens up on you. In traffic, this is the most important bend on the circuit because it gives you an overtaking opportunity coming out onto Clark Curve. I would say Paddock and Surtees are the other corners that can set you up for great overtaking manoeuvres."

1980

■ Over the winter, 'dumpling kerbing' was installed at the corners to dissuade competitors from hooking wheels over the track edges. Debris fencing was also erected along Cooper Straight and around Surtees. A £45,000 medical centre was to be built on the perimeter of McLaren Bend in time for the Grand Prix and a new £40,000 administration block was also planned for the paddock area.

■ The 'Superfinal' of the opening round of the Brands Hatch Shell Oils Southern Rallycross Championship was won by John Welch, although his Ford Escort Mk3 4WD turbo had caught fire during one of the earlier races.

■ The track hosted Britain's first major International race of the year on 16 March, with the six-hour World Championship for Makes race. The entry included the three top women drivers in Europe – Desiré Wilson, Divina Galica and Lella Lombardi, all of whom had been backed by John Webb during their careers. The race was marred by an accident which claimed the life of Martin Raymond. The race had been running for almost three hours when Raymond lost control of his Chevron and spun to a halt at Dingle Dell on the outside of the track. Marshals helped to push the car onto the grass and Raymond then attempted to free a seized gearbox. Several laps later, the Osella of Marco Rocca moved out to pass the Porsche of Paul Edwards and the two cars collided. The Porsche, and possibly the Osella as well, hit the stationary Chevron, killing Raymond instantly. The race was red-flagged and it only continued for an hour after the restart, in order to exceed the 60 per cent distance necessary for it to qualify for the World Championship. It was won by Riccardo Patrese/Walter Rohrl in a Group 5 Lancia Beta Montecarlo from their team mates, Eddie Cheever/Michele Alboreto. Alain de Cadenet/Desiré Wilson were third in a Group 6 De Cadenet.

■ Brett Riley in a March 783/793 became the third different winner in as many races in the Vandervell F3 championship round on 30 March.

■ Desiré Wilson became the first woman to win an F1 race, albeit against a small field, when she took Theodore Racing's Wolf WR3 to victory in the Aurora AFX British F1 round on Easter Monday, 7 April. Former motorbike World Champion Giacomo Agostini finished fourth with a Williams FW06.

■ After a strong showing in 1979, the Aurora F1 series was clearly in decline, prompting Webb, as its originator, to issue a statement. He blamed rising costs coupled with the state of the economy, pointing out that to run a competitive car required an investment of between £80,000 and £100,000, and about the same in running costs for a season. He said that high interest rates meant that potential sponsors had been unable to commit,

LEFT *Desiré Wilson became the first woman ever to win an F1 race by taking her Wolf WR3 to victory in the Aurora event at Brands Hatch on 7 April 1980. (Phil Blume/LAT)*

leaving competitors high and dry, but that he hoped for more cars on the grid soon.

■ Stars turned out in force to pay tribute to Stirling Moss at the Pace Petroleum Race Day on Bank Holiday Monday, 5 May. Former World Champions Juan Manuel Fangio, Jackie Stewart, John Surtees and Denny Hulme were among the guests at the meeting, which featured a parade of famous cars raced by Moss in the fifties and early sixties. The first event was meant to be a demonstration of 500cc cars but soon turned into a full-bloodied race, Moss taking the 'victory' in a Cooper Mk9 JAP.

■ Roberto Guerrero in an Argo JM6 finished just 0.2sec clear of team mate Thierry Tassin in the Vandervell F3 race on 29 June.

■ In the Marlboro British Grand Prix on 13 July, Didier Pironi and Jacques Laffite were on the front of the grid in their Ligiers and took an early lead. New wheels, however, led to a tyre failure on each JS11/15, allowing Alan Jones to take the victory with his Williams FW07B from the Brabham BT49 of Nelson Piquet and Carlos Reutemann in the second Williams. In the BMW Procar race, Reutemann and Jones finished first and second, ahead of Pironi and Laffite. Kenneth Acheson won the Vandervell F3 event in his March 793, narrowly beating Stefan Johansson's newer

BELOW *Commentator Raymond Baxter interviews John Bolster during the special 'Tribute to Stirling Moss' day in May 1980, while Innes Ireland (right) looks on. (Author)*

March 803, while Nick Whiting beat four Capris to win the Tricentrol British Saloon Car championship round with a works Rover 3500 V8.

■ The Aurora F1 series seemed to be back to rude health for the Bank Holiday meeting on 25 August. Emilio de Villota scored a last-minute win in his RAM Williams FW07B in the Pace Petroleum Trophy race. He shadowed the Arrows A1G of Guy Edwards all race, until Edwards's engine blew on the penultimate lap. The bright red Ford Capris of Gordon Spice and Andy Rouse dominated the Tricentrol saloon race.

■ A feature of events on these days was the £50 awarded by MCD to the Brands 'man of the meeting'. On 14 September at the MG Car Club event, it went to Midget driver Steve Everitt, who commented at the presentation in the Kentagon that it would go towards repairing his car in time for the winter 'clubbies'. Everitt had been on pole for the race for Modified Midgets and Sprites, and enjoyed a tremendous battle with David Sheppard. The pair took it in turns to dive inside at Paddock and hold the line all round to Graham Hill Bend, where whoever had the outside line would gain the advantage. At Paddock on the last lap, there was contact and Everitt flew off onto the infield, demolishing three layers of catchfencing before hitting a marshal's car.

■ In September it was announced that the Aurora F1 series would be suspended at the end of the season due to the current economic situation.

■ Roberto Moreno won the Marlboro World Cup Formula Ford Festival on 2 November in a Van Diemen RF80. Moreno won each of his qualifying heats, established a new lap record at 49.4sec, 87.18mph, and then won the final by just over 2sec from Tommy Byrne's Van Diemen.

1981

■ In February, Brands Hatch Racing took delivery of three brand new Royale RP29 Formula Ford 1600 cars and the first of 20 new Talbot Sunbeam Ti saloons. The school had run a trio of RP26s for the previous two years.

■ A proposed non-championship F1 race on 4 May was dropped after the San Marino Grand Prix was included on a clashing date in the World Championship calendar.

■ Ray Mallock won the first round of the British Formula Atlantic championship on 15 March in his Ralt RT4 on a treacherously wet track. At the same meeting, Ayrton Senna da Silva (as he was known then) took his first single-seater victory in only his third FF1600 race. A few weeks later, on 4 May, it was Ian Flux's turn to win the Atlantic race with the Ehrlich RP5, again in torrential rain. Flux's victory brought to an end Mallock's previous domination of the championship, which had replaced Aurora F1 as the national single-seater series.

■ Despite incessant rain, Barrie Williams took his Colt Lancer to victory in the 1600cc race for the Tricentrol British Saloon Car championship on 25 May, ahead of David Morgan's Colt. Nick Whiting's Capri won the bigger class in front of Win Percy's Mazda RX-7.

■ The BARC organised a seven-race meeting on 7 June, supported by the *Sun* newspaper, with free admission for all spectators plus a lunchtime 'pits walkabout'.

BELOW *Ray Mallock won the British Formula Atlantic Championship race on 25 May 1981 in his Ralt RT4. (Author)*

■ Thierry Tassin in a Ralt RT3/81 scored his third F3 victory of the year on 12 July, beating championship leader Jonathan Palmer's Ralt.

■ On 26 July, after a five-race BRSCC-organised programme, attention moved to the Clearways oval, which Promotasport Raceway International took over for its annual Festival of Speed, featuring Bangers and Superstox.

■ It all came good for Rover V8 driver Jeff Allam on Bank Holiday Monday, 31 August, when he won the British Saloon Car Championship race on the Grand Prix circuit. Win Percy in a Mazda RX-7 was second, ahead of Pete Lovett's Rover V8.

■ There was nearly a fairytale debut for the new Ford C100 in the Flying Tigers 1000 race on 27 September, the final round of the World Endurance Championship for Drivers. Driven by Manfred Winkelhock/Klaus Ludwig, the 3.9-litre Cosworth DFL powered car took pole position and led for the first hour before a broken gearbox caused its retirement. The race was won by the Lola T600 of Guy Edwards/Emilio de Villota. Another potential winner, evoking memories of the classic BOAC 1000 races in 1970 and 1971, was the Kremer team's replica Porsche 917. The car, driven by Bob Wollek/Henri Pescarolo, unfortunately retired soon after the Ford.

■ Tommy Byrne in a works Van Diemen RF81 won the Formula Ford Festival and Marlboro World Cup on 1 November. Byrne beat the works Royale RP29 of Rick Morris in a thrilling final.

■ In December, it was announced that the first-ever British Rallycross Grand Prix would take place the following year on a new course designed by Trevor Hopkins. From the start-finish line, cars would turn 90deg right at the top of Paddock, down a steep shale and grass slope towards Graham Hill Bend. They would then slew left-right over mud to rejoin the track on the climb up to Druids Bend. After rounding the hairpin, the cars would turn left, where a section of Armco barrier was removed and a ramp created to launch them across the top of South Bank. A tight downhill right then took them the wrong way along Cooper Straight to a zig-zag through the rear pits entrance and up the pit exit road to rejoin the track at the top of Paddock.

RIGHT *Series Champion Ayrton Senna da Silva (as he was then known) waits on the grid for the start of the Formula Ford 1600 Championship race on 29 September 1981. (sutton-images.com)*

1982

■ In February, new hospitality suites were completed, offering an almost uninterrupted view of the Indy circuit.

■ On 31 January, Graham Hathaway, in an Escort, won the inaugural meeting on the new rallycross circuit.

■ The proposed Brands Hatch 1000, the opening round of the World Endurance Championship for Drivers, scheduled for 14 March, was postponed when it became clear just a couple of weeks beforehand that there would not be enough entries. The situation arose because the sport's governing body, FISA, was late in finalising regulations for the championship. Only 14 entries had been received and a replacement date of 17 October was granted.

■ Niki Lauda might have won the Marlboro British Grand Prix on 18 July in his McLaren MP4B, but the hero of the huge crowd was Derek Warwick in the lumbering Toleman TG181 – nicknamed the 'Belgrano' after the ageing Argentine battleship that had recently been sunk in the Falklands conflict. Keke Rosberg was on pole in a Williams FW08 but failed to get off the line on the

BELOW *Derek Warwick, in his Toleman TG181C chases second-placed Didier Pironi's Ferrari 126C2 during the 1982 British Grand Prix on 18 July. (Phipps/Sutton)*

parade lap, so he started from the back. He flew through the field but had to pit twice for tyres and finally retired with low fuel pressure. Nelson Piquet took an early lead, his Brabham BT50 BMW running light on fuel and the team planning to make a fuel stop – unheard of in those days in Formula One. Alas, the Brazilian retired before they had the chance to see if the strategy would work. Warwick, meanwhile, charged from 16th on the grid, taking Didier Pironi's Ferrari 126C2 for second place at Paddock Bend, to huge cheers from the grandstands, before a CV joint broke. Lauda took the win ahead of the Ferraris of Pironi and Patrick Tambay.

■ Other Grand Prix attractions included Derek Bell demonstrating his Le Mans winning Rothmans Porsche 956. Pete Lovett in his Rover 3500 V8 won the supporting saloon car race, while Tommy Byrne in a Ralt RT3 won the F3 event.

■ Dave Scott in a Ralt RT3D beat Martin Brundle's similar car in the Marlboro F3 encounter on 15 August.

■ It rained on Bank Holiday Monday, 30 August, in the middle of the RAC British Saloon Car Championship race, catching out a number of the slick-shod competitors. Early leader Jeff Allam had a moment at Druids in his Ford Capri, allowing through Vince Woodman (Capri) and Brian Muir (Rover 3500 V8).

RIGHT *Mike Wilds (Can-Am BRM P154) leads Ray Mallock (Lola T70) and the rest of the Historic sportscar field around Paddock during the 1982 British Grand Prix meeting on 18 July. (Author)*

MIDDLE *Vince Woodman's Capri leads the pack into Paddock Bend during the 1982 Grand Prix supporting British Saloon Car Championship race on 18 July. (LAT)*

BOTTOM *Jacky Ickx (Porsche 956) battles spectacularly with Riccardo Patrese (Lancia Martini LC1) to snatch an aggregate victory in the 1982 Shell Oils 1000 on 17 October, taking the WEC Drivers' title. (sutton-images.com)*

■ In September, John Webb announced the creation of Thundersports, a series for unrestricted sports-racing cars, designed to fill the gap left after the demise of the Aurora F1 series. The only regulation was to be that each car must have a minimum of two drivers. Races would be up to 150 miles in length and each event would have a total prize fund of £15,000. It was emphasised that the cars would race in a series, not a championship.

■ Dave Scott's Ralt RT3D again won the F3 event on 10 October ahead of Martin Brundle, who had been on pole and set fastest lap.

■ The postponement of the World Endurance Championship race at the beginning of the season meant that Brands played host to the season-closing FIA Group C event instead on 17 October. The Shell Oils 1000 produced a sensational drive in the wet from Jacky Ickx in his factory Rothmans Porsche 956, pursuing the more nimble works Martini Lancia 'barchetta' of Teo Fabi/Riccardo Patrese in the closing stages to snatch both the overall race win and the WEC Drivers' title. The race was stopped early on and run in two parts after a guardrail had been badly damaged. If the Lancia had won, Patrese would have taken the title, so Ickx, partnered by Derek Bell, threw caution to the wind. In fading light, he hunted down the Lancia, finishing less than 2sec behind it on the road but winning on aggregate.

■ Julian Bailey in a Lola T640E beat Rick Morris in a Royale RP31M in a dramatic finale to the Formula Ford Festival and Marlboro World Cup on 31 October. Mauricio Gugelmin rolled his Van Diemen while challenging for the lead.

■ Sweden's Rolf Nilsson won the first-ever British Rallycross Grand Prix on 12 December in his Porsche, after the Escorts of John Welch and Martin Schanche had run into engine problems. Nilsson was unchallenged in the atrocious conditions. Trevor Hopkins finished second in a Fiesta.

■ The award presented annually by FOCA for the best Grand Prix was won by Brands Hatch. It was presented to John and Angela Webb by FISA president Jean-Marie Balestre at the FIA prizegiving ceremony in Paris just before Christmas.

1983

■ Derek Bell/Siggi Brunn won the first of the new Thundersports challenge races on Easter Monday, 4 April, in the German driver's Porsche 908/3 Turbo. The pair finished three laps ahead of the rest of the field after heavy rain had affected the 58-lap race.

■ There was a poor entry of only 13 F1 cars for the Marlboro Race of Champions on 10 April. Some teams had withdrawn and others substituted lesser drivers for their regulars, unhappy about taking part in a non-championship race having only just returned from Long Beach and only a week before the French Grand Prix. The race developed into a two-car battle between the Williams FW08C of Keke Rosberg and the Tyrrell 011 of Danny Sullivan. The Finn kept the American at bay for lap after lap to claim the win by 0.49sec, with Alan Jones (Arrows A6) third. The Honda V6 turbo, which would become one of the most successful F1 engines, made its debut in the back of Stefan Johansson's Spirit. The Rover V8s of Steve Soper and Jeff Allam were 1-2 in the saloon car race.

■ Rob Gibson in a Porsche 911 won the second round of the British Rallycross Championship on 17 April, ahead of the Ford Fiesta of Trevor Reeves.

■ A heavy rain shower failed to stop Ayrton Senna da Silva from winning the Marlboro British F3 championship race on 8 May. Martin Brundle chased the Brazilian's Ralt RT3E in his similar car to take second place. Senna was sensationally fast through

Paddock Bend, just dabbing the brakes, flicking down a gear and throwing the car into the corner, hard on the throttle. "It's right on the limit at that corner and I can tell you it feels quite dangerous," he commented afterwards.

■ John Brindley/Brian Cocks in a Lola T530 Chevrolet beat Martin Birrane/David Kennedy in a Ford C100 by a clear lap in the Thundersports encounter on 30 May. Mauricio Gugelmin won the supporting FF2000 race in a Van Diemen RF83.

■ News in June that the New York Grand Prix, scheduled for 25 September, had been cancelled fuelled speculation about a second Formula One race in Britain, either at Brands Hatch or Donington Park. Later that month, it was confirmed that a Grand Prix of Europe would be held at Brands on that date. It was the first time that Britain had been awarded two World Championship Formula One races in the same season. The race would also mark the return of tobacco manufacturer John Player as the title sponsor. Advance ticket buyers would receive a free £7.00 entrance ticket to the preceding weekend's 1000km Group C endurance race.

■ At the *Sun* Free Race Day on 31 July, Nigel Mansell demonstrated his JPS Lotus 92 F1 car in front of 30,000 spectators, second only to a Grand Prix crowd. The total requests for free tickets, using a coupon from the newspaper, exceeded 25,000, and the tickets were dispatched by the Brands booking office staff. Page 3 girl Linda Lusardi was in attendance, while the feature FF2000 race was won by Julian Bailey in a Reynard SF83.

BELOW *The works Porsche 956s lead the field away at the start of the 1983 Grand Prix International 1000kms race on 18 September. (LAT)*

BELOW *Keke Rosberg (Williams FW08C) and Danny Sullivan (Tyrrell 012) battle it out during the 1983 Race of Champions. (LAT)*

ABOVE *A panoramic view of Druids during the 1983 Grand Prix of Europe on 25 September – note the crane-mounted TV camera.* (*Phipps/Sutton*)

■ A popular addition at some of the meetings in 1983 was Radio Brands, operated under the direction of BBC Radio One producer David Atke. Jingles and pop music were used as fillers during quiet periods, such as delays due to catchfencing or barriers having to be rebuilt.

■ The Bank Holiday meeting on 29 August featured a round of the British Saloon Car Championship, which was won by Peter Lovett in a Rover Vitesse. The race was led for the first few laps by Steve Soper's Rover until Lovett passed him. Hans Stuck was third in a BMW 635CSi.

■ A week before the Grand Prix of Europe, on 18 September, Brands played host to the FIA European Endurance Championship with the *Grand Prix International* 1000km race. There were shades of 1970 and the Porsche 917s in the wet, because the track was flooded before the noon start. Jacky Ickx led away in a Rothmans Porsche 956, ahead of Derek Warwick in JFR's privately entered car and Derek Bell in the other works entry. Warwick moved into the lead but, after 40 minutes, clerk of the course Peter Browning deemed conditions too dangerous and deployed the Safety Car for 10 minutes. Warwick pressed on until he was nearly a lap ahead and then handed over to co-driver John Fitzpatrick, who maintained the lead until handing back to Warwick for the final stint. Stefan Bellof, co-driving Bell's car, tried hard to catch him but had to make an unscheduled pitstop five laps from the end, handing second place to his team mates, Ickx/Jochen Mass. Warwick took the flag after six hours of racing, having covered 975km. Despite the free ticket offer associated with the Grand Prix, only 12,000 spectators turned out.

■ With John Player returning to sponsor the Grand Prix of Europe in September and only 10 weeks in which to prepare, it took 2200 litres of paint to change the colours of the kerbing around the circuit to black and yellow, from the red and white of the previous sponsor, Marlboro.

■ Nelson Piquet won the John Player Grand Prix of Europe on 25 September in his Brabham BT52 BMW after early leader Riccardo Patrese (Brabham) and Elio de Angelis (JPS Lotus 94T Renault) had touched and spun off after 10 laps. In front of a 65,000-strong crowd, Alain Prost in a Renault RE40 took second place ahead of the Lotus of Nigel Mansell. The race marked the F1 debut of Jonathan Palmer, who drove a third Williams FW08C and finished 13th. The 40-car, 30-lap Thundersports race was won by Ray Mallock/John Cooper (Lola T280 DFV) under pressure from John Foulston/John Brindley in the former's Lola T530 Chevrolet. Mallock also finished fourth, co-driving Mike Salmon in a Nimrod Aston Martin.

■ A 'first' at the Grand Prix of Europe was the provision of a giant Diamond Vision television screen at the back of South Bank, allowing around 55 per cent of the 96,000 spectators basking in the autumn sunshine to follow the race *via* the BBC's televised pictures. John Webb secured sponsorship from Unipart to fund the £50,000 required. Other attractions included a pit-lane 'walkabout' on race morning and displays from a Flying Fortress and Avro Lancaster during the lunchbreak.

■ At the Formula Ford Festival and World Cup on 28–30 October, Andrew Gilbert-Scott scored a clear victory in the final with a Reynard 83FF.

■ The second running of the British Rallycross Grand Prix on 11 December produced a win for Olle Arnesson in an Audi Quattro.

1984

■ Despite a combination of rain, hail, sleet and snow at the Giant 500 Car meeting on 1 April, spectators were able to see over 400 cars lined up for the lunchtime start-finish line walkabout. Race entries for the meeting were free to encourage as many as possible, and Jack Brabham presented the prizes at the end. Maurizio Sandro Sala won the feature EFDA FF2000 event in his Reynard 84SF.

■ John Foulston/John Brindley won the Thundersports race on Easter Monday, 23 April, in their Lola T530 Chevrolet.

■ John Harper in a Monza Lister-Jaguar just beat Willie Green's Lotus 16 in the FIA European Historic Championship round on 20 May. Green had been left on the line with a dead engine but stormed through to second place.

■ On a streaming wet track, the 2-litre Toj SC205 BMW of Tom Dodd-Noble/John Morrison emerged the winner of the Spring Bank Holiday Thundersports race on 28 May. Julian Bailey in his Reynard 84SF won the FF2000 race from Martin Donnelly's Van Diemen RF84 and Anthony Reid's Argo JM14B.

■ In June, the International Racing Press Association awarded its 'Prix Orange' for the best-organised Grand Prix media centre to Brands Hatch for its 1982 and 1983 Grands Prix.

BELOW *In June 1984, the International Racing Press Association awarded its Prix Orange for the best-organised Grand Prix media service to Brands Hatch for its 1982 and 1983 Grands Prix. Depicted on the certificate are John Webb with Ann Bradshaw and Robin Bradford from the Brands Hatch press office. (John Webb Collection)*

L'ASSEMBLÉE GÉNÉRALE DE L'INTERNATIONAL RACING PRESS ASSOCIATION
A DÉCIDÉ, À LA MAJORITÉ, DE CONFÉRER SON

PRIX ORANGE
AUX ORGANISATEURS DU GRAND PRIX D'EUROPE À
BRANDS-HATCH

1982 1983

MONACO
LE 1ER JUIN 1984

■ Niki Lauda in a Marlboro McLaren MP4/2 TAG was the winner of the John Player British Grand Prix on 22 July. The race was stopped after 11 laps when a steering arm broke on Jonathan Palmer's RAM and he crashed at Clearways. An accident on the opening lap had also left two cars in a dangerous position and so the red flags were shown. When the race was restarted, Nelson Piquet, who had started from pole and led in his Brabham BT53 BMW, was beaten off the line by Alain Prost's McLaren, with Lauda third. After 19 laps, Lauda passed Piquet and looked settled in second until Prost slowed and retired in the pits. Piquet also retired a little later, leaving Derek Warwick a popular runner-up in a Renault RE50, ahead of Ayrton Senna's Toleman TG184 Hart.

■ Andy Rouse in a Rover Vitesse won the supporting British Saloon Car Championship race at the Grand Prix, from James Weaver (BMW 635CSi) and Dave Brodie (Colt Starion). A huge field for an HSCC Atlantic Computers Historic GT race was led home by Mike Wheatley's Can-Am BRM P154 and Ray Mallock's Lola T222 after John Foulston's McLaren M8C had been penalised 10sec for jumping the start.

■ More than 162,000 people attended the Grand Prix over the three days, the race day crowd being around 109,000. On the Thursday before the Grand Prix, John Webb announced that advance ticket sales had exceeded the £1 million mark for the first time.

■ Brands Hatch promoted another World Championship double-header when the 238-lap British Aerospace 1000 for Group C cars was held the following Sunday, 29 July. This time 24,000 people turned up, the largest crowd for a sports car race in Britain for many years, due in part to another free ticket offer from the Grand Prix. Unfortunately, the race was not as exciting as previous years when far fewer spectators had attended. Jonathan Palmer/Jan Lammers dominated the event in Richard Lloyd's Canon Porsche 956, thanks to an ingenious nose-wing which cured the car's inherent understeer. Incidents and mechanical problems afflicted the other Porsches and the works Lancia LC2-84, leaving Jochen Mass/Henri Pescarolo the runners-up in Joest Racing's Le Mans winning Porsche 956B, three laps behind the winners.

■ The now-traditional *Sun* Free Race Day on 12 August drew a crowd of 30,000 to see Maurizio Sandro Sala win the FF2000 feature race in his Reynard 84SF.

■ Win Percy gave the Toyota Supra its maiden Group A win in the Bank Holiday Monday Trimoco RAC British Saloon Car Championship round on 28 August, beating the Rover Vitesse of Andy Rouse and the Colt Starion Turbo of Dave Brodie. Ian Taylor/Peter Lovett won the Thundersports race with a Lola T594C Mazda.

■ A joint car and motorbike meeting was organised by Brands Hatch Racing Club and the British Motor Cycle Racing Club over 29–30 September. A total of 28 races were held and revisions made to the gravel traps and run-off areas to accommodate the

ABOVE *The Race Control tower and commentator's box in 1984. (Author)*

BELOW *Niki Lauda obviously didn't think much of the toilet facilities at Brands Hatch in 1984. He preferred to relieve himself behind the transporters in the Formula One paddock during the Grand Prix meeting. (Michael Hewett)*

two disciplines. Damon Hill rode a Yamaha, winning three races, and also drove a Van Diemen in the FF1600 events but crashed out of both races.

■ The last-ever FIA Formula 2 event, before it was replaced the following season by Formula 3000, was held at the track on 23 September. The race was won by Philippe Streiff in an AGS JH19C BMW after torrential rain had caused it to be stopped and restarted, only to be stopped again as conditions worsened. Michel Ferté was second in a Martini 002 BMW and early leader Roberto Moreno's Ralt RH6 Honda was third. The supporting F3 event was won by Ross Cheever in a Ralt RT3 VW.

■ Formula 2 cars had not raced at the circuit since 1971, John Webb not being a particular fan of the formula. Explaining the change of heart, Webb said: "In a good Grand Prix year, we can afford to take the chance on races that would otherwise not be a safe financial risk."

■ Damon Hill won the JPS Champion of Brands FF1600 race at the BRSCC 14 October meeting, beating more experienced rivals in his Van Diemen RF84.

■ Dutchman Gerrit van Kouwen totally dominated the Formula Ford Festival and World Cup over 2–4 November in his Lola T644E, smashing the FF1600 lap record along the way, leaving it at 48.889s, 88.62mph.

■ European champion Martin Schanche won the Motaquip Rallycross Grand Prix in style on 9 December in his 4WD Ford Escort Mk3 Turbo, watched by a huge crowd.

RIGHT *Ayrton Senna in the Hart turbo engined Toleman TG184. The Brazilian qualified seventh and finished third in the 1984 John Player British Grand Prix on 22 July. (Author)*

1985

■ At the Brands Hatch Giant 500 club meeting on 31 March, the lunchtime display allowed spectators to go onto the track to see the cars at close quarters. Competitors who presented their machinery got part of their entry fee returned, resulting in an impressive turnout, with the parade stretching most of the way around the Indy circuit.

■ A controversial incident overshadowed a thrilling Thundersports event on Easter Monday, 8 April. Neil Crang in a Tiga was black-flagged for overtaking the pace car, despite being convinced he had been waved past. This left an easy win for Tiff Needell/Richard Piper in their Chevron B36.

■ The Truck Superprix on 21 April was won by Italian Gaudenzio Mantova, in a Scania 142. A variety of sideshows, including aerial displays, a jet-propelled truck and a funfair, kept the 40,000 crowd entertained.

■ The Atlantic Computers International Historic Weekend over 8–9 June featured the FIA Historic Championship, and £20 million worth of cars contested 18 races over two days. The weekend had an Italian flavour, the paddock brimming with exotica from Club Italia and Scuderia del Portello.

■ Ross Cheever, brother of American F1 driver Eddie, won the Marlboro British F3 round on 23 June, driving a Ralt RT30 VW.

■ On 24 July, the main access road from the A20 entrance behind the start-finish grandstand was named Colin Chapman Way, in honour of the late founder of Lotus Cars and Team Lotus. The ceremony was performed by Chapman's widow, Hazel, along with his son, Clive, and daughters, Janet and Sarah. Chapman's association with the circuit dated back to 1954 when a Lotus 8, driven by Nigel Allen, was the first car on the new Druids hairpin extension.

■ The highlight of Lotus Raceday on 28 July was an appearance by Ayrton Senna, driving a JPS Lotus 97T F1 car. The main event of the meeting was the Thundersports race, won by Ian Taylor/Pete Lovett in a Tiga TS85 BMW, after the Lola T530 of John Foulston/John Brindley, the winners on the road, had been disqualified in post-race scrutineering. A celebrity race, using identical Ford Escort XR3is, was won by Sir Jack Brabham from Divina Galica.

RIGHT Nigel Mansell scored his maiden Grand Prix victory in the 1985 Shell Oils Grand Prix of Europe, driving his Canon Williams FW10B Honda. (Michael Hewett)

■ The *Sun* Free Race day on 11 August attracted a huge crowd. MCD circuit director Peter Todd finished third in the celebrity event, his first ever race.

■ The Failsafe Battle of Brands took place on Bank Holiday Monday, 26 August, and was won comfortably by John Brindley in his Lola T530. Indy-style qualifying, with one car out at a time, was used: the cars completed one out-lap and three flying laps.

■ A large number of spectators turned up mid-week for two days of tyre testing for F1 teams over 28–29 August, in preparation for the Grand Prix of Europe. Ten teams were present. Stefan Johansson led the way in his Ferrari from the Williams-Honda of Keke Rosberg.

■ Derek Bell/Hans Stuck clinched the first FIA World Endurance Championship of Drivers by winning the Shell Gemini 1000 on 22 September in their Rothmans Porsche 962C. The event lived up to its title when the two works Lancias qualified on the front row, with two works Porsches and then the two works Jaguars behind. At the finish, the Porsches had a 1-2 with the Lancias 3-4 but, to the dismay of a 26,000 crowd, the green Jaguars were parked with broken engines.

RIGHT *Derek Bell/Hans Stuck took victory in the first FIA World Endurance Championship for Drivers by winning the Shell Gemini 1000 on 22 September 1985. (LAT)*

■ Future Brands Hatch boss Jonathan Palmer was unable to take part in the Shell Grand Prix of Europe on 6 October, as he was recovering from a broken leg sustained during the 1000km Group C race meeting at Spa. Nigel Mansell scored his first-ever F1 victory, driving a Honda V6 turbo powered Williams FW10B. Pole man Ayrton Senna (Lotus 97T Renault) and Keke Rosberg in the other Williams also stepped onto the podium. When Michele Alboreto's Ferrari 156/85 caught fire, fourth place by Alain Prost's McLaren MP4-2B TAG was enough to clinch the first FIA World Championship won by a Frenchman.

■ In the supporting Europa Cup Renault Elf Turbo race, guest driver Barrie 'Whizzo' Williams demolished the series regulars. The CanAm Lola-Chevrolet of John Foulston/John Brindley broke a driveshaft in the Thundersports event, leaving the win to Mike Wilds/James Wallis with the locally entered Otford Group Lola T286 DFV. Andy Rouse led a 1-2-3 for the Ford Sierra Turbo in the saloon race.

■ Pre-event favourite Johnny Herbert planted his Quest FF85 into the Paddock Hill catchfencing on his first flying lap of qualifying for the First Edition Formula Ford World Cup and Festival over 25–27 October, so he had to start his heat from the very back of the grid, with a 10sec penalty. He picked his way through the field, though, to finish sixth. In his quarter-final, he was fourth, and he finished second in his semi-final. He led away from the start of the final and, despite the best efforts of Jonathan Bancroft in a Van Diemen RF85, took the victory.

Damon Hill in another Van Diemen finished third, just holding off the similar car of Mark Blundell.

■ The Formula Ford World Cup meeting was marred by the death of a 26-year-old marshal who was fatally injured when a car cartwheeled over the barrier at Paddock Hill Bend during the heats, demolished an advertising hoarding and came to rest within a marshalling area.

■ Mark Blundell's last-lap victory, driving a Reynard 84SF in the final round of the BBC Grandstand FF2000 Trophy on 1 December, clinched the title.

■ John Welch became the first British competitor to win the British Rallycross Grand Prix when he took his 4WD Ford Escort Turbo to victory on 8 December. Welch was knocked off on the first lap but was soon back up to second place and challenging the leader, Martin Schanche. When Schanche retired with damaged steering, Welch was left out in front to take a hugely popular win.

ABOVE *Johnny Herbert crosses the line to win the 1985 Formula Ford Festival in his Quest, closely followed by second-placed Jonathan Bancroft in his Van Diemen. (sutton-images.com)*

1986

■ At the BRSCC annual dinner and dance, the prestigious BRSCC Trophy, awarded annually to the person or body who has done most to further British motor sport during the year, was presented by the Minister for Sport, Richard Tracey MP, to John Webb. It recognised Webb's achievement in staging five successive Grands Prix at Brands Hatch.

BELOW *John Foulston, a regular competitor in Historic GT and Thundersports racing, bought Brands Hatch, Oulton Park and Snetterton from Eagle Star Holdings in a £5.25 million deal in May 1986. (Author)*

BELOW *A nine-car accident at the start of the 1986 Shell Oils British Grand Prix on 13 July triggered the red flags to be waved and the race to be stopped. Behind the Arrows of Thierry Boutsen and the Zakspeed of Jonathan Palmer in the foreground, Jacques Laffite is trapped in his Ligier JS27 Renault. (LAT)*

■ The Can-Am Lola T530 of John Foulston/John Brindley won the Thundersports event by a full three laps on Easter Monday, 31 March, having also taken victory in the Oulton Park Gold Cup race on Good Friday.

■ Following the success of Radio Brands at the European Grand Prix the previous year, the Home Office granted its approval for an extension of the service for 1986. It was announced in April that Radio Brands would cover six key events, broadcasting on 1594KHz medium wave. The station would be on the air for the Truck Superprix, the British Grand Prix, the Cellnet F3 Superprix, the Powerbike International and the British Rallycross Grand Prix. As well as race commentary, the broadcasts would feature interviews, news bulletins, music, weather and local traffic information.

■ Sweden's Rolf Bjork emerged the winner of the Lucas Truck Superprix over 12–13 April, driving a Scania 142. BBC presenter and racing driver Mike Smith, who eventually finished eighth, commented that it was "like driving a block of flats from the fourth floor up". Other competitors included Willie Green, Rod Chapman, Barry Sheene, Steve Parrish and Barry Lee. A full weekend of entertainment included a low flypast by a British Airways Concorde.

■ Andy Wallace won the 30-lap British F3 race on 20 April, after holding off a challenge from the similar Reynard 863 of Dave Scott. Gary Brabham set a new class record on his way to fifth in his Ralt RT30.

■ New circuit owner John Foulston, partnered as usual by John Brindley, cruised to an easy victory in the 82-lap Thundersports race on Bank Holiday Monday, 26 May.

■ 'Mansell Mania' was the headline after the Shell Oils British Grand Prix on 13 July. Nigel Mansell's CV joint broke on the startline, but a first-corner accident, in which Jacques Laffite suffered serious leg injuries, meant a restart. This time Mansell, in the spare car, had no problems. His team mate, Nelson Piquet, was on pole position and led the first 22 laps, but Mansell passed the Brazilian on the run to Hawthorn Bend. The Williams pair went on to lap the entire field. The event was typical of a Brands Hatch spectacular. Apart from the on-track action, the 115,000 crowd, the biggest ever seen at a British Grand Prix, was treated to a Vulcan bomber and Concorde flying low overhead. *Autosport* reported that the organisation had been superb, and that the marshalling and rescue work had been an object lesson to the rest of the world. It also noted that the traffic arrangements had worked better than anyone could remember. "This cannot, must not, have been the last British Grand Prix at Brands Hatch for five years," was the closing line of its editorial.

■ The traditional RAC British Saloon Car Championship support race was won by Jeff Allam in a Rover Vitesse, from the similar car of Jean-Louis Schlesser. The non-championship Cellnet F3 race was won by Andy Wallace in his Reynard 863, from the Ralt RT30 of Gary Brabham. The John Foulston/John Brindley show once again dominated the event-closing Thundersports race.

■ The staff at Brands Hatch barely had time to sweep up from the Grand Prix before the following weekend's Shell Gemini 1000 World Sports-Prototype Championship race meeting over 18–20 July. Grand Prix ticket holders again had free entries and it

BELOW At the restart of the 1986 British Grand Prix, the field swoops down from Druids and around Graham Hill Bend. South Bank is packed with spectators. (Michael Hewett)

worked, despite poor weather on race morning. The crowd's favourites were the pair of Silk Cut Jaguar XJR-6s but victory went to the RLR team's Porsche 956 GTI, raced by Bob Wollek/Mauro Baldi. Derek Bell was second in the Rothmans Porsche 956 he shared with Hans Stuck and Klaus Ludwig.

■ The Cellnet Formula 3 Superprix over 2–3 August was billed as the world's richest F3 event, with a £25,000 prize fund. Fifty drivers from 15 nations competed in a seven-race, three-round knockout competition over two days, using both the Indy circuit and the Grand Prix circuit. The weather was not kind but it did allow the spectators to witness a dominant display of wet-weather driving from Andy Wallace, whose Madgwick Reynard 863 VW won the final, 43sec clear of Martin Donnelly, with Johnny Herbert third.

■ At the Lucas British F3 race on 31 August, Andy Wallace became the first F3 driver to lap the Indy circuit at over 100mph, earning himself a £1000 bonus, on his way to taking pole position. He went on score a lights-to-flag victory in his Reynard 863 from the Ralt RT30 of Martin Donnelly.

ABOVE *Ever the showman, Nigel Mansell looks more exhausted than usual after winning the 1986 British Grand Prix in the spare car, which did not have a drinks bottle fitted. (sutton-images.com)*

■ An extra Thundersports race was organised at short notice for 14 September to replace one rained off from the August Bank Holiday Birmingham Superprix meeting. Brands Hatch arranged to allocate some of its profits from the Grand Prix to an additional 100-mile race over the full Grand Prix circuit for the competitors. When it came to the weekend, it was nearly a case of *déjà vu* because the racing on the Saturday was curtailed due to poor visibility. Sunday was brighter, though, and Andrew Radcliffe/Mike Wilds took their Lola T530 to victory after battling with the John Foulston/John Brindley Lola until the latter's throttle linkage snapped.

■ The Formula Ford Festival on 24–26 October produced a head-to-head in the final between Austria's Roland Ratzenberger and the Swiss, Philippe Favre. Each had dominated his heat, quarter-final and semi-final and lined up on the front of the grid. The pair pulled away from the pack, with Ratzenberger ahead, and

remained nose-to-tail for the duration. Favre waited until the last corner before attempting to dive inside his rival and the pair were side-by-side as they crossed the line, Ratzenberger just holding on to win by 0.05sec.

■ In November, outline planning permission for the construction of a hotel adjacent to the circuit's entrance was approved by Sevenoaks District Council. The £7 million, 140-room hotel was expected to be operational by early 1988. The hotel was to be owned and operated by Brands Hatch Leisure plc. The circuit also received planning permission for the construction of a further 10,000sq.ft of industrial units.

■ The Shell Oils Rallysprint on 8 November featured a three-discipline challenge between F1 and rally drivers, with Martin Brundle, Johnny Dumfries and Derek Warwick taking on Stig Blomqvist, Russell Brookes and Jimmy McRae. Also taking part were a team of 'young thrusters' comprising Damon Hill, Gary Brabham and Mark Lovell. Tests included a 10-lap race in Toyota MR2s on the Indy circuit, a one-mile rally stage on the gravel service roads above Druids using Group A Toyota Corollas, and an autotest on a wet course in front of the main grandstand. Entry to the event was free and the surprise (and surprised) winner was Damon Hill.

■ During August to October, Brands Hatch Leisure distributed questionnaires to spectators at both car and bike meetings. About 3700 were returned and the results showed that, for car meetings, 64.75 per cent of spectators were aged between 21 and 40. Saloon car racing was the favourite part of the sport, ahead of Formula One, Formula Ford 1600 and Formula 3.

■ Nigel Mansell attempted to break Keke Rosberg's unofficial Indy circuit lap record at a special 'Tribute to Williams' day on 30 November, which featured a parade of all the Williams F1 cars and a pit-lane 'walkabout' for the public. With the track cold and slippery, Mansell could not better Rosberg's 35.85s, managing only 37.4s. Even so, he entertained the 12,000 crowd by performing tyre-smoking doughnuts and signing autographs. Topping the racing bill in this season-closing meeting was the final round of the BBC Grandstand FF2000 championship, which Dave Coyne won, thereby clinching the title.

■ BHL announced that it was to cut the cost of spectating for the following year by introducing a 'Circuitsavers' discount scheme. Visitors to Brands, Oulton Park and Snetterton could save up to 57 per cent on admission, paddock, grandstand and pit-lane 'walkabouts' by using a combination of coupons throughout the year. The book of coupons, worth £50 at face value, cost £30; a book worth £100 cost £50; and one worth £150 cost £65. It was also announced that child admission (under 16) would be free at most race meetings in 1987.

■ Andy Bentza in an Audi Quattro was the surprise winner of the Motaquip British Rallycross Grand Prix on 7 December, from Seppi Niittymaki's Xtrac Escort and the similar car of John Welch.

RIGHT *Bob Wollek/Mauro Baldi won the 1986 Shell Gemini 1000 World Sports Prototype Championship race in their Porsche 956GTI. (LAT)*

MIDDLE *Ross Cheever spins his Ralt RT30 at Druids during a very wet Cellnet Formula 3 Superprix on 3 August 1986. (Author)*

BOTTOM RIGHT *Brands Hatch organised a special 'Tribute to Williams' day on 30 November 1986, during which Nigel Mansell attempted to break the unofficial Indy circuit lap record, held by Keke Rosberg at 35.85s, in his Williams FW11 Honda. On a cold and slippery track, Mansell could only manage 37.4s, but kept the crowd entertained. (Author)*

BELOW *John Foulston's McLaren M8D leads the BRM P154 of Mike Wheatley and the rest of the Historic GT field around Paddock at the 1986 British Grand Prix meeting on 13 July. (Author)*

1987

■ The Van Diemen Formula First car was unveiled in January. This new formula was designed to provide a low-cost entry into motor sport and BHL estimated that a minimum operating budget for a year's racing would be just under £4000.

■ Jyrki Jarvilehto won the first round of the Mobil 1 British Formula Ford 2000 championship on 1 March. A free ticket offer at the Racing Car Show boosted crowd numbers, despite the rain.

■ Mark Rennison in a Ford RS200 won the opening round of the British Rallycross Championship on 15 March.

■ Damon Hill took pole in his Ralt RT31 Toyota for the Lucas F3 race on 5 April but Johnny Herbert won a processional race on the Grand Prix circuit in his Reynard 873 VW. The inaugural Formula First race was won by Eugene O'Brien, after being restarted due to a number of first-lap accidents.

BELOW *The winning Jaguar XJR8 of Raul Boesel/John Nielsen passes the Brun Porsche 962C of Jochen Mass/Oscar Larrauri at Paddock Hill Bend during the 1987 Shell Gemini 1000 on 26 July. (LAT)*

■ Mike Wilds/Ian Flux took a dominant victory in their Lola T530 at the Easter Monday Thundersports encounter on 20 April, after the similar car of John Foulston/John Brindley had been retired.

■ It was the turn of Bertrand Gachot in his Ralt RT31 Alfa Romeo to win at the Lucas F3 meeting on 17 May, ahead of the Reynard 873s of Johnny Herbert and Martin Donnelly.

■ Another mixed car and bike meeting took place on 24 May at the four-day Treasure Competition & Caravan Festival over the Bank Holiday weekend with a 15-race programme, five of which were for cars.

■ There was a quality field for the International Historic Superprix on 6–7 June, with BHL chairman John Foulston taking four victories out of four. After winning the pre-1971 single-seater race in a McLaren M19A, the Historic GT race in a McLaren M8D and the 'historically interesting' race in a McLaren M23, he also won the main event, the Steigenberger Hotels Trophy, in his Can-Am Lola T260.

■ Ian Flux/Ian Taylor in a Lola T530 Chevrolet took pole and won the Thundersports encounter on 28 June. Jyrki Jarvilehto repeated his win of earlier in the year in the FF2000 supporting race.

■ In July, proposals were announced for changes to the circuit. Westfield Bend was to be realigned, making it tighter, to gain more run-off area, while Dingle Dell Corner was to be made into a right-left-right chicane.

■ A crowd of 35,000 turned out to see the Silk Cut Jaguar XJR8 of Raul Boesel/John Nielsen take victory in the Shell Gemini 1000 Group C enduro on 26 July, after a hard-fought battle with the Porsche 962 GTI of Mauro Baldi/Johnny Dumfries. John Watson/Jan Lammers finished third in the other Jaguar ahead of the Joest Porsche 962C of Derek Bell/Hans Stuck. Tim Harvey won the supporting British Touring Car Championship round in his Rover Vitesse.

■ The Cellnet Formula First race on 9 August was stopped twice and a spectator hospitalised, despite competitors having been warned about driving standards by clerk of the course John Nicol in the pre-race briefing. Jonathan Bancroft won the FF2000 race in a Reynard.

■ Julian Bailey dominated the FIA International Formula 3000 race on 23 August in his Lola T87/50 DFV, chased hard all the way by the Ralt RT21 Hondas of Mauricio Gugelmin and Roberto Moreno.

■ Martin Donnelly won a wet and ultimately red-flagged F3 round on 6 September. Damon Hill, driving the other Intersport Ralt RT31, led at first from pole man Johnny Herbert (EJR Reynard 873), with Donnelly third. Herbert was passed by Donnelly who hounded Hill and overtook him into Paddock. The race was stopped after 12 laps with a number of cars off the track.

■ Nigel Mansell smashed the unofficial Indy circuit lap record while testing his 'active' suspension Williams FW11B Honda on Wednesday 9 September. Mansell set a time of 34.9s, 124.153mph.

■ On 29 September, John Foulston, the chairman of Brands Hatch Leisure, was killed at Silverstone while testing his McLaren Indycar.

ABOVE *Third-placed Roberto Moreno approaches Druids in his Lola T87/50 DFV during the FIA Formula 3000 race on 23 August 1987. (sutton-images.com)*

■ Johnny Herbert won the rain-soaked Cellnet F3 Superprix on 11 October. Run along the lines of the Formula Ford Festival, the event consisted of heats, semi-finals and a final. The first semi was won by Herbert in his Reynard 873 VW, while Martin Donnelly took the restarted and shortened second semi in his Ralt RT31 Toyota. With darkness rapidly approaching, the final was shortened from 30 laps to 20. Herbert won, ahead of Bertrand Gachot (Ralt) and Donnelly.

■ The great storm which swept across south-east England on Friday 16 October caused around £100,000 worth of damage at the circuit. In addition to a number of trees being blown over, the main grandstand and the scrutineering bay both suffered roof damage, while the ticket booths at the entrances were totally destroyed.

■ Eddie Irvine was in dominant form at the Formula Ford Festival and World Cup meeting between 30 October and 1 November, winning the final in his Van Diemen RF87, ahead of Alain Menu (Reynard 87F).

■ Eddie Irvine followed his FF1600 success with victory in the BBC Grandstand Formula Ford 2000 round on 15 November, again in a Van Diemen RF87, and repeated the feat a week later on 22 November. Both races were run in the rain.

■ Jonathan Palmer avoided the mayhem to win the Toyota MR2 race at the Rallysprint event on 28–29 November after pole man Martin Brundle was hit by Paul Warwick on the first lap. The three-disciplined event pitched rally drivers against F1 drivers. Unsurprisingly, Juha Kankkunen won the rally stage, but Brundle took victory in the autotest. Palmer's race victory ensured that the Grand Prix drivers won the event overall.

■ A huge crowd watched Mikael Nordstrom take victory in the sixth Motoquip Rallycross Grand Prix on 5–6 December in his Ford RS200E. Will Gollop finished second in his MG Metro 6R4.

1988

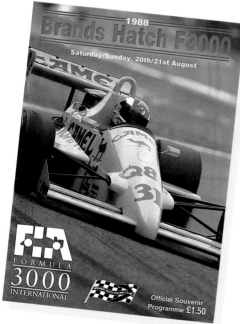

- Will Gollop won the first Rallycross event of the year on 17 January in his Metro 6R4.

- The Easter Monday meeting on 4 April was the first occasion on which the modified Grand Prix circuit was used, with the reprofiled Westfield and Dingle Dell corners. These were the first changes made to the track since 1976. Mike Wilds/John Brindley won the feature Thundersports event in their Lola T530.

- John Alcorn's Reynard 883 Toyota beat Damon Hill's Ralt RT31 Toyota in the F3 race on 17 April.

- In April, it was announced that Mary Foulston, the widow of John Foulston, had been appointed as the chair of Brands Hatch Leisure plc, the position her late husband had held. She succeeded John Tompkins, the chief executive of Atlantic Computers, who had held the post since Foulston's death.

- Damon Hill took pole position with his Intersport Ralt RT32 for the F3 race on 22 May by a large margin, but was stopped by a transmission failure. JJ Lehto scored a convincing victory with the Pacific team's Reynard 883, over Eddie Irvine in his Ralt.

BELOW Brands staged a 'Cars of the Century' event mid-week in July 1988. It was attended by HRH Prince Charles, seen here with the victorious Jaguar team from the previous month's Le Mans 24 Hours. (Author)

- The Historic Sports Car Club put on a memorable display of racing over 4–5 June. Alo Lawler took an ex-Alain Prost McLaren M30 to victory in the Historic F1 encounter.

- In July, BHL sold its new hotel, which had been built at the entrance to the circuit and was due to be opened on 1 September, to Thistle Hotels Ltd. Money raised from the sale was to be put towards upgrading facilities at the circuit, including building new pits, a new F1 paddock, media centre and hospitality suites.

- An unusual event took place at the circuit on Thursday 21 July, with a parade of 'Cars of the Century' attended by HRH the Prince of Wales, who drove around the circuit. The event was held in aid of the Prince's Trust and included a variety of different

BELOW Marshals and the medical team attend the severely injured Johnny Herbert after his 150mph crash during the FIA International Formula 3000 race on 21 August 1988. It was over two hours before the race could be restarted, and only six cars took part. (Author)

cars which were driven around the track, including that year's Le Mans winning Jaguar.

■ It was Jaguar *versus* Sauber-Mercedes in the Brands Hatch 1000 event on 24 July, when the XJR-9 of Martin Brundle/John Nielsen/Andy Wallace won in front of a 30,000 crowd. Pole man Mauro Baldi messed up his start with his Sauber C9, allowing team mate Jochen Mass to contest the lead with the Klaus Ludwig/Bob Wollek Porsche 962. As the leaders came up to lap backmarkers, Steve Hynes moved his Tiga out of the way at Clark Curve but lost control, collecting Mass's Sauber and sending it hard into the barriers as Baldi spun to a halt in avoidance. This left Ludwig ahead of Nielsen. The lead was contested by these two and Jan Lammers/Johnny Dumfries, until the second Jaguar was stopped by electrical problems. Brundle eventually took the flag ahead of Ludwig/Wollek with Baldi/Jean-Louis Schlesser third for Sauber. The C2 class victory by Gordon Spice/Ray Bellm in their Spice SE88C Cosworth clinched the World title in the class.

■ The FIA International Formula 3000 event over the weekend of 20–21 August was not a happy occasion. First, Michel Trollé was badly injured during practice when his Lola crashed at the new Dingle Dell corner almost head-on. In the race the following day, Johnny Herbert suffered severe leg injuries when he was involved in an 11-car pile-up. Herbert and Martin Donnelly dominated qualifying in their Reynard 88Ds and Herbert led their 1-2 for the EFR team from the start, the pair pulling away from the rest of the field. Then the race was stopped when Roberto Moreno's Reynard 88D crashed at Paddock. At the restart, Donnelly and Pierluigi Martini (March 88B) got the drop on Herbert. As they went down Pilgrim's Drop on the long part of the circuit for the first time, Herbert touched Gregor Foitek's Lola T88/50 at 150mph, hitting the bridge and triggering a multiple accident. Foitek barrel-rolled down the track while Herbert's car rebounded into the path of Olivier Grouillard's

Lola. The track was blocked and the race again red-flagged. It was over two hours before it was started for the third time, with just six cars on the grid. Donnelly scored a hollow victory from Martini and Mark Blundell (Lola).

■ Andy Rouse in his Ford Sierra Cosworth RS500 took victory in the supporting BTCC race, but Frank Sytner's Class B win in his BMW M3 left him ahead in the championship.

■ Gary Brabham's Ralt RT32 VW beat Damon Hill's Ralt-Toyota in the F3 event on 4 September, with Paul Warwick's Reynard 883 VW third.

■ Dave Pinkney/Tim Harvey triumphed in the 300km Uniroyal Tyres race for production saloons in their Ford Sierra RS Cosworth on 25 September.

■ The Cellnet F3 Superprix on 8–9 October comprised 45 laps of the Indy circuit with compulsory tyre changes. Competitors started with tyres with red sidewalls and changed to blue-walled tyres so that spectators could easily see who had made their pitstops. Gary Brabham won in his Ralt RT32 from Jason Elliot's Reynard 883.

■ The Formula Ford Festival and World Cup over 28–30 October was won by Van Diemen RF88 driver Vincenzo Sospiri, who passed the similar car of Derek Higgins with a lap to go. On the run to the flag, Jose Cordova in a Reynard 88FF just beat Higgins to second place.

■ Will Gollop in his Metro 6R4 won the Rallycross Grand Prix on 11 December, becoming the seventh different winner in the seventh running of the event.

1989

■ A large crowd witnessed the opening round of the British Rallycross Championship on 12 February, where John Welch won the Superfinal in his Opel Kadett GSI 4x4.

■ A range of modifications were made to the circuit during February. The barriers at Paddock Bend were moved back and the catchfencing removed in order to lengthen the gravel trap there. At Druids, the barriers were also repositioned and the gravel trap lengthened. More run-off area was provided at Graham Hill Bend, as requested by the FIM, motorcycling's governing body. The gravel trap at Clearways was also doubled in width and continued through Clark Curve along to Brabham Straight.

BELOW *A huge crowd turned out for the 1989 Brands Hatch Trophy race on 23 July, a 300km sprint which counted towards the World Sports Prototype Championship. The race provided a win for Kenny Acheson and Mauro Baldi, who is seen here leading the field around Paddock Hill Bend in his Sauber-Mercedes C9/88. (LAT)*

■ The Indy circuit official lap record, which had been held by Indycar driver Danny Ongais at 41.4sec for over a decade, was finally broken by Gary Brabham in a Reynard 88D in the opening round of the British F3000 championship on 19 March. Brabham set a time of 40.08sec, 108.10mph. The race was won by Andrew Gilbert-Scott in his Reynard ahead of Roland Ratzenberger (Reynard), with Brabham third.

■ In April, Brands Hatch Ford, a Ford dealership run by Jackie Epstein, was opened by the Paddock entrance.

■ David Brabham was the winner of the Lucas British F3 event on 23 April in his Ralt RT33 VW. The race had to be started three times after a number of incidents. Brabham was victorious again a few weeks later on 21 May, beating the Reynard 893 of Mika Häkkinen.

■ The Historic Sports Car Club attracted around 400 entries for its Superprix on 3–4 June. The main race was won by David

Franklin's McLaren M6B. A new permanent catering facility, named Hailwoods and located at the lower end of the paddock, was opened for the first time at this meeting.

■ Over the weekend of 24–25 June, the circuit hosted a new concept in family entertainment. Sky-Track '89 combined a race meeting, an air show and a military display. The event included truck racing, Superkarts, Formula Ford, saloons, hot air balloons, parachute displays, flypasts by Vulcan and Vampire aircraft, and

ABOVE You can always rely on Brands Hatch to produce close racing, as can be seen in this shot as Julian Bailey tries to put his Nissan R89C inside the Toyota 89CV of Johnny Dumfries during the 1989 Brands Hatch Trophy race on 23 July. (Author)

army displays. The Brabham name continued its winning ways in the feature British F3000 race, when Gary Brabham took his Reynard 88D to victory, beating Roland Ratzenberger's similar car.

■ A huge crowd turned out for the Brands Hatch Trophy on 23 July, a round of the FIA World Sports Prototype Championship. The event was a 300km sprint over 115 laps of the Grand Prix circuit and was described as one of the best sportscar races ever seen. It provided a win for Kenny Acheson/Mauro Baldi in a Sauber-Mercedes C9, ahead of the Porsche 962 of Bob Wollek/Frank Jelinski. The race marked the debut of the new turbocharged Jaguar XJR-11, in which Jan Lammers/Patrick Tambay took pole but dropped to fifth in the race with exhaust damage. The supporting BTCC race was won by Robb Gravett in a Ford Sierra RS500.

■ Eddie Jordan's team of Martin Donnelly and Jean Alesi took their Reynard 89Ds to a resounding 1-2 at the FIA International Formula 3000 round on 20 August.

■ Philippe Adams scored his maiden F3 victory in the Lucas championship round on 3 September with a Ralt RT33, ahead of Bowman team mate David Brabham.

■ Gary Brabham secured the inaugural British F3000 title on 10 September by winning the final round in his Reynard 88D after the other title contender, Andrew Gilbert-Scott, had crashed his EJR Reynard at Dingle Dell, causing the race to be halted. Perry McCarthy was second in a Lola T88/50.

■ The Cellnet F3 Superprix on 22 October was again run as a stand-alone, 45-lap event over the Indy circuit with compulsory tyre changes. Mika Häkkinen won with a Ralt RT33.

ABOVE *Robb Gravett's Ford Sierra RS500 leads the similar cars of Andy Rouse and Mike Smith up Hailwood Hill towards Druids during the British Touring Car race on 23 July 1989. (Author)*

■ Any one of six drivers could have won the Formula Ford Festival and World Cup on 28 October, but it was Nico Palhares in his Van Diemen RF89 who emerged the winner, from Michael Vergers and David Coulthard, also in Van Diemens.

■ BHL announced in November that it was discontinuing its Thundersports category due to dwindling grids.

■ Also in November came the shock news that John and Angela Webb were to leave Brands Hatch Leisure in February 1990 and that Nicola Foulston would become chief executive. Rumours concerning the future of the circuit abounded, including a sale and a multi-million pound facelift. Foulston stated: "As long as I am chief executive officer, the circuit, or any part of it, is not for sale."

■ Fog descended on Brands for the British Rallycross Grand Prix meeting over 2–3 December, causing the event to be run as a series of shortened 1.75-lap qualifying runs. As the fog closed in even more, hopes of running the final faded and the results were declared from the qualifying runs, Will Gollop becoming the first ever double winner of the event. The previous occasion on which a Brands Hatch event had been cancelled due to fog had been in late November 1975.

RIGHT *A very wet crowd watches the action from Druids during the 1989 Formula Ford Festival. (sutton-images.com)*

1990s

THE FOULSTON YEARS

John Webb's departure from Brands Hatch, at the risk of using a cliché, signalled the end of an era. With hindsight, it is easy to see why there was a clash between two such strong personalities. Webb was a product of his time – a post-war age when your word was your bond, there was no need for written contracts, and a helping hand might be given to a business colleague or friend in need. And so was Nicola Foulston. She grew up in the years of Thatcherism, when 'professionalism' was the order of the day and business was business, devoid of sentiment. There was a clash of cultures, which today she readily recognises.

"Absolutely," she said. "We were arrogant, and I believed I could do anything I wanted to do. And my father was in the middle, because he had a lot of time for John Webb because of what he had done in terms of creating some of the racing opportunities, all of which I was very sceptical about. So my father sort of bridged that gap. When he'd gone, that gap was unbridgeable."

The first thing Foulston did in her new role as chief executive was to change the management structure at the circuit. "Because of the cultural differences, the way the business had been run was dated in the fifties and sixties," she explained. "It was a very flat management structure and needed changing into a more modern structure. I took a year to do it, and I should have done it pretty quickly, overnight. At the time my mother was still chairman and she wanted me to do things slowly – not to upset the apple cart. So we did things slowly and that was a mistake, because everything had to happen in the end. If you're going to make a big change, make it all and get on with it.

"So after I came in it took me a year to clear it out, and in the end most of the old management went. A few of the key ones I kept, but I had to start getting the right people for the jobs and that was the first thing I did.

RIGHT *Jenson Button on his way to winning a wet Formula Ford Festival in a Mygale on 25 October 1998. (sutton-images.com)*

"I felt that my father had bought Brands to save it from property developers, which had been a very real threat in the eighties, and I wanted to prove that he hadn't made a mistake. Because it was such a handful, my mother did look at proposals from developers, and a car company, Nissan, who wanted to take it over as a private track. My job was to protect the family's interests, but I was also protecting Brands and to carry on what my father had started."

Although she was learning fast and beginning to develop the business in new directions, at that stage Foulston did not really have any particular vision for the circuit. "I had a vision of Brands Hatch Leisure," she said. "The word 'leisure' was already in there, but the precise nature of what that would be, I didn't have a good feel for. And to be frank, if it had been left just to me, I'm not sure how far it would have gone."

At an early stage, another person who was to play a major role in the future development of the circuit came on the scene. "I had an excellent salesman," explained Foulston. "He is now my husband. He was very low down in the organisation and he had a vision of what Brands should be able to do. I promoted him quite quickly because he was one of the few people I saw eye-to-eye with on a business level."

The person in question was Richard Green, who had been selling track days and racing school days out. But while some rose up in the new organisation, for others, like operations director John Symes, life was very different without the Webbs around.

Symes observed: "Many people asked me: 'How on earth can you work for John Webb? It must be bloody impossible!' In reality, John was a very easy person to work for – you just had to understand the rules. I'm an early morning person, he's an early morning person. So I would always be at my desk for eight o'clock. What he was very good at, not only with me but with everybody else, was drawing out the football pitch, letting you know what the rules of the game were, tossing you the ball and expecting you to get on with it. He wouldn't interfere. But he would always want to have a finger on the pulse. He did this with me by pitching up soon after eight o'clock in the morning, perching on the corner of my desk, lighting up a cigar and saying: 'What's going on then, Symesy?' We'd have a five-minute chat about what was going on, and then he'd womble off and go and find someone else to chat to. And with people in my sort of position, he'd do that throughout the day. So he always knew what was going on, but he was very good at not interfering.

"The other thing he was always good at was supporting his staff. If you'd made a cock-up, in private you'd get the biggest bollocking ever, but to the outside world he would support you two hundred per cent, always.

"When John and Angela left, I thought: 'This is going to be interesting, and I suspect that I won't be here forever.' It was an interesting time. I'm a fairly reasonable character, and I'm a fairly straightforward character, as well, but at that time there were a lot of people cosying up to Nicola, who seemed to work on the basis: 'Yes Nicola, no Nicola, that's a wonderful idea Nicola.' I was a director of the company, and I didn't feel it was my position to do that. If I felt she was wrong, then part of my responsibility as a director was to say: 'Hang on, I'm not sure that's in the best interests of the company.'

"I was recognised as about the only person who stood up to her, and explained the logic behind my thinking. And interestingly I survived longer than all the yes-men.

"She called me back after one board meeting and asked what the matter was, because normally I contributed a lot in board meetings, but this time I'd hardly said a word. I told her I'd felt it was probably better if I kept quiet on this occasion because, at the previous board meeting, her reaction to a suggestion of mine had been to storm out and slam the door so hard the bloody thing fell off its hinges. And she'd cancelled my maintenance budget, so I couldn't afford for that to happen again because I'd no money to put the door back on!"

Symes's direct approach was not always appreciated. When the new Foulston Centre administration building was being planned over the winter of 1990–91, he was forbidden from having anything to do with it. "Nicola decided she didn't want me involved, because we'd already had a disagreement as to the basic philosophy of the Foulston Centre, which I felt was wrong," Symes explained. "I felt we should build an administration block on the payline, so that people could access it from outside, but you could access the circuit through the offices. I also wanted to build the hospitality suites where the Grovewood Suite had been. I acknowledge that this would have been a more expensive way of doing it because, if you combine two facilities, it's always going to be cheaper. But I felt it was fundamentally wrong to do what she was proposing to do. Because of that, she made it very clear I was to have nothing to do with the building or its construction in any way, shape or form.

"However, when they'd done the basic groundworks, the project director came and asked if he could talk to me. I asked him: 'Are you aware that I've been instructed not to have any involvement in this project?' He said: 'Yes, but it was Nicola who told me to come and talk to you.' He said they were a bit puzzled because they'd got the foundations in, but the front of the building was about 10 metres nearer to the track than it should have been. Could I have a look at the drawings? It wasn't that difficult. If they'd had current, up-to-date drawings, they'd have been OK. But they'd based the site plan on an out-of-date drawing which didn't show where the barriers had been moved back and the run-off area at Clearways extended. And that's why the Foulston Centre is so tight up to the track. It was based on an out-of-date drawing."

The £3.5 million, 25,000sq ft Foulston Centre was to house the circuit's administration office and international media facilities, with corporate hospitality facilities on the upper levels.

"What I did was to persuade my mother, because she was still in the chair at that time, that we needed a corporate centre and that we would pay for the admin side of the building by having corporate hospitality facilities above," explained Foulston. "The project would become the mainstay of our expansion of all the other activities. The corporate facilities would allow us to do lunches for corporate days, briefings for the racing school, whatever the activity was we were selling. So they would be multi-purpose – they could be sold all the time. It was my mum who wanted it to be called the Foulston Centre."

By this time, another member of Webb's team who had departed was Jackie Epstein, unhappy with some of the management decisions that were being taken. "We'd built the industrial suites at the back of the circuit and I took the one on the corner at the back entrance as a showroom, because by this time we'd acquired a Ford franchise," he explained.

"It had always been our ambition to have a Ford dealership at Brands. A retail dealer had to come under a main dealer and our main dealer was KT at Dartford. They were very nice people. We got to know them well and established a good friendship. There are certain regulations, laid down by the Ford Motor Company, and the retail franchise down the road failed to meet its company target five years running. So Ford foreclosed on their dealership and gave it to me. Well, I met our target in the very first year.

"What upset me was that, within two or three months of Nicola taking the reigns, she wanted to close down Brands Hatch Ford. We'd signed a five-year contract and could be sued, but I went to KT and explained the whole position and they said: 'OK, we'll let you go.' So I got her out of it, but I was very unhappy about it. Eventually we came to a shouting and bawling match and she said: 'Let's do a face-save. I'll promote you upwards and you can

ABOVE *Nicola Foulston. (LAT)*

retire. As far as the press are concerned, it's not a rowing matter.' So I left in 1990."

In response, Foulston claimed that the business was in fact run by Jackie and Isabel Epstein and that Brands Hatch Circuits only received a flat fee. "Naturally, I sought to bring all businesses in-house so that the company could benefit from the profits and not a select few old friends of Brands Hatch," she said.

Construction of the Foulston Centre meant that the spectator banking at Clearways was inaccessible to spectators for many months during 1991. The centre was eventually opened by BRSCC president John Cooper on 27 September. Now housing Brands Hatch Leisure's administration offices and international media facilities, it had been designed by London architects Rolfe Judd, under the direction of Historic racer Don Hands. The Kentish suite, on level one, could house up to 580 people for briefings or 300 for a formal meal. The Canterbury Suite on the top level catered for 300 people for banquets or 500 for buffets. The building also had a roof terrace. The old Atlantic (Grovewood) Suite and the old BRSCC office buildings would be demolished over the winter.

Also during 1991, extensive safety work was carried out to the circuit. The gravel trap at Paddock Hill Bend was extended around the outside of the old circuit/tarmac run-off area, so that it ran right to the bottom of the dip before Hailwood Hill. All the way from this point up to Druids, the bank was moved back on the outside of the track and new, triple-layer Armco barrier installed. Similar work was also carried out at McLaren and Clearways and all other areas where two-layer Armco was in place were upgraded to three-layer. Some of the earth excavated in the course of this work was used to provide increased height for the spectator banking on the entry to Druids. Moving the bank provided extra run-off area at Druids, allowing the gravel trap to be extended.

At Hawthorn, the run-off area was extended by over 20 metres in width and lengthened along the Derek Minter Straight. The gravel trap at Westfield was also extended and the barrier running from the inside of the Dingle Dell chicane to the outside of Stirling's was moved back. Debris fencing was strengthened and installed at more points around the circuit. Operations director John Symes explained at the time: "The continuing modifications and improvements not only ensure we are given track licences by FISA and the FIM, but enable us to keep pace with the ever-increasing performance of racing cars and motorcycles in safety terms." In addition to the safety work, a new public address system was installed during the year around the Indy circuit.

At the end of March 1992, Symes, one of the last key people from the John Webb era to still be *in situ*, finally departed. "I became Nicola Foulston's 17th directorial reject," he said. "Sixteen directors got fired in 27 months before she fired me. There were directors she inherited, then she brought in other people and made them directors, and so on. It was an interesting time.

"I was still running the Brands Hatch Racing Club until Nicola took the decision to kill it off. She had a philosophy which I sum up as: 'If John Webb had ever declared that black was black, you must now understand that it is white.' Whatever JW had done or was responsible for, Nicola set out to destroy and do exactly the opposite. That was her basic principle. Her philosophy was that John Webb was an idiot, hadn't known what he was doing, so whatever he'd done, she basically undid."

Foulston disputes that her philosophy had anything to do with Webb. "I had a strapline," she said. "Everybody in the office knew it. It was: 'If it doesn't make money, we don't do it'. And 'if it's on your desk and it doesn't make money, it goes in the bin' – that was another little motto."

"A lot of people left and she bounced a lot of people," continued Symes. "I knew it was coming. She tried to do it in a slightly subtle way, in that she wanted me to resign and then she was going to give me another contract and we'd work the details out in due course. I wasn't playing that game. John

Webb had left me with an eight-year fixed-term contract and I'd only run three years. She didn't say anything to me for a few months. Then she went off skiing and took the other directors with her, leaving a memo saying that I was the only company director in the UK for that period, and that I had her full confidence to act on behalf of the company. She came back on a Monday afternoon, and there was a board meeting on the Tuesday morning. As we filed out, she asked me to stay behind and Paul Smith, who was the financial director at that time, came back into the room and closed the door behind him. I thought: 'This is interesting …'

"She said: 'You and I have not always agreed.' I said: 'That's true, but irrespective of that, I've always carried out your instructions to the letter.' And she said, 'That's absolutely correct but I'm not prepared to tolerate the situation any longer, so I'm terminating your contract.'

"She told me I was leaving that night and that I wasn't to tell anyone. I tried to sort out my desk so that other people could easily pick things up and, about half an hour later, one of the juniors said: 'I'm sorry to hear you're leaving.' I found a note had gone round to say I'd resigned. I chose to tell people that I'd been dismissed. And I felt the world had been lifted off my shoulders."

Prior to this, in February 1992, it was announced that the 24-year-old Nicola Foulston was taking full executive and managerial control of the Brands Hatch group.

"In the first year, 1990, I worked for my mother and the advisers," she explained. "But it became clear, probably for the same reasons as with John, that there were going to be clashes, because my mother didn't have the same vision for Brands as I did, and as my father had. She's far more cautious and she was also quite steeped in the tradition of motor racing. She'd driven, she'd raced herself and many of her friends were racing drivers.

"Over the course of that year my mother became increasingly nervous and I became increasingly frustrated, because to me it was obvious – charge people for their tickets, charge people for testing. So my mum and I became estranged. In the meantime, having worked with Richard for a year, my views and my visions of what could be done at Brands had become much bigger."

Foulston's answer to her frustration was to offer to buy the circuit from her mother, a proposition that Mary Foulston eventually agreed to but with a price tag of of £6 million. Perhaps she never expected her daughter to be able to rise such a large sum, but if this was the case then she had reckoned without the sheer determination of Nicola Foulston, who approached one of her father's old bankers and persuaded them to back her.

Rather than agree to sell the entire business, however, Mary Foulston and her advisers decided to spilt up the assets. They retained the freeholds to the land but transferred the operating business, Brands Hatch Circuits Ltd, which owned leases on the freeholds, to Nicola Foulston's Trust for £6.1 million. All this took place throughout 1991, so by the beginning of 1992 Nicola Foulston now owned Brands Hatch. The question now was, what could she do with it?

Later that year, Foulston admitted in an interview with *Autosport* that it was not viable to think in terms of getting the Grand Prix back to Brands Hatch. "Circuit work would need £8 million," she said. "I'm told that it used to be possible to make around £1 million from a Grand Prix but that the figure isn't realisable any more. Even if it was, we'd be looking at an eight-year pay-off.

"The technical problems are immense. The pits need £5 million and the infrastructure is a problem. I would have to close the circuit. The ramparts go right out to the M20 and there's a valley running through the woods. To take the track away from the village area [West Kingsdown] would mean putting in thousands of tons of earth. Then we'd have to construct tunnels and exits. The aim now is to run it as a high-grade international venue."

Part of Foulston's strategy was to introduce a controversial, six-tier grading system in September 1992, which rated national racing championships from A to F, depending on their perceived spectator appeal. It was also decreed that no Grade F races (the least popular, or least profitable) would be run on BHL circuits. This meant that 29 club series were effectively banned and the traditional five-round Winter Series was cancelled for that year. The system sparked further controversy when both the British Formula 2 and Formula 3 series were given Grade C classifications, putting them below club formulae such as the VW Beetle Cup.

According to BHL's market research among spectators, the only events which were placed in the top Grade A category for 1993 would be the British Touring Car Championship and the FIA Truck Superprix. Grade B included Formula Ford open series, Formula Vauxhall Lotus, Group N production saloon cars, Thundersaloons, TVRs, Ferraris, Rover GTis and VW Beetles. Group C comprised British F2 and F3, Citroën 2CVs, Minis, Caterham-Vauxhalls, Porsches, Formula Vauxhall Junior, Formula First and others. Down in Grade D, surprisingly, was rallycross, along with Supersports, HSCC series and BHL's own Formula Forward. Grade E included most of the 750 MC series and Silhouette Specials.

The categories which lost out in Grade F included the BARC Sports/Saloon Challenge, Formula E and Pre-74 Formula Ford.

An immediate casualty of the scheme was the rallycross schedule planned for February and March 1993. Because the hire fees for the circuit were linked to the grades, being inversely proportional to an event's status, it meant a £4000 hire fee for the British Rallycross Drivers Association, rendering its events loss-making. An additional clause was a cancellation penalty of up to £12,000, even in the event of bad weather, so the association felt the risk was too great.

With unprofitable club racing squeezed out, Foulston set her sights on higher-profile events. That April, she visited the Valvoline 200 IndyCar race at Phoenix, Arizona, for talks with Bill Stokkan, the chairman of the IndyCar board, about the possibility of holding a race at Brands. Her interest had been sparked by Nigel Mansell's participation in the 1993 series and the interest it was generating with the British public. In July, she visited the Toronto race amid rumours that she was trying for a non-championship October date that same year.

Later that month, indeed, Stokkan made a proposal to a meeting of team owners for an extra race to be run at Brands in October. The proposal included a US$1 million prize fund, together with a percentage of television, gate and merchandising revenue. In addition, the promoter, Brands Hatch, would pay all transportation and hotel costs. However, the proposal went against an agreement between FISA

(the world governing body) and IndyCar that the latter would only race outside North America on oval tracks. FIA vice-president Bernie Ecclestone stated at the time: "They have two options – either they race on a banked oval, as our agreement states, or they run without an RAC or FISA licence. If Nicola Foulston runs an event contrary to the agreement with FISA, the RAC would have to pull the plug on other events at the circuit and I imagine that IndyCar will run into trouble from the American governing body, which is part of FISA."

It left the circuit in an impossible situation. If Brands was to push ahead and hold a race without the sanction of the RAC, it would run into all sorts of problems regarding safety, marshalling, insurance and licences. The following week, however, the IndyCar board rejected the proposal anyway, although no official reason was given. It was thought that the timing of the proposed race, one week after the championship finale at Laguna Seca, would have given little time for preparation, as well as causing problems for IndyCar with FISA.

Despite this setback, plans were unveiled at the end of August 1993 for a new £2.5 million pits complex, to be built over the winter. Foulston said at the time that the plans marked the final phase in: "The enormous reinvestment we have been forced to undertake as a result of the demands placed upon us by the governing body." She went on to say

that the circuit could now concentrate on what she described as: "The more important task of upgrading spectator facilities."

Foulston explained in 2006: "The pits were very old. This is the hardest part of motor racing and fundamentally why, in my opinion, the business is flawed and always will be. The fact that the capital expenditure required to keep the circuits up to spec for the core product, which is motor racing, far exceeds the money that can be made from that core product. So you're always investing in something that doesn't give you a return, and that's a real problem. We did the most basic job we could get away with at the time."

The new pits complex was to have 36 garages – 17 double and two single – and was to include a new control centre. All this was designed so that the view of the Indy circuit would not be spoiled from the grandstands.

"What we are doing in building this facility," said Foulston at the time, "is achieving an international standard which will enable us to run whichever championships are available at International level that we believe are in demand by the public. I want to provide motor sport that the public wants to see. At the moment that includes rallycross, truck racing, motorcycles and the British Touring Cars." The old pits complex, which had been constructed in 1976, was demolished in September.

BELOW *Russell Ingall on his way to victory in the 1993 Formula Ford Festival in his works Van Diemen.* *(sutton-images.com)*

In April 1995, a consortium of investors led by Apax Partners, the venture capital firm, acquired 90 per cent of the equity in Brands Hatch Leisure from the Foulston family interests for £15.5 million. The reasoning, as Nicola Foulston put it, was: "To strengthen the Leisure group's commercial future." The other investors were former racing driver Adrian Chambers, who became the non-executive chairman of the group, and racing enthusiast Peter Rickitt. Foulston retained a 10 per cent share and her role as the chief executive.

Around this time, Rob Bain, then a group senior manager with the accountancy firm Ernst & Young, specialising in mergers and acquisitions, was brought in by Foulston to act as her financial adviser on a flotation of BHL on the London Stock Exchange. "The reason for the flotation was principally to raise money to buy the leasehold of the business," Bain explained. "The way it was structured was that the leasehold was held offshore and the majority of the proceeds went on securing the freehold."

Foulston explained: "I needed to raise money to buy my mother out of the land. Having done the initial deal, which was fine for our needs then, I had given myself independence from the family and therefore I was free to do what I wanted with the business. My financial constraint was that I could only borrow the value of the leases, not the value of the land, and so I was massively curtailed in the investment plan. I could never have more than £3.2 million debt. For a business which was growing the way we were, and with the capital expenditure requirements laid on us by the MSA and the FIA, that was a joke.

"I'd done a deal already with Apax to bring in some money, and they had further re-endorsed that we needed the land. In order to raise the money to buy out my mother – and bear in mind that she hadn't wanted originally to sell me the land – going public, where I would not be the only shareholder, was a way of securing the family out of whatever folly I might be doing."

In August 1996, BHL acquired for shares the freehold interests in the land occupied by its circuits and facilities, which it had previously leased from the Foulston family interests. Subsequently 6,370,000 shares (equal to 29.18 per cent of the enlarged outstanding equity share capital) were placed and admitted to the official list of the London Stock Exchange to raise £9.3 million after costs. Dealings commenced on 7 November 1996. BHL's market capitalisation at the placing price was £34 million. The principal shareholders were Apax Partners with 12,370,000 shares (equal to 56.66 per cent of the share capital) and Awak Limited with

3,231,735 (14.8 per cent). Awak, a company incorporated in Guernsey, was owned by the trustees of the 'Nicola Fund', which formed part of the J G Foulston Children's Trust and of which Nicola Foulston was the beneficiary.

It had not been an easy time. Prior to the acquisition of the land and the flotation, Mary Foulston had been in the process of suing her daughter. "She felt that we weren't maintaining the circuits the way they should be," explained Nicola Foulston. "As the landlord, she cared about how much money we spent on it. But we were totally hampered because we only had leases, so we couldn't borrow more money to spend on the circuits. So it was kind of a circular problem."

Mary Foulston was not alone at that time in feeling that the circuits were getting rather shabby, as her daughter admitted was the case: "They were shabby, and it was a very difficult situation, because I'd actually given myself too little financial leeway. I didn't have the balance sheet to borrow, to invest, so effectively I'd made the business too small in real terms. When I'd realised that mistake, I'd gone to venture capitalists to borrow money and that's when we looked at buying the circuits back out."

One outcome of all this activity was that Foulston was named the Veuve Clicquot Businesswoman of the Year in 1997. "I was told at the time by Veuve Clicquot that what they really loved was looking at family businesses, because that's what Madame Veuve Clicquot was all about," she explained. "She took over her husband's business when he died and was the first woman entrepreneur in the 1800s.

James Thompson

"My first memory of Brands would probably have to be racing a Vauxhall Junior, back in 1992. I remember it before they changed Graham Hill Bend, which was much better before. I also have fond memories of the Grand Prix track.

"The long circuit was very special for the simple reason that, before they changed Dingle Dell, there was nowhere else where you got airborne in a racing car. You still feel so

James Thompson leads through Paddock Bend in his SEAT Leon during the 9 April 2006 BTCC meeting at Brands Hatch. (sutton-images.com)

closed in by the trees and everything out the back, and the low bridges. It's quite an imposing circuit to drive on and it really is one of the best tracks around. It's got a bit of everything – fast corners, slow corners, enough to tantalise the tastebuds.

"I've won a few races there and generally Brands has brought me a lot of good memories, with a few bad ones as well. One weekend, Jason Plato hit me twice, and I didn't make the hairpin either time. Once, in Ford 2000, I had a massive accident at Dingle Dell and ended up in the trees. But generally they're fond memories."

They looked at all the candidates that year and they liked the fact I had taken on a family business and resolved family controversy."

In September 1998, it was announced that planning permission was being sought to realign the Grand Prix loop to move it away from the houses near Dingle Dell. Nicola Foulston said at the time that the move was part of a scheme to improve community relations. The revisions meant that the straight between Stirling's and Clearways would be moved away from West Kingsdown village, and a 21-foot noise barrier erected. The cars would then flick left and right to rejoin the track at Clearways. Brands was also hoping to gain permission for a number of new buildings around the Indy circuit, including a new grandstand and hospitality complex.

At the end of November 1998, further details of the proposed developments were released. Levels, gradients and some bends on the circuit would be changed in order "to maximise the racing line and to ensure safety" and a state-of-the-art pit and paddock facility would be built on the start-finish straight. The existing main grandstand was to be demolished and replaced by a new, 15,000-seat grandstand on the infield, banked two ways to overlook the pits and the Indy circuit. Other work included new service roads, guardrails and kerbing, and extended gravel traps, while a new connector loop would enable separate use of the Grand Prix loop and the Indy circuit.

During the winter of 1998–99, extensive work was carried out at Paddock Bend, where the gravel trap was vastly increased, and at Graham Hill Bend, where the track was completely reprofiled, the descent from the exit of Druids becoming longer and the corner itself becoming a tight, 90deg left, requiring harder braking and creating overtaking opportunities. The change added 130 feet to the length of the circuit and meant that all existing lap records were consigned to the history books. The length of the Indy circuit was now 1.2262 miles and that of the Grand Prix circuit 2.6228 miles.

In January 1999, a bizarre period in the history of Brands Hatch began. News broke that Nicola Foulston had made a bid to buy Silverstone, and had entered negotiations with Formula One impresario Bernie Ecclestone to get the British Grand Prix returned to Brands Hatch if she was unsuccessful in her attempts to acquire the Northamptonshire circuit.

It had been Richard Green who had first persuaded Foulston that they should start talking about having the Grand Prix, on the simple basis that it all boiled down to money and that if they were prepared to pay more than Silverstone then they would be in with a chance. It was also a case of necessity – Brands Hatch's motor racing portfolio at that time was not impressive and they needed an event that would generate large income. They knew roughly the amount that Silverstone was paying to host the Grand Prix and were confident that they could make it more profitable and therefore afford to spend more in order to acquire the rights to run it.

Foulston and Green first discussed the idea around 1994-95, but hosting a Grand Prix was beyond their capacity at that time. Not only did they lack the wherewithal to improve the circuit to the required standard, but Foulston was also aware of the impression held by many people that her father and Bernie Ecclestone had fallen out at some point. She was reluctant, therefore, to make an approach based simply on an idea, but felt that a cast-iron business plan was required before even making contact.

In 1997, though, with the company now successfully floated, she realised that the simple act of even just having a conversation with Ecclestone about the Grand Prix would be good for the share price and arranged for Green, initially alone, to meet him. Green returned from a promising meeting in which Ecclestone apparently said that he had no problem with the Foulston family and that he was happy to talk. At this point Foulston herself took over the negotiations.

Prior to going to Ecclestone, Foulston had already been in contact with the British Racing Drivers' Club at Silverstone, about a possible merger. These discussions continued concurrently to her talks with Ecclestone because the Formula One boss was initially sceptical that Brands could accommodate the FIA requirements for a British Grand Prix. Foulston was pursuing Lord Hesketh, who at that time was chairman of the Silverstone board, with a view to making a takeover bid.

It was good business sense. As a public company, Brands had to be seen to be expanding and the most obvious move was to acquire other motor racing activities. It was not feasible to grow the business organically, just through price and volume; the only way was to buy in profit from other businesses. Because Silverstone was a cooperative – owned by the BRDC members – Foulston was in the position of being able to make a 'blind bid'. If she obtained a certain percentage of the vote there would then be nothing the management could do.

However, she decided to make an initial approach to Lord Hesketh for a behind-the-scenes chat and found him quite receptive to her ideas. The BRDC was apparently already taking advice about restructuring because the board was aware that they couldn't keep up with the financial requirement of the Grand Prix without changing the way they ran their business. They were therefore looking to separate the BRDC itself, the non-profit making members' club, from the operation that needed to make money. The board had seen how much Brands Hatch had raised through floatation – it was capitalised at £40 million plus – and were wondering what they might achieve.

Apparently unbeknown to the members, the board was already considering inviting bids, which is why Foulston's approach was welcomed and Brands was invited to tender.

By this time Rob Bain, who had been involved as an adviser during the flotation in 1996, had come on board as the finance director of BHL. He took up the story: "When we made our approach to the BRDC, one of its members also made an approach. He was a property developer, and then all of a sudden we were hearing about various media groups being interested. The only way we could take those other options away from the table was by securing a Grand Prix contract. That would effectively close the door on any other bidder."

What Foulston and her team knew, but others apparently did not, was that Silverstone's contract to hold the British Grand Prix contained a change-of-ownership clause. In other words, if Silverstone changed hands, Bernie Ecclestone could take the Grand Prix away. Anyone thinking of bidding for the track needed his approval.

Foulston therefore arranged another meeting with Ecclestone to inform him that Silverstone was inviting bids. Ecclestone, unaware of the situation despite having a contract with the circuit, was apparently less than happy. Foulston told him that she was aware of the change-of-ownership clause and realised that there was obviously no point in her making a bid for Silverstone if he wouldn't sanction holding a Grand Prix there under her ownership. She offered to negotiate with him to run the Grand Prix on the basis that he would only accept her bid for the circuit. In other words, anyone else bidding for Silverstone would be wasting their time because Ecclestone would take the British Grand Prix away if anyone other than Foulston bought it. It was a bold move, but it paid off.

Despite there being no other FIA-sanctioned circuit in Britain where Ecclestone could have taken the British Grand Prix, he agreed to give Foulston exclusivity on her bid – a measure perhaps of his frustration with the way Silverstone had handled the situation. Indeed, Ecclestone was reportedly very angry that they had been considering selling the operating arm of their business, 90 per cent of

which was the Grand Prix, without even discussing it with their major client.

The meeting had been a success. Foulston had many ideas about how the British Grand Prix could be better run and they tallied with those of Ecclestone. The pair quickly realised that they spoke the same business language.

In April, the 31-year-old Foulston lodged a formal bid to host the British Grand Prix in 2002. She stated at the time that the ideal scenario would be for Brands Hatch and Silverstone to be part of the same organisation and for the Grand Prix to remain at Silverstone. Silverstone, though, had been heavily criticised by Ecclestone, who had already threatened that Britain was in danger of losing its Formula One event.

Foulston was also quoted at the time as saying that Brands Hatch would require between £9 million and £12 million to bring it up to the standard required to host a Grand Prix. Sceptics pointed out that Brands had less than half the land that Silverstone had available to it on a race weekend and that, since the circuit had last hosted a Grand Prix 13 years previously, it could not accommodate all the hospitality that now accompanied such an event.

An *Autosport* editorial at the time supported Foulston's actions. It acknowledged that she had been regarded as "the pariah of British motor sport" because she had ruffled feathers when she had taken control of Brands and had appeared to care little for national racing. It went on, however, to point out that she had run national motor sport on a supply and demand basis and made it work. It added that Brands only ran one fewer club racing event than it had a decade before, and that, across the BHL group, club racing events had grown by 26 per cent.

In April 1999, Foulston published an open letter to the BRDC members in the form of a double-page advertisement in *Autosport*. The letter outlined Brands Hatch Leisure's proposal to take over Silverstone Circuits, together with the freehold of Silverstone. It stated that the BRDC would retain its independence and maintain its position as a members' club, while becoming BHL's motor sport organiser.

The letter went on to point out that BRDC members would retain all their existing benefits at Silverstone and that these benefits would be extended to other circuits owned by the group. It promised that the British Grand Prix would remain at Silverstone. It ended with an emotive promise to safeguard motor sport at Silverstone for as long as it remained within BHL ownership.

In its 13 May issue, *Autosport* reported that Brands was close to securing the Grand Prix from

ABOVE *Allan McNish crosses the line in his DAMS Lola T90/50 Cosworth DFV to win the International Formula 3000 Championship race on 19th August 1990. (sutton-images.com)*

2002 onwards and that the FIA had approved an £18 million improvement plan for the circuit. Earlier that week, Foulston had met with Ecclestone who said afterwards that he saw no reason why the race could not be held at the Kent circuit.

The plan the FIA had approved involved moving the start-finish line from its present site out onto the Grand Prix circuit, and the construction of a new pits and media complex on the straight between Surtees and Hawthorn. Foulston hit out at sceptics who claimed that the deal did not make economic sense. "People who hold that view tend not to be financial entrepreneurs," she said. "We have the know-how to put together a financial proposition of this type. If anyone can source a lot of money, spend a lot of money and make a lot of money, it's BHL."

Foulston's proposal was discussed at a meeting of the BRDC but was rejected, and the Club's board was not authorised by the membership to proceed with negotiations. As a result she had to push ahead with plans to hold the Grand Prix at Brands from 2002 onwards and the deal for BHL to run the race was confirmed on 14 May. On 17 May, she announced that she was no longer pursuing the Silverstone option.

"I've insisted all along," she said, "that we're interested in buying any race circuit in the world but, as of today, we're withdrawing our formal offer to purchase Silverstone. We have a lot of work to do down at Brands Hatch and that's what we'll be concentrating on. At today's date, I can put my hand on my heart and say with certainty that the 2002 British Grand Prix will be run at Brands Hatch."

She went on to state that the £20 million project to upgrade the circuit would enable the track to stage "the biggest and best Grand Prix ever". She claimed: "We anticipate having a far bigger Grand Prix in 2002 here than Silverstone ever has." Bernie Ecclestone was fully supportive of the plans, saying: "If by chance she manages to secure Silverstone, she can put it [the Grand Prix] on there. If not, it will be at Brands."

At that time Foulston had what was internally referred to as 'the Silverstone contract', which took priority. In other words, if Silverstone was sold it had to be sold to her, because that was the only way it could retain the Grand Prix. She also had 'the Brands Hatch contract', which simply stated that Brands had the rights to the British Grand Prix from 2002. What it meant, as Foulston stated publicly, was that she could decide where the race would be held. If she was successful in buying Silverstone, it would be run there. If the BRDC didn't sell to her, she'd run it at Brands Hatch. Foulston now owned the rights to the British Grand Prix and was in a win-win situation.

It demonstrated a huge confidence on the part of Bernie Ecclestone in Foulston's ability to deliver because, effectively, she now owned something she hadn't paid for or had to operate. But it gave her value in the business because the important thing was ownership of the contract, which was reputed to be for £11 million a year, with an annual increment of six per cent – said by some to be double what was being paid by Silverstone under its existing agreement. On the announcement of the deal, nevertheless, BHL's share price reached an all-time high.

Foulston claimed at the time that planning permission for the changes at the track was not an issue. "We've received planning permission for every single building and circuit change that we've ever applied for," she said. "All the changes are totally consistent with our existing planning permission. We expect it to be passed without problem."

The proposals not only included the revisions to the Grand Prix loop which had been proposed the previous September, but also included extended run-off areas all around the track and more temporary grandstands, both around the Indy circuit and the Grand Prix loop. A large number of trees would have to be felled to accommodate the new pits and paddock complex, but new trees were to be planted elsewhere and earth banks erected to provide sound-proofing. It was claimed that racing on the Indy circuit would be unaffected while work on the Grand Prix loop progressed.

The BRDC members at Silverstone, meanwhile, regarded the whole thing as a bluff and dismissed the plans for the circuit as "impractical". Even McLaren's Ron Dennis described Foulston as a "piranha" and said the deal she had done with Ecclestone was merely "designed to destabilise the situation at Silverstone". The BRDC issued a statement saying: "Silverstone is the only circuit currently capable of staging it [the Grand Prix] in Great Britain. The BRDC is aware of several significant difficulties facing any potential rival. These difficulties include the cost of a competitive contract, the expense and extent of the reconstruction and investment that would have to be committed by a new entrant, and the complications inherent in gaining the planning approval vital to building a circuit capable of replacing Silverstone."

In July 1999, Foulston made a public bid for Silverstone, by offering directly to the membership, as opposed to her original proposal, which had been to the BRDC board and had been rejected. The offer would provide each member with a £60,000 windfall and give the club responsibility for administration of all BHL's motor sport activities. In return, BHL would acquire a 50-year lease on Silverstone, together with the BRDC's commercial activities. In addition, Foulston pledged £2 million to establish an academy to find the next British F1 star if her bid of £43 million for the Northamptonshire track was accepted; Bernie Ecclestone had apparently agreed to match Foulston's £2 million if the sale went ahead. BRDC insiders regarded the move as an indication that BHL's chief executive was beginning to get desperate, as she had a deadline to meet to get planning permission for the timely start of the work at Brands.

"This was simply the next stage in the strategy," she explained. "My preferred option was always to merge with or acquire Silverstone. My original strategy had been to negotiate with the board, who then consulted the membership. The membership had said they didn't want to negotiate and so the board was not authorised to continue. The second prong to my strategy, therefore, was to make a public bid directly to the membership and appealing to each member."

By September, all the replies from the BRDC members had been received and it was clear that the offer had been rejected, prompting Foulston to announce that she had abandoned plans to take over Silverstone, claiming: "We have bigger fish to fry." Revised plans for the changes to Brands were revealed, with a tight hairpin right at Hawthorn (which would become the first corner) and then a sweeping left-hander to rejoin the original layout. The design was submitted to the local district council for planning permission.

"It was another step to turn up the heat on Silverstone," explained Rob Bain. "We'd knocked all the other bidders away from the table but they still wouldn't come to the negotiating table with us, so we decided to raise the pressure. We had two Grand Prix contracts, one to run at Silverstone, one to run at Brands Hatch, and then we pursued planning permission. Obviously we were confident. We were spending a vast amount of money trying to secure planning permission and we were successful."

Never a fan of Silverstone, Bernie Ecclestone was hoping that Foulston would be successful in obtaining the necessary planning consent. "I thought she'd get the job done," he said. "You've got to remember, I'm a Brands supporter. So maybe a little bit was hope that she would, as much as thinking that she would. But I hoped and thought she would get it. I never wanted it to be at

Silverstone. Brands is a bit special."

However, the plans to upgrade the track came under fire in November from a group of conservationists. The Woodland Trust, the Forestry Commission and the Council for the Protection of Rural England joined forces to oppose the plan to remove 15 hectares of woodland. The group argued that the area contained endangered flora and fauna. BHL countered that the area was poor-quality woodland and that it had a relatively low nature conservation interest.

While all this was going on, Foulston was also considering her personal life, particularly her wish to retire and start a family.

"I had a plan almost from the beginning," she explained. "My father died at 40 in a racing car after building up his own business and, when I started working and went to Brands Hatch, I had very much a plan that I wouldn't work for my whole life in the same way. I didn't necessarily have the plan that I would do what I've done, which is to retire and have a family and live abroad. But I was worried about getting stuck in a rut. At the time, I thought I'd do something else career-wise, or go into politics, or something completely different. As it happens, I got to know Richard over that decade and we developed a view that it's very easy not to smell the coffee any more. It's very easy to lose sight of the simple things in life."

Enter the Interpublic Group, one of the largest advertising and marketing communications groups in the world. The company was listed on the New York Stock Exchange and had a market capitalisation at the time of approximately US$11.0 billion. Octagon was the sports marketing and entertainment division of Interpublic, and one of the leading sports and event marketing and television distribution agencies in the world. Through its specialist motor sport division, Octagon Motorsports, the company already owned and managed several International series, including the Superbike World Championship.

"They came to us," explained Rob Bain. "They were obviously in the sports marketing area and they acted as agents effectively for many sporting properties. They decided their strategy was to acquire sporting properties. They owned a number of other assets, like World Superbikes, and they owned the rights to strange things like beach volleyball and beach soccer. They were buying all sorts of things."

It was not quite as simple that, though. Through the World Superbike events that were held at the circuit, Foulston knew Maurizio Flammini, who ran an advertising and marketing business in Rome and who owned the rights from the FIM (the world governing body of bike racing) to World Superbike events. Flammini was already in contact with Interpublic about a possible partnership and Foulston felt that this was a company which might not only have the financial clout to buy BHL but also finance its commitments. Meetings were arranged and the BHL nucleus of Foulston, her managing director Green and finance director Bain planned everything to the nth degree.

The upshot was that, on 9 November 1999, BHL recommended to its shareholders that they accept a share-for-share offer by Interpublic, to acquire all the share capital. On the basis of the closing price on the last practicable date prior to the announcement, the offer valued each BHL share at £5.46 and the existing share capital at approximately £120 million. If the bid was successful, said the statement, Foulston would remain as the chief executive of Brands Hatch and join the board of Interpublic's sporting division, Octagon.

On 30 November 1999 the board of Interpublic announced that acceptances had been received in respect of 19,931,486 BHL shares (91.3 per cent) and that, accordingly, the offer had become unconditional.

The sale had gone through. Nicola Foulston had achieved her true objective.

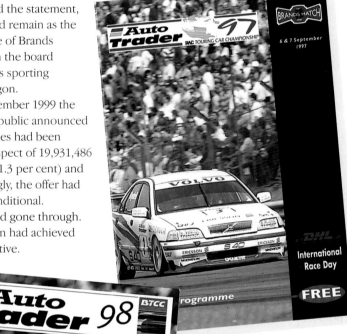

1990

■ Rickard Rydell dominated the opening round of the British F3000 championship on 1 April from pole position with GP Motorsport's Reynard 89D.

■ Mika Hakkinen was proving the man to beat in Formula 3, taking his West Surrey Racing Ralt RT34 to a clear victory in the 29 April race ahead of Peter Kox (Bowman Ralt) and Paul Warwick (Superpower Ralt).

■ In May, it was announced that the circuit was to have a new administration and media centre, to be built on the outside of Clark Curve. There had been rumours that the track would be

BELOW *During the FIA International Formula 3000 meeting on 19 August 1990, Eric van de Poele (Reynard 90D), Andrea Chiesa (Lola T90/50) and Gianni Morbidelli in another Lola try to go three abreast around Druids. (Author)*

redeveloped with a new Grand Prix circuit that would omit the current loop, instead leaving the Indy circuit at Clark Curve to loop around the top of the hill on the other side. A new pits and paddock area would have been included in the extension, according to these rumours.

■ A Mika also won the 20 May F3 encounter, but this time it was Salo with Alan Docking's Ralt RT34, ahead of Häkkinen and Steve Robertson (Bowman Ralt).

■ The circuit's 40th anniversary was marked by the HSCC's Historic Superprix meeting over 2–3 June. As well as the International Supersports Cup and the Historic F1 race, the event included the Ken Tyrrell Trophy for 500cc F3 cars. A celebrity race, featuring a dozen Brands drivers from the fifties onwards, used the circuit's new fleet of Ford Fiesta XR2is and was won by Gerry Marshall, despite starting from the back.

During the lunch break, Mary Foulston cut a celebratory birthday cake.

■ In June, Brands regular Nick Whiting was kidnapped following a car theft at his All Car Equipe garage in Wrotham, close to the circuit. The body of the 43-year-old former Super Saloon champion was found three weeks later on the Rainham Marshes in Essex. Whiting competed in rallycross in the late sixties but found success on track in Special Saloon and Super Saloon racing. He was particularly known for his bright yellow All Car Equipe Ford Escorts.

■ Allan McNish scored his second FIA International F3000 win of the year on 19 August on a soaking wet track, driving the DAMS team's Marlboro Lola T90/50. Damon Hill (Middlebridge Lola) led initially from second on the grid, ahead of McNish and Eddie Irvine (EJR Reynard 90D), but lost out during a series of pitstops to change to slick tyres and had to settle for the runner-up spot. Ford Sierra RS500s took the top six places in the supporting Esso British Touring Car race, headed by Robb Gravett's Trakstar entry.

BELOW Andy Rouse (left) and Robb Gravett head into Druids Bend side-by-side in their Ford Sierra Cosworth RS500s at the start of the 1990 FIA International F3000 Championship BTCC support race. (sutton-images.com)

■ Mika Häkkinen all but clinched the British F3 title on 2 September by winning the race after his championship rival, Mika Salo, crashed out.

■ Dave Coyne was the popular winner of the Formula Ford Festival over 26–28 October, which boasted a record entry of almost 200 cars. Coyne, driving a Swift FB90, achieved the feat despite starting his heat from the back of the grid with a 10sec penalty.

■ Planning permission was granted on 1 November by Sevenoaks District Council for the construction of a new administration and hospitality building. The 25,000sq ft, fully air-conditioned facility would be sited on the outside of Clark Curve, next to the track, and would cost an estimated £3 million. The basement and ground floor would comprise office space and catering facilities, while the first and second floors would house hospitality suites and media facilities. Work was due to be completed in spring 1991.

■ A pile-up on the third lap of the 'A' final of the British Rallycross Grand Prix, on 2 December, took out the cars of Will Gollop, Steve Palmer and John Welch. The incident brought out the red flag, leaving Martin Schanche the winner of the shortened event in his Ford Escort RS200E.

■ The final meeting of the Winter Series had to be cancelled due to freezing weather.

1991

■ The track was designated as an official testing venue for the FIA International F3000 championship.

■ A major row broke out in March over television rights in British motor racing. Brands Hatch Leisure controlled Motor Video Productions, a company formed late in 1990 by Nicola Foulston and Videovision's Brian Kreisky. MVP was to be responsible for filming at all BHL circuits, plus Thruxton and Donington. However, Barrie Hinchcliffe Promotions (BHP) had the rights to film the British Touring Car Championship and, when its application to film the opening meeting at Oulton Park on Good Friday was turned down, the RAC MSA switched the meeting to Silverstone. Foulston claimed that her desire to control TV coverage at the BHL circuits went back to the first meeting she had attended with John Webb. At that meeting, Hinchcliffe had told Webb it would cost the circuit £150,000 in production costs

BELOW *Three abreast around Druids agan, but this time it's the Citroën 2CVs of David O'Keeffe, Richard Dalton and Roy Eastwood performing the trick on 14 April 1991. (Michael Hewett)*

to get British F3000 onto television. Foulston had apparently regarded this as a joke and had vetoed the idea.

■ David Coulthard won the British F3 race on 28 April in his Paul Stewart Racing Ralt RT35, becoming the first double winner of the season. Rickard Rydell (TOM'S-Toyota) was second ahead of Rubens Barrichello (WSR Ralt).

■ Paul Warwick, the younger brother of F1 star Derek, maintained a 100 per cent winning record in the British F3000 championship in the third round on 12 May with the Mansell-Madgwick team's Reynard 90D.

■ Gil de Ferran (Edenbridge Reynard 913) won the 19 May F3 race, ahead of David Coulthard's PSR Ralt.

■ The Racefest 91 meeting over 29–30 June featured British F3000, BTCC, trucks, karts, Historic cars, cycle racing and an air display. Advance ticket buyers could get a weekend pass for just £10. Tim Sugden in Prodrive's BMW M3 won the BTCC race from

Will Hoy's similar VLM team car, while Paul Warwick's Reynard again won the F3000 encounter, under pressure from Dave Coyne's similar car. Warwick was to lose his life a few weeks later in a crash at Oulton Park.

■ Brands did not have a round of the FIA World Sportscar Championship but it had the Interserie Cup instead on 27–28 July, with two 33-lap sprints on the Indy circuit. Joest Racing Porsche 962 drivers 'John Winter' and Bernd Schneider took a win each.

■ The only round of an FIA championship to run at Brands in 1991 was the International F3000 meeting on 18 August. Alessandro Zanardi set the fastest ever F3000 lap of the circuit on his way to pole position, at 1m 12.44s, 129.22mph. Zanardi was an unreserved fan of the track, although he claimed: "You have to commit yourself to the corners before you can see them." Shortly after taking pole, he crashed the Barone Rampante team's Reynard 91D heavily at Dingle Dell. Damon Hill in Eddie Jordan's Lola T91/50 led the first few laps before Emanuele Naspetti took the lead and went on to win in his Forti Corse Reynard ahead of Zanardi and Christian Fittipaldi (Pacific Reynard).

■ It was announced afterwards that Brands would not be applying for a round of the FIA F3000 championship the following year. The circuit stated that FISA, the sport's governing body, demanded too much money for the event. The circuit claimed that it was not economically viable and that the F3000 race had been run at a loss for the previous three years. "We didn't have a sponsor last Sunday and we had to pay out a prize fund of

ABOVE *Damon Hill (Lola T91/50) led the first few laps of the 1991 FIA International Formula 3000 Championship race on 18 August.* (sutton-images.com)

approximately £137,500," said Nicola Foulston. "We had an estimated 5000 paying spectators at £15 per head, which compares with 5359 last year and 5882 in 1989. We stuck our neck out again this year, but we needed a gate of more than 10,000."

■ In contrast, at the Esso British Touring Car Championship meeting on Bank Holiday Monday 26 August, 30,000 spectators saw Andy Rouse take his Kaliber Toyota Carina to victory ahead of the BMW M3 of Will Hoy in the first race, while Hoy took victory ahead of the Trakstar Ford Sapphire of Robb Gravett in the second.

■ King Hussein of Jordan was a guest of Jackie Stewart at the circuit to see Paul Stewart Racing's Ralt RT35, driven by David Coulthard, take victory at the F3 meeting on 1 September, ahead of the Reynard 913 of Gil de Ferran and the Ralt of Rubens Barrichello.

■ Sweden's Fredrik Ekblom won with a Team AGS Lola T90/50 at the British F3000 race on 8 September. A new public address system was officially handed over at this meeting, TOA UK presenting the equipment to BHL's Nicola Foulston, who said the next phase would include the installation of a closed-circuit TV surveillance system. It was noted in *Autosport* that there was now no PA system on the long circuit.

■ BRSCC president John Cooper officially opened the new John Foulston Centre on Friday 27 September.

■ Marc Goosens won the Formula Ford Festival over 25–27 October with a Van Diemen RF91.

■ Pat Doran raced his Ford RS200E to victory in an action-packed British Rallycross Grand Prix on 1 December after early leader Will Gollop had suffered a puncture.

1992

■ The run-off area between Westfield and Dingle Dell, where three-tier barriers were erected, was extended.

■ Kelvin Burt won a wet F3 encounter on 26 April in Fortec's Reynard 923 from pole man Gil de Ferran, in Paul Stewart's similar Reynard. When the teams returned on 17 May, de Ferran was beaten by Philippe Adams in Alan Docking's Ralt RT36.

■ Yvan Muller won the British F2 championship round on Bank Holiday Monday, 25 May, in the Omegaland team's Reynard 91D.

■ A record entry of 365 competitors took part in the HSCC Historic Superprix on 30–31 May, competing in 16 races.

BELOW *John Cleland (Vauxhall Cavalier GSI) and Andy Rouse (Toyota Carina) race side-by-side into Druids during the 1992 August Bank Holiday BTCC meeting. (sutton-images.com)*

■ A huge crowd saw John Cleland and Jeff Allam make it a Vauxhall 1-2 in Vauxhall Sport's Cavaliers in the Esso BTCC round on 7 June, with Steve Soper third in VLM's BMW 318is. Toyota Carina team mates Will Hoy and Andy Rouse collided at Westfield on lap two, taking each other out.

■ The 15-event programme at the Capital FM Racefest on 28 June featured races for cycles, motorcycles, superkarts, cars and trucks. Races included the Lords *versus* Commons race in Ford XR2is and Champion of Brands solo and sidecar races. Yvan Muller won the headlining British F2 race again and a large crowd enjoyed good weather.

■ The Capital FM Bug Prix on 4–5 July, promoted in association with the *People* newspaper, included a head-to-head contest between the top Beetle Cup drivers and those in VW Formula Vee. Attractions included a have-a-go rally stage, karting, four-wheel-

ABOVE *The 1992 Formula Ford Festival on 23–25 October provided close racing as always, especially as much of the meeting was wet. (LAT)*

drive and parascending. John Webb might have left the circuit, but the tradition of offering all-round entertainment by taking a small event and promoting it as a big one was continuing.

■ Twenty-five years of Formula Ford racing was celebrated in style at the *Evening Standard* Free Car Race Day on 19 July. Jan Magnusson won the feature event with his yellow Van Diemen RF92.

■ In August, Nicola Foulston denied that a consortium of racing drivers and property men had put in a bid to buy the circuit. She categorically denied that it was for sale or that a bid had been received, saying: "I've only just taken full control of the company, so I'd hardly wish to give it up now."

■ In September, as part of its evidence to a local planning enquiry for the Swanley area, BHL submitted a concept plan for a new Grand Prix loop to be built. The track would leave the Indy circuit at Clark Curve and would contain a new pit and paddock area. It was stressed that the plan remained at the

conceptual stage and that the project would require considerable investment were it to proceed.

■ Tim Harvey won both BTCC races on Bank Holiday Monday, 31 August, in Vic Lee's Listerine BMW 318is, with Will Hoy second on both occasions in his Toyota Carina.

■ Yvan Muller took his fourth British F2 victory of the season on 6 September.

■ At the Formula Ford Festival over 23–25 October, Jan Magnussen started his heat from the back of the grid with a 10sec penalty and yet still managed to emerge the eventual winner, setting a new lap record along the way.

■ It was announced in November that the 1993 Kart Grand Prix meeting would be held at the circuit over 31 July and 1 August. It meant that Brands would have three 'Grands Prix' – Rallycross and Truck being the other events.

■ Will Gollop took his MG Metro 6R4 to a record third victory in the British Rallycross Grand Prix over 5–6 December, heading a British clean sweep with John Welch and Barry Squibb completing the podium.

1993

In February, work was progressing on a £500,000 facelift to the circuit. A second access tunnel was being constructed between the main paddock and the pits to allow constant two-way flow of traffic. Prior to this, a system of traffic lights and marshals had controlled the flow of traffic through the narrow tunnel under the track at Paddock Bend. In addition, a FISA-specification chicane was installed at the entry to the pit-lane to slow cars as they entered the pits. At the far end of the pits, a large new assembly area was constructed on the site of the old post-race (Grand Prix) scrutineering bay. Cars would assemble here prior to a race and then be directed around the Clearways loop and onto the grid.

Kelvin Burt raced Paul Stewart Racing's Reynard 993 to victory in the F3 meeting on 18 April, his second win from three starts. Burt was again the winner at the 16 May meeting.

Cyclists returned to the Kent track when Brands hosted a stage of the Milk Race in May. Competitors completed one and a half laps of the Indy circuit in an anticlockwise direction.

A record 410 cars and motorcycles took part in the Historic Superprix meeting over 6–7 June, in blazing sunshine. The theme of the event was a 'Tribute to John Surtees', who performed demonstration runs with many of his old cars and bikes.

Works BMW team mates Jo Winkelhock and Steve Soper took a win each at the BTCC double-header on 13 June, with Keith Odor runner-up each time in his works Nissan Primera. The two BMW drivers were made to work hard for their wins, both races providing plenty of nose-to-tail racing.

The *Daily Express* and *Auto Express* Free Day meeting over 26–27 June drew almost 26,000 spectators to a sun-drenched circuit. Johnny Herbert demonstrated his F1 Lotus 107B, setting an unofficial Indy circuit record of 35.88s, 120.76mph. The circuit also staged a tribute to James Hunt, who had died earlier in the month. The 1976 World Championship winning McLaren M23 was placed on the grid and a minute's silence observed. Red flags interrupted proceedings during the racing, but many spectators stayed until 7.00pm to watch the closing Truck race.

Two drivers were killed during the British Kart Grand Prix on 1 August in two separate incidents, causing the meeting to be abandoned. Gordon Ellinor died when his 210 National Stratos kart rode over the wheel of another competitor and was thrown

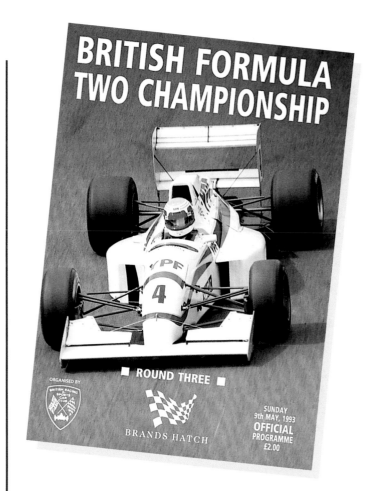

into the barriers on the right of the track during the rolling start of the third heat. Kenton Owen's Zip Bullit rolled at Paddock on the third lap of the 125 National final following a multiple collision.

Paul Radisich scored his maiden BTCC victory on 22 August and the first for the Ford Mondeo. It also marked Ford's 200th race win in the series. Dario Franchitti clinched the Formula Vauxhall Lotus title.

Russell Ingall won the new Zetec class at the Formula Ford Festival on 24 October with the works Van Diemen RF93, while Andrew McAuley took victory in the Kent class with a Reynard FF92.

Martin Schanche took his Escort RS2000 4x4 Turbo to victory in the British Rallycross Grand Prix on 5 December.

RIGHT *Paul Radisich scored Ford's 200th BTCC win on 22 August 1993, the first win for the Ford Mondeo. (LAT)*

1994

■ Nicola Foulston made herself unpopular in a *Sunday Times* interview, by accusing the Brands marshals of being rude to the public. She said she found it intolerable that she had 300 volunteer marshals over whom she had no control, and that she would be inviting them to undergo customer care training at BHL venues. She later apologised for the remarks. She also proposed that marshals should be linked to the public address to give a running commentary of accident clear-ups in order to keep spectators informed of what was going on.

■ The new control tower at the circuit, the first part of the £1 million pit complex to be completed, was used for the first time on Good Friday, 1 April.

■ Gabriele Tarquini won both rounds of the double-header BTCC meeting on 17 April in his works Alfa Romeo 155TS. Team mate Giampiero Simoni finished second in the first race ahead of John Cleland's Vauxhall Cavalier, but was disqualified next time out for overtaking under yellow flags, which promoted Cleland to second place.

■ Jan Magnussen in PSR's Dallara F394 and Vincent Radermaker in WSR's similar car took a win apiece in the F3 double-header on 24 April. Two weeks later, on 8 May, the F3 contingent was back, this time on the Grand Prix circuit, and Magnussen won again in a Paul Stewart Racing 1-2 with Dario Franchitti.

■ Gabriele Tarquini and team mate Giampiero Simoni delivered an Alfa Romeo 1-2 in both BTCC rounds held on the Grand Prix circuit on 26 June. Patrick Watts finished third in each race with a works Peugeot 405.

■ Former Formula First racer Richard Green was appointed to the board of Brands Hatch Leisure as its sales and marketing director. Green had already worked for BHL for seven years.

■ The track hosted a tribute to 60-year-old John Surtees, the only man to win World Championships on two wheels and on four, with cars and bikes from all over Europe and America converging in Kent on 3 July. American racer Dan Gurney was one of the great drivers who attended.

■ Jo Winkelhock dominated the BTCC races on 29 August, taking both victories in his works BMW 318i, ahead of the Alfas of Gabriele Tarquini and Giampiero Simoni.

■ In October, Nigel Mansell signed a 10-year contract with Brands Hatch Leisure for the racing school to be renamed the Nigel Mansell Racing School. The 1992 F1 World Champion said he was intending to host some classes himself.

■ Jason Watt, who had already won the British FF1600 crown with his Vector TF94, added the Zetec title at the Formula Ford Festival on 23 October, while Gavin Wills took the prize for the older, Kent engined cars with a Swift SC92F.

■ When the 1995 Brands Hatch fixture list was announced, there were only 18 meetings – a major reduction. There would be eight headlining events, including three BTCC rounds and the Rallycross Grand Prix. There were also plans for a 'Christmas Bash' in the spirit of the Boxing Day meetings run until the late seventies. Five events would be club meetings and the remaining four bike events.

■ Martin Schanche was fined US$2000 for causing an accident in the Division 2 'A' Final of the British Rallycross Grand Prix on 4 December, which resulted in the Subaru Impreza of Per Eklund catching fire and the race having to be stopped. Kenneth Hansen won the event, the ninth different winner in 13 years.

RIGHT *Per Eklund (Subaru Impreza) erupts in a ball of flame, as Barry Squibb (Ford Escort Cosworth) passes during the British Rallycross Grand Prix in 1994. (sutton-images.com)*

1995

■ Forty jobs at the circuit were axed in early January.

■ The Racing Ahead initiative got under way on 19 March with a 5000-strong crowd paying just £1 for entry, with free paddock transfers and grandstand seats, to watch a club meeting. The crowd exceeded the circuit's expectations: only 1000 programmes had been printed and they soon ran out. An 18-race programme was run smoothly by the BRSCC.

■ Rain helped to produce what *Autosport* described as "the most incredible couple of tin-top races seen in years" at the British Touring Car rounds on Easter Monday, 17 April. This year's BTCC featured cars from Alfa Romeo, BMW, Ford, Honda, Peugeot, Renault, Toyota, Vauxhall and Volvo, and a damp track produced plenty of mayhem for a massive crowd. Tim Harvey managed to take TWR's Volvo 850 to victory in both the races.

■ Three red flags severely delayed the action at the wet BTCC double-header on the Grand Prix circuit on 11 June. Tim Sugden rolled Team Toyota's Carina at Clearways in the first race, while Nigel Smith's HMSO Vauxhall Cavalier got beached in the gravel trap at Stirling's in the second race, and then Rickard Rydell rolled his Volvo 850 at Westfield. None of the drivers was injured. Clerk of the course Pierre Aumonier told the drivers that the event would be cancelled if there was one more stoppage. Alain Menu (Renault Laguna) and John Cleland (Vauxhall) were the race winners.

■ Swede Kenneth Hansen took his Citroën ZX 16v 4x4 Turbo to victory at the British Rallycross Grand Prix meeting over 17–18 June.

■ Controversy marred the BTCC rounds on 14 August. Both Rickard Rydell and John Cleland received endorsements to their licences for two separate clashes with each other. Will Hoy (Renault) and Cleland (Vauxhall) were the winners of the two races and the meeting drew a crowd of 32,000.

BELOW *John Cleland gets airborne at the Dingle Dell chicane in his Vauxhall Cavalier during the BTCC round on 14 April 1995. (LAT)*

ABOVE *The British Touring Car Championship made three visits to Brands Hatch during 1995, with plenty of action and controversy. (LAT)*

■ Ralph Firman swept the board at the F3 meeting on 28 August, winning both rounds of the double-header event with PSR's Dallara F395.

■ Brands teamed up with *Autosport* to offer spectators entrance for just £1 at the 'Racing Ahead Pound Day' on 24 September, with children free. The club racing bill featured 12 races on the Grand Prix circuit, including Formula 4, Formula Vee, Roadsports and Thoroughbred Sports Cars. The organising club, the 750 MC,

received a massive 293 entries. Unfortunately the weather was unkind, the rain lashing down, but the quality of the racing provided a showcase for club motor sport.

■ Works Van Diemen RF95 driver Kevin McGarrity emerged the winner of an enthralling final of the Formula Ford Festival on 22 October in the Zetec class, while Finnish driver Topi Serjala in Apollo Motorsport's Swift SC95F won the Kent class. Commentator Brian Jones was presented with a cake bearing a microphone to mark his 20th successive Festival.

■ The Saloon Car Festival planned for 10 December was cancelled because the circuit was under snow.

1996

■ In January, John Nicol, the chief executive officer of the BRSCC, became the group motorsports director of the Brands Hatch Leisure Group, with specific responsibility for its motor racing strategy and calendar planning.

■ Interserie returned to Brands after a four-year break on 8 April. Robbie Stirling, driving a Lola-Judd V10 sports-prototype, took the honours by winning both 40-lap races on the Indy circuit from Ranieri Randaccio's Fondmetal-Cosworth V8.

■ Frank Biela in Audi Sport's A4 and Jo Winkelhock in BMW Team Schnitzer's 320i took the honours in the 21 April BTCC double-header, with Alain Menu second in both races in the Williams team's Renault Laguna. Just over two months later, on 30 June, it was Menu's turn, and he landed a double on the Grand Prix circuit.

■ Endurance racing returned to Brands on 8 September with a four-hour Global GT race over 166 laps of the Grand Prix circuit. The factory team's new Porsche 911 GT1 blitzed the opposition, drivers Hans Stuck/Thierry Boutsen finishing over a lap ahead of the McLaren F1 GTR of Andy Wallace/Olivier Grouillard.

■ The final two rounds of the 1996 BTCC on 22 September provided much banging and barging. The first race was red-flagged on the first lap, after a clash between Alain Menu (Renault) and Roberto Ravaglia (BMW) caused mayhem on the approach to Druids. Menu, however, won the restarted race while Frank Biela, who had already secured the Drivers' crown, won the second with the Audi A4.

■ In October, the circuit was coming under pressure from a local anti-noise lobby to cut back its activities. Nicola Foulston said that the circuit might consequently have to reduce the number of race meetings in 1997, but she wanted to press ahead with plans to increase other commercial activities, such as the race, rally and off-road driving schools. The protesters, however, said that it was these activities, held on weekdays, that were causing the problem, rather than the weekend race meetings.

■ At the 25th Formula Ford Festival on 20 October, Mark Webber stormed to victory in a rain-soaked final in his Van Diemen RF96. A Brands regular and senior instructor at the Nigel Mansell Racing School, Mark Marchant won the Kent-engined class in his Jamun M96.

BELOW *The Porsche 911GT1 of Hans Stuck/Thierry Boutsen leads a huge field of 43 cars at the start of the 1996 BPR Global Endurance GT race on 8 September. (sutton-images.com)*

1997

■ After his Formula Ford Festival success the previous year, Mark Webber made Brands his own again with a strong victory in the British F3 championship round on 27 April for Alan Docking's team, ahead of PSR drivers Peter Dumbreck and Jonny Kane, all in Dallara F397s.

■ The BTCC was enjoying a high profile these days, with live television coverage, and a large crowd turned out to see Alain Menu (Williams Renault Laguna) and James Thompson (Prodrive Honda Accord) take a win apiece on a sunny 18 May.

■ The 30th anniversary of Formula Vee was celebrated at the circuit over the weekend of 30–31 August with eight former champions among the 100 or so competitors who turned out for the 750 MC organised event.

■ All racing activities in the UK were postponed or cancelled on Saturday 6 September as a mark of respect for the funeral of Diana, Princess of Wales. It meant that the grids for the BTCC and supporting races, to be held the following day at Brands, would be decided from championship positions. In the event, the BTCC teams decided that the grid for the first race should be decided on the basis of the warm-up lap-times, and for the second on the fastest laps during the first. Frank Biela took victory in the first event in his Audi, while Rickard Rydell won the second with TWR's Volvo S40.

■ The traditional end-of-season Formula Ford Festival was renamed the World Finals, and there was plenty of Dutch support for Jacky van der Ende who claimed the title in his works Duckhams Van Diemen RF97 on 19 October.

BELOW *Alain Menu won the first of the British Touring Car Championship encounters on 18 May 1997 in his Williams Renault Laguna. (LAT)*

1998

■ Enrique Bernoldi took Promatecme's Dallara F397/8 to victory in the first F3 encounter on 26 April, while Luciano Burti won the second in his Paul Stewart Racing Dallara.

■ Rickard Rydell took his Volvo S40 to two dominant victories in the BTCC races on 17 May, with Anthony Reid (Nissan Primera) and James Thompson (Honda Accord) finishing second in the respective races. Jenson Button was excluded from first place in the Formula Ford support race for overtaking under waved yellow flags.

■ Brands played host to the 50th birthday party for Lotus on 7 June with a nine-race programme, including events for F1, F2 and F5000 cars. Demonstration cars included Graham Hill's Gold Leaf Lotus 49B, Gold Leaf and JPS 72s and Lotus 87 and 91 cars. The event was attended by Colin Chapman's widow, Hazel, and son, Clive. The line-up also included classic models such as the 25, 33, 49, 72 and 79. This was a fitting venue, because Chapman often used the traditional Boxing Day meeting at the circuit to show new models for the first time.

■ There was talk that the Grand Prix circuit could return to the BTCC in 1999, having been dropped from the schedule in 1997 because the cars went out of the view of spectators in the Indy circuit area. It was reported that restrictions on the use of the Grand Prix loop, due to complaints from local residents, might be a sticking point.

■ Barrie Williams and Norman Grimshaw were the stars of the three-hour endurance race at the HSCC Superprix meeting over 4–5 July, winning their class in their Mini Cooper S.

■ BTCC title contenders Anthony Reid (Nissan Primera) and Rickard Rydell (Volvo S40) won a race apiece on Bank Holiday Monday, 31 August, but only after Reid had been handed a 2sec penalty for his move on Rydell in the feature race. Rydell made his feelings about the move known to Reid in no uncertain terms in *parc fermé*

BELOW *Mario Haberfeld suffers an engine failure allowing team-mate Luciano Burti to take victory in the April 1998 British Formula 3 Championship race. (sutton-images.com)*

afterwards, and the incident was caught by the television cameras, earning Rydell a £2000 fine. A big attraction for the huge crowd was the presence of Nigel Mansell, driving a third Ford Mondeo. The former F1 World Champion failed to finish either race.

■ The Formula Ford Festival over 24–25 October had lost the backing of Ford itself and the name reverted to the Festival once more, after a year as the 'World Finals'. It was won by 18-year-old Jenson Button in a French-built Mygale, the first victory by a non-British marque.

BELOW *The start of the BTCC feature race on 31 August 1998 and the cars head towards Paddock, with 50 laps of the Grand Prix track ahead of them. (Author)*

BOTTOM *Anthony Reid (Nissan Primera) and Rickard Rydell (Volvo S40) enter the pit-lane nose-to-tail at the end of the BTCC feature race on 31 August 1998. Rydell was fuming after a robust overtaking manoeuvre by Reid during the race and made his feelings known in* parc fermé, *earning himself a £2000 fine. (Author)*

1999

■ There was eastern promise in the F3 double-header on 25 April. Luciano Burti (Stewart Racing Dallara F399) narrowly beat Narain Karthikeyan (Carlin Dallara) to win the first race, but the Indian driver won the second 25-lapper and Malaysia's Alex Yoong, driving Alan Docking's Dallara, came through to demote the Brazilian to third place.

■ Yvan Muller scored his maiden BTCC victory in Vauxhall Motorsport's Vectra in the Sprint race on 16 May, while works Nissan Primera driver Laurent Aïello took the spoils in the Feature race.

■ Narain Karthikeyan repeated his dominant F3 victory from earlier in the year on the Grand Prix circuit on 20 June, snatching the lead from pole man Luciano Burti on the run to Paddock and never looking back, despite a safety car period.

■ Martin Stretton took his 1977 six-wheel Tyrrell P34 to victory in the Thoroughbred Grand Prix race during the HSCC Historic Superprix meeting over 3–4 July.

■ Rickard Rydell (Volvo S40) and Laurent Aïello were the winners at the BTCC meeting on Bank Holiday Monday, 30 August. Aïello edged closer to the title with a 22 point lead over his Vodafone Nissan team mate, David Leslie.

■ In October, the Millennium Superprix, a showcase British Rallycross event scheduled for 5 December, was cancelled because track alterations required to stage the event could not be completed in time.

■ Ricardo van der Ende mimicked his older brother, Jacky, by winning the Formula Ford Festival on 24 October in his Van Diemen. His brother had won the title two years earlier. The pair became the first siblings to win the prestigious event.

BELOW Pole man Luciano Burti (Stewart Racing Dallara F399) is about to be beaten into Paddock Hill Bend by eventual winner Narain Karthikeyan (Carlin Dallara F399) at the start of the British F3 Championship round on 20 June 1999. (LAT)
RIGHT Nicolas Kiesa leads the pack during a wet Formula Ford Championship World Cup race in October 1999. (Batchelor/Sutton)

2000s

NEW CENTURY, NEW BEGINNING

On 11 January 2000, Brands Hatch Leisure plc announced that Nicola Foulston had resigned as its chief executive and as the chair of the Brands Hatch Leisure Group. Foulston also confirmed that she would not be taking up the position offered by the Octagon Group to become its director of motorsport, and departed the next day. Rob Bain, who had joined BHL in March 1998 as the group finance director, was appointed as the chief executive.

According to *Autosport*, Foulston had tendered her resignation before Christmas, as soon as Octagon's purchase of the circuit was completed, "to pursue a personal life". From £1.50 at its flotation on the London Stock Exchange in 1996, Brands Hatch shares rose to a peak of £8.00 at the time of the takeover. Asked how she would answer critics who claimed she was "cashing in her chips and running away", Foulston told *Autosport:* "I'm a professional whose job it was to maximise value for my shareholders. If that's what you mean by cashing in, that's exactly what I've done, because that was my job. In terms of my role as a member of the motor sport fraternity, when I joined Brands Hatch 10 years ago its future was in huge jeopardy and there was much doubt whether it would remain a motor sport circuit. Its future is now secure. I believe the last thing I've done is betray the sport."

John Webb denied that there was ever any doubt over the circuit's future and was following events from his home in Spain with interest. He remained sceptical as to whether planning permission for a Grand Prix would be granted and even whether Interpublic had executed sufficient due diligence when it purchased the company.

Foulston insisted that Interpublic had conducted due diligence and that the only mistake it had made was to disregard the parachute clause in the service contracts, which allowed her to leave immediately. "We were a public company and Interpublic is a public company," she said. "There is no way a public

RIGHT *This aerial view of the circuit shows the colourful scene on race day at the inaugural A1GP meeting on 25 September 2005. (MSV)*

company could be sold to another public company while keeping any secrets. Every single number, every single contract, every single word in the Brands Hatch contract had to be disclosed, whether I liked it or whether Interpublic wanted it."

The one thing that Interpublic apparently did overlook, however, was the break clauses which Foulston, Green and Bain all had in their service contracts. These were fully disclosed and Foulston had expected them to be disputed, on the grounds that Interpublic was buying a company worth a certain amount of money, based on the trio's vision of the future and deals which they had negotiated. It would not have been unreasonable for them to have turned round and said 'you've got to see these through, otherwise we're not buying you', which is what Foulston herself admitted she would have done under the circumstances. Interpublic's board, however, ignored the break clauses, perhaps not even considering the possibility that the three would wish to leave.

The service contracts terminated automatically under law on the day Interpublic bought the company and Foulston immediately telephoned Interpublic's main board to inform them. The response was for the MD to jump on Concorde and fly to London to try and talk Foulston out of leaving. He and her immediate boss, Frank Lowe, are reported to have offered her a quarter of a million pounds a year to stay and were staggered that she repeatedly refused their ever-increasing offers of better positions within the group. Foulston had always intended to leave and she stuck to her guns.

With Foulston's departure, the man in the hot seat now was 33-year-old Rob Bain who, despite also having a break clause in his contract, decided to stay on. "That was a mistake on his part, in my opinion, and one I think he now feels the same about," said Foulston. "In fairness, when we had recruited him in 1997, I had told him my plan was not to remain at BHL in the longer term but to start a family.'

"So I told Interpublic straight away that Rob was prepared to stay on and be the MD, because he wanted that role. I was very sceptical that he would get the support from Octagon. I thought he wouldn't get the investment and it would be a real mess – which it was. But Rob said he wanted to give it a shot. He felt confident and he stayed on."

Rob Bain himself recalled: "I was going to leave but they requested that I stayed on. Sometimes when I'm in a positive frame of mind, I think it was a good thing. When I'm in a negative frame of mind, I think it was a bad thing."

Under Bain's leadership, BHL pressed ahead with its plans to run the British Grand Prix at Brands Hatch. On 26 June 2000, Sevenoaks District Council's planning sub-committee voted 12–6 in favour of approving plans for the redevelopment of the venue. However, the plans still had to be approved by John Prescott, the Secretary of State for the Environment, Transport & the Regions. BHL had promised that holding the Grand Prix would bring more than £30 million to the area and create 3000 temporary jobs. It had also pledged to replace the 15 hectares of ancient woodland that would have to be felled with 40 hectares of new trees. To appease local residents, the company promised to reduce activities on the track and even to buy local houses from residents at twice the market price. Bain said at the time: "We feel sure he [Prescott] will take into full consideration the extensive public consultation we undertook and the huge benefits that will come to Britain, Kent and Sevenoaks."

The Formula One teams, however, were not so happy at the proposal to take the Grand Prix to Brands. Indeed, three of them wrote to the local council to oppose the plans. A letter from Williams Grand Prix Engineering read: "Principally the site is too small to meet the needs of today's Grand Prix. The proposals provide inadequate space for essential hospitality, for helicopter movements, for the race teams and for spectator parking." It continued: "The design principles to which the proposed modifications to the circuit have been made significantly underestimate the speeds that we are likely to achieve. For us, safety is a paramount issue, and on this point alone we find the proposals unacceptable."

In September, Prescott's department decided to review the application, rather than just rubber-stamp it. The government does not usually get involved with local planning applications unless it believes them to be of national significance. In this case, it was thought that it was because the track lay within a greenbelt area. BHL insisted the delay would not affect its ability to run the 2002 Grand Prix, but Bernie Ecclestone described it as: "A non-event now."

It was obvious that, even if it got the go-ahead, the work required at Brands could not be completed in time. Octagon was faced with the problem of having a contract to run the British Grand Prix, but no circuit on which to run it.

Rob Bain was particularly disappointed by the decision of John Prescott's department. "We had a suitable circuit, designed by Herman Tilke," he said. "It would have been great for the local area, and it would have been great for Formula One. It would have been a modern-day circuit to rival Bahrain with the track infrastructure, the grandstands and everything else. And yet the government called it in, which forced a situation to arise where the only way the Grand Prix could be saved would be for the Brands Hatch Group to lease the Silverstone circuit under what I would describe as favourable terms. That happened. Then the government called that in, so we had to go through a Competitions Commission process.

"This was because the Office of Fair Trading wondered whether it was against the public interest because we were consolidating track hire, and a lot of racing clubs and track hire companies were involved. It was the most nonsensical thing I've ever been involved in. We spent six months doing that.

"And then it came back to the government

paying, because the only way that the Grand Prix was going to be kept was if the main road at Silverstone, the A43, was upgraded to a timetable that suited Formula One – not Northamptonshire County Council. So the government had to throw money at getting the road complete. If the government had stayed out of the Brands Hatch thing, they would have saved a couple of million, but it was the nature of that government at that time to be interfering."

Finally, on 18 December 2000, it was announced that a deal had been struck between Octagon and the BRDC for the race to be run at Silverstone, and

BELOW 'Indycars' returned to the circuit for the first time since 1978 for the London Champ Car Trophy on 5 May 2003. Here the field runs down from Druids and around Graham Hill Bend on the first lap. (LAT)

for Octagon to take over the operation of the circuit. Under the terms of a 15-year lease, Octagon would manage Silverstone with a view to significantly developing corporate hospitality and racing school activities at the circuit.

The decision meant that the changes planned for Brands Hatch in order to accommodate a Grand Prix would not now take place. Rob Bain announced that the planning application had been withdrawn and that a revised application to update the circuit would be submitted. In February 2001, Brands Hatch Leisure was renamed Octagon Motorsports, with Bain as its chief executive.

In April 2003, the name was changed again to Brands Hatch Circuits Ltd, apparently to distinguish the company from its parent, the Octagon Group. By this time, however, Interpublic was looking for a way out of its motor sport activities. The previous month, it had published its fourth quarter report for 2002, in which it had said that it had employed business analyst Goldman Sachs "to evaluate exit strategies relative to its motorsports assets". The report valued Octagon's assets, for which it had paid £119 million, at just £44 million.

The company's financial report for 2004 explains the situation at the time. "Beginning in the second quarter of 2002 and continuing in subsequent quarters, certain Motorsports businesses experienced significant operational difficulties. Some of the impairment indicators included significantly lower than anticipated attendance at the British Grand Prix race in July 2002 and a change of management at Motorsports in the third quarter of 2002."

The financial report goes on: "We performed an impairment test and concluded that certain asset groupings of Motorsport had a book value that exceeded their fair market value. As a result, we recognised an impairment loss of $127.1 [million] which is composed of $82.1 [million] of goodwill impairment, $33.0 [million] of fixed asset impairment and $12.0 [million] of other impairment."

The book value was what Interpublic had paid for the company. If, after two years, the profits were depressed, which they were, then the actual value of the company was below what it was on the books, necessitating a write-off. Interpublic had bought something which at the time was making £8 million PBIT [profit before interest and tax] and was forecast to increase this to £10, £12 and £14 million over subsequent years. That forecast of PBIT had been based on expansion of the business through a plan written by Foulston and Green and which Bain had endorsed. But now that the company had lost

its principal business maker and key sales director, fulfilment of that forecast was always going to be a struggle.

Part of the problem facing Interpublic had been the Grand Prix contract that Nicola Foulston had negotiated with Bernie Ecclestone. She had agreed to pay £7.1 million per year, and an annual increment of 10 per cent. Up until that time, the BRDC had been paying £3.1 million per year. When the planning application was called in, Interpublic had held the rights to the Grand Prix, but had nowhere to run it. In December 2000, it had struck a 15-year deal with Silverstone to run the Grand Prix there in return for agreeing to develop Silverstone at massive cost.

In addition, the company was investing heavily in work at Brands Hatch which was required in order to host headline events such as World Superbike and Champ Car racing.

The latter event, held on 5 May 2003, was the biggest car race to take place at the track during this period. It was run on the Indy circuit rather than the longer Grand Prix circuit, apparently at the request of CART, the series promoter. Unfortunately, the race was rather processional because the drivers had to conserve fuel – due to the confined nature of the pit-lane, they were only allowed to make two pitstops rather than the three demanded by the allocated race distance. CART's senior manager of technology, John Anderson, said at the time that the Brands pit-lane was a big concern and that wholesale changes would be needed to bring it up to standard if the series was to return. A 35mph pit-lane speed limit was enforced during the event, which attracted 60,000 people over the weekend with a claimed race-day crowd of some 40,000.

Long before this, Rob Bain had resigned on 8 July 2002, the day after the British Grand Prix at Silverstone, following a row with Bernie Ecclestone over facilities at the Northamptonshire circuit. His place as managing director had been taken by Andrew Waller.

By the time of the Champ Car race, over 70 applications had been received to purchase Brands Hatch Circuits Ltd, which included not only Brands but also Cadwell Park, Oulton Park and Snetterton. Estate management firm Jones Lang LaSalle was handling the sale and, although the tracks were being sold as licensed motor sport venues, the fear was that there would be no guarantee that any new owner might not redevelop them for other uses. However, Interpublic was to have the final say on the sale.

In October, the short list of bidders had been narrowed down to five. Binding offers had to made by 8 November, after which a buyer would be chosen.

Finally, following months of speculation, it was

Jason Plato

"The first year I drove at Brands Hatch was 1999, my first year in cars, in Formula Renault. It was amazing – and that was just the short circuit. Later in the year, we drove the long circuit and I thought: 'This is a proper track – it's dangerous, it's edgy.' Paddock is still an amazing corner. Graham Hill used to be – particularly in the wet, when it was flat provided you were on the right line.

"The Grand Prix circuit was unbelievable. There are few circuits in the world where you don't want to get out of the car because it's such good fun, but the Brands long circuit was certainly one of those. It still is now – a little less so, but it's still is a big challenge. You look at some corners and think: 'It's a bit tight and a bit narrow here, and if I go off, I'm going to hurt myself.' But ultimately, I think, that's what turns us on. You need corners where you can hurt yourself. It sorts the men out from the boys.

"In terms of outstanding memories, this was where I won the 2001 British Touring Car Championship. It was a very, very bleak October day and, to be honest, we shouldn't have been out there, the weather was that foul. It was the climax to a very tense season, with a lot of infighting within the team, and it was an amazing event for lots of different reasons. Most of them political!

"It will always stick in my mind. The weather was that bad, the podium celebration was held in darkness. The race was delayed but they couldn't *not* run it, because it wasn't only the final race of the year – it was the title decider. So they just had to do it. And it got to the point where it was dark and we needed headlights.

"I aquaplaned on standing water at Surtees but managed to get back onto the track. Yvan [Muller] aquaplaned three times and never lost it, but he hit the kerb and damaged the underside of his car. As it turned out, his car caught fire and he failed to finish, but it wouldn't have made a blind bit of difference. I would have ended up third in the race, which would have given me enough points anyway. But it looked from the outside that it had cost him the championship.

"There was a lot of bad blood between us that year, and I came through to win. I remember the podium celebrations and it was lashing down with rain, but funnily enough I didn't care one bit. It was an amazing experience."

Jason Plato in his Seat Leon leads during the 24 September 2006 BTCC meeting. (LAT)

announced on 5 January 2004 that MotorSport Vision (MSV), a new company headed by former F1 driver Jonathan Palmer, had been successful in its bid to acquire the circuits. Across the country, motor sport enthusiasts breathed a sigh of relief.

The 47-year-old Palmer already owned and operated PalmerSport, a facility at Bedford Autodrome, providing prestige motor sport events for the corporate market. His partners in MSV were John Britten, who had founded and developed the Morse computer group and had also been a sportscar race team owner, and Sir Peter Ogden, formerly the managing director of Morgan Stanley, and who had founded Computacenter in 1983.

Palmer's acquisition did not include the rights to run the British Grand Prix, which Interpublic retained. Again it renamed its motor sport arm, from Brands Hatch Circuits Ltd to Silverstone Motorsports Ltd.

Palmer explained: "To start with, apparently there were about 70 other potential buyers who expressed interest when Jones Lang LaSalle first marketed the business in the middle of 2003. I applied for details, looked at them carefully, and worked out what we could do with the circuits with my partners, John Britten and Peter Ogden.

"We believed the numbers that people were talking about were far too high, but we thought it could be interesting and put in a bid. Although our indicative bid was pretty low, the vendors certainly felt that we had the credibility – I'd had the experience of running circuits and a reputation from that, and my partners were wealthy businessmen, so they thought the combination was likely to perform.

"There was a short list of five people in the end, of which we were at the bottom, to start with anyway. The agents initially ran with Roger Bennington, Richard West and John Batchelor. For some reason they failed to perform, the agents came back to us, and we ended up buying it."

Palmer's bid was evidently not the highest. Former British Touring Car Champion Robb Gravett, for one, claimed that he made a higher bid. "The reason I got in involved was that I felt we needed some assistance in this country in trying to make motor racing available to people more cost-effectively," explained Gravett. "We had some very good ideas, so we went out and raised money which was substantially more than I believe it was sold for. I think the plan we had was a very good plan, but for some reason it didn't happen."

Among the other interested parties had been Bernie Ecclestone, making it his third attempt to acquire Brands Hatch. "Yes, I did try to buy all the circuits," he said. "I negotiated with them but I think it was over a Christmas period. I was away and perhaps Jonathan was fortunate enough to get the guys there on the back foot. In all fairness, I would have given a lot more money.

"They knew me well enough because I'd negotiated the deal with Silverstone, and they knew that my word was enough. If they'd have bothered to find me and asked me if I would have given more, I'd have said: 'Yes'. And they would have got more. So good for Jonathan."

And what would Ecclestone have done to the track, had it been third time lucky? He replied: "I don't know. I'd have thought about it and done something, because I wanted to preserve Brands."

Palmer had been unaware that he had been bidding against Ecclestone. "The day after we'd bought it – we exchanged on 27 December 2003 and completed on 12 January 2004 – was pretty manic," he said. "I remember being here in the office, having just taken over the business, thinking: 'Well, here we are, where do we start?' My mobile rang and it was Bernie Ecclestone. He said: 'Just to let you know, congratulations. I knew you were the best person to buy the circuit and I'm very pleased. I've told Interpublic it was the right thing to do.' And we had a bit of a chat about values and he did say that he'd had a look at it."

It is hard to imagine Bernie Ecclestone being outbid if he really wanted something, and even harder to imagine that he lost out on the deal because he had been away over Christmas. In conversation with Ecclestone, it is clear that he has a soft spot for Brands Hatch: "A bit special – one of those magic places." This is supposition on the author's part, but is it possible that he was staying

in the background, waiting to see who the successful bidder might be? If he thought the circuit might go to a property developer and be lost to motor sport, might he have been ready to step in? If someone else was willing to spend their money to retain it for motor racing, might he have been quite happy to let them?

Another individual who put in a bid at the time was Nicola Foulston herself. "Yes, I made a bid," she laughed. "It was the lowest bid. They said they wouldn't sell it to me if I was the last person on earth. They don't like me very much."

Veteran commentator Brian Jones was particularly interested in the figures surrounding the sale of the circuit by Interpublic to Palmer's company. "Nicola Foulston had sold the company to Interpublic for £119 million," he said. "I went onto the Interpublic website and there, buried in the figures, was that they had not sold to the highest bidder. They had sold to Jonathan Palmer, and he had paid £15.5 million. So Interpublic took a hit of over £100 million. If those figures are accurate, they're staggering. I'll leave you to work out how and why a company could lose over £100 million in this way."

"I think Interpublic bought the Brands Hatch Circuit group largely because they thought it was the meal ticket to have the British Grand Prix," Palmer said. "Nicola had sold it to them with the rights, albeit subject to considerable modifications that had to be done. In reality, I think there was a very slim chance that the substantial planning permission they needed would ever get granted in the available time scale.

"As soon as it was called in by John Prescott's office, the whole time scale was delayed. So what Interpublic thought was an asset became a liability, because now they had to place the British Grand Prix somewhere, and the circuit they bought to hold it couldn't actually do so. I imagine there was a bit of a panic and I'm sure the BRDC at Silverstone realised Interpublic had little other choice, and put a pretty hefty price tag on leasing Silverstone.

"But that meant that the economics for Interpublic totally went to the wall. They lost money on the British Grand Prix and they were also losing money on the circuits. From the accounts, Brands, Cadwell, Oulton and Snetterton were losing about £3 million a year over the two years before we bought them, which obviously depressed their value. Certainly we paid a lot less than Interpublic had paid Nicola Foulston."

Interpublic must have rued the day it ever took over Brands Hatch Leisure. Not only did it lose out on the sale of the circuits but, having decided to withdraw from motor sport altogether, it had to buy its way out of its contracts to promote the British Grand Prix and to lease Silverstone Circuit. Its financial report for 2004 stated: "On January 12 2004, we completed the sale of a business comprising four motorsports circuits ... owned by our Brands Hatch subsidiaries to MotorSport Vision Limited. The consideration for the sale was approximately $26.0 million. An additional contingent amount of approximately $4.0m may be paid to us depending upon the future financial results of the operations sold. We recognised a fixed asset impairment loss related to the four owned circuits of $38.0m in the fourth quarter of 2003. Additionally, we recognised a fixed asset impairment of $9.6m related to the other motorsports entities and a capital expenditure impairment of $16.2m for

outlays that Motorsports was contractually required to spend to upgrade and maintain certain remaining racing facilities."

Palmer confirmed that there had been a performance clause in the contract. "Our deal was that there was a base of about £15.5 million, then a further payment according to how well we do with the circuits," he said, but declined to comment on whether the clause had kicked in or not.

The report went on to say that Interpublic paid a total of $93.0 million to Formula One Administration in two instalments of $46.5 million each on 19 April 2004 and 24 May 2004 in order to terminate its agreement relating to the British Grand Prix. It also paid $49.0 million in three instalments to the BRDC to terminate its lease on Silverstone. In total, the company recorded a pre-tax charge in the third quarter of 2004 of $33.6 million in motor sport contract termination costs.

Palmer was clearly delighted with his acquisition. "Race driving, commentary and the motor sport business have dominated my life and I'm thrilled to have been successful in acquiring four of the most famous motor racing circuits in Britain," he commented at the time. "We are totally committed to developing motor sport at the MotorSport Vision circuits and believe that, through innovation and quality enhancement we can revitalise one of the UK's most exciting sports.

"The future of these historic venues as motor racing circuits is now assured. Central to our plans is continued ownership of all four circuits and development of the motor sport business at each of them in accordance with their character and [the] opportunities they present. In four years, Bedford Autodrome has become the most successful corporate motor sport venue in the country, although it was never designed to hold motor racing

BELOW *The A1 Team Lebanon car of Khalil Beschir is launched into a series of rolls at Paddock Hill Bend during the inaugural A1 Grand Prix race on 25 September 2005, after making contact with the A1 Team Italy car of Enrico Toccacelo. Beschir emerged unscathed. (LAT)*

events. The addition of these four major circuits provides a most valuable complementary portfolio of venues.

"There is clearly a great deal of work ahead and the challenge of successfully developing the new business is substantial. However, I'm very excited about the prospect of providing spectators with more entertaining motor racing and competitors with circuits that become even better to race at."

Meanwhile, in Spain, John Webb was also delighted at the outcome. "For the first couple of years after I'd left, when I saw the team being dismantled, I'd been very upset," he said. "Then I thought: 'Forget it.' But when Jonathan bought it, I dropped him a line and said: 'Well done.' He came out to Spain and I realised that he knew what he was doing and I said I'd be pleased to help in any way, particularly when I found out that, in buying from Interpublic, he'd bought the freeholds, not just

the companies. He had no records at all. When I left, I didn't take all the records with me, but I had a little, plus a lot up here in my head. So he asked Angela and me if we'd become consultants.

"We're helping him in any way he wants, principally on the ideas front – promotional ideas, profitability. Plus, if I have an idea, I'll just send him an email and quite often he'll adopt it.

"Jonathan is very similar to me, very determined, but he'll listen to other people. I'm not sure I always did. He's a good ideas man. He's very meticulous. It would annoy him to see something out of place and he would do something about it immediately. He wouldn't fire somebody but he would certainly bollock them. Like me, he goes round with notebooks looking for anything wrong. If you can't find something that's wrong, then you can't put it right."

Palmer said of the relationship: "It was just

BELOW *An aerial view of the track in 2001. (LAT)*

Andy Priaulx

"A lot of the modern circuits have massive run-offs and are quite featureless, but Brands has masses of character, especially with Paddock Hill dropping away as it does. When you go round the back on the Grand Prix circuit, it feels like a mini [Nürburgring] Nordschleife. When I drove at the WTCC meeting in 2006, not having raced there for three or four years, I hadn't really remembered quite how close the barriers were. And it still had that feeling of being a circuit with a massive history.

Andy Priaulx slid wide through the Paddock Hill Bend gravel trap in his BMW 320si, losing the lead of the WTCC race on 21 May 2006. (LAT)

"I think my favourite Brands memory is winning so often in the Renault Spyders. I would like to say it was the World Touring Car race of 2006, but that's probably one of my worst memories of the place. I was best BMW, the heaviest car on the whole grid, and I was leading the race, but Paddock Hill Bend is one of those corners that can really catch people out. I was still trying to come to terms with the standing water and low tyre pressures after the Safety Car, and I went off. But my win in 2007 made up for it. That was one of my best-ever wins in my career. It was a tough weekend for me, with a lot of distraction and a lot of pressure, but I channelled my thoughts and my mind in the right direction and I got the end result that I was after. So I have very fond memories of Brands Hatch now."

sensible business thinking really. I'd come in from motor racing, with the points of view of a driver and somebody running a corporate events circuit. That's very different from operating a race circuit, where you're running race meetings and attracting spectators. I'd never done that in my life. Clearly John Webb was the person who knew the most about Brands Hatch, and who had made the biggest success of it on an ongoing and consistent basis.

"When I was racing my Sprite, and Gerry Marshall and Tony Lanfranchi would be holding forth in the bar, John was always there and he and Angela were very much revered as 'Mr and Mrs Brands Hatch'. He was always very smart on the promotional side and clearly he always had an eye as to what would work. I was very quick to realise that John was the person I needed on board for the benefit of his experience. I went to see him and his mind is as sharp as ever.

"A lot of things in business don't change. What it takes to attract a person to come and watch motor racing probably hasn't altered for a long time. John knows. And if he watches a race meeting on TV, he'll send me an email the next day and guess the number of spectators. He'll be within 10 per cent of the actual figure.

"We meet up about two or three times a year and he has given us input on how to arrange calendars, which events to have when, the kind of events that worked, the ones that didn't work, pricing policies, things that are important to people when they come, marketing and promotion, new championships, and all sorts of things like that."

Some people have remarked that Webb and Palmer appear to be out of the same mould. "It's difficult for me to say," said Palmer. "We both passionately care about Brands Hatch and motor racing. We both are pretty entrepreneurial, so we're not just going through the routine of running an efficient track. We both like thinking of new ideas and being creative in how we go about attracting people. And I suppose we're both pretty shrewd and also confident in doing things and doing them our way."

Palmer's first task was to look carefully at his acquisitions. "I think Interpublic's focus had been very much on the British Grand Prix, and sorting that out," he said. "So the other circuits were relatively peripheral issues, and you have to say that the management wasn't doing a great job. Maybe they didn't have the support from head office, maybe they didn't have the funding, I don't know. But when we took them over, the circuits were pretty scruffy. Oulton Park had had some money spent on it, to be fair. The new pits buildings there were very good, but Brands was in

a rather sorry state, and Cadwell Park and Snetterton were very neglected.

"We haven't touched the actual asphalt at Brands," he continued, "but there was just an awful lot of tat around – scruffy access roads, old bits of hard-standing here and there, grass overgrown, fences falling over, litter everywhere. The Brabham and Stewart buildings looked awful in the old brick and there was a tatty old toilet block on the end.

"We completely refurbished the Brabham and Stewart hospitality buildings, and we put in a new, enclosed staircase and built a new toilet block with a terrace on top.

"We've also done a great deal of safety enhancement work. We've improved the run-off areas round most of the circuit, Druids, Graham Hill and Clearways are all much safer now on the Indy circuit, and we also spent around £500,000 upgrading the Grand Prix circuit to obtain an FIA Grade 2 licence for the A1 Grand Prix, with major works at Hawthorn, Westfield and the run to Sheene."

Two years after MSV acquired Brands Hatch, in fact, it had undergone a transformation. Palmer: "I want people to walk in and think: 'Gosh, this looks smart.' Basic things matter enormously. Things like good food, and making sure the loos are always clean. The old airfield entrance was as scruffy as hell – it used to look awful."

Speaking in 2006, Palmer still felt there was room for improvement. "I still think we're only 70 per cent of the way to smartening it up," he said. "There's another 30 per cent to go to make it as neat and tidy as I'd like it to be. In time, I'm talking about five years, you'll probably see a redevelopment of the Kentagon and Hailwood's restaurant into something else. Hailwood's really needs something to be done, maybe with a grandstand on top of it, but it's a question of where you can see a return on your investment. The hard thing is to make money out of it.

"I wouldn't rule out some circuit modifications, either. We'll have a look at that. I don't have a clear idea, but maybe we should be trying to make more overtaking opportunities around the circuit."

Any changes would probably be restricted to the Indy circuit. "The amount of use of the Grand Prix loop is limited to 24 days racing a year, so there's not really a lot of scope for doing much," Palmer explained.

After MSV had moved in, more than the infrastructure underwent improvements. The quality of the racing on offer also stepped up a gear. It was Palmer's expressed intention to bring back top-class International events to Brands Hatch, and his first step was the inaugural A1 Grand Prix event on 25 September 2005. A1GP, billed as the 'World

ABOVE *Massive
hospitality stands
provided a good
vantage point at
Paddock Hill Bend
during the DTM race on
2 July 2006 ... (MSV)*

Cup of Motorsport', pitches nation against nation in a series of far-flung races during the northern hemisphere winter, using identical cars. Then as now, driver quality was varied but the Brands opener proved a tremendous success, drawing crowds in numbers not seen for many years. A colourful opening ceremony on the main straight preceded two exciting races, both won by young Brazilian Nelson Piquet Jr, who pulled off an outstanding pass around the outside of Surtees Bend.

The following year marked another landmark for the circuit, because an FIA World Championship event took place for the first time in many years. The competitors in the World Touring Car Championship races had to endure some fairly unseasonal weather in the middle of May, but rain at Brands has always meant spectacular racing and this was no exception. While the spectators huddled together in the rain and wind, the WTCC competitors provided two entertaining races, including a first win for Chevrolet, courtesy of former BTCC champion Alain Menu. The Swiss, who had won many times before at Brands, regarded it as his greatest win there.

A few weeks later, in July, the Kent amphitheatre echoed to the sound of the flame-spitting DTM 'silhouette' touring cars. With former F1 drivers like

Mika Häkkinen, Jean Alesi and Heinz-Harald Frentzen present, the meeting drew a large crowd of around 21,000.

Palmer is clear that the future of Brands Hatch lies with this sort of event, and will not even try to win back a Grand Prix. "Brands Hatch is very unlikely to hold a Formula One race," he said. "I think everyone's pretty clear about that. It doesn't have the space. Where its niche lies is as a second-tier circuit and to hold some of the International races one step below F1. That means World Touring Cars, DTM, A1GP, World Superbikes, that sort of thing. In 2005, we brought the Truck Grand Prix back here.

"We've got the FIA Grade 2 licences for the Indy circuit and for the Grand Prix circuit and the fact that we're not suitable for F1 cars is actually an asset, really. It has a smaller capacity than Silverstone and it's a more intimate circuit. When you get 20,000 people here, it looks absolutely heaving. When you get 20,000 at Silverstone, it looks pretty empty. So it has a much better atmosphere than Silverstone for anything other than F1.

"Brands is also perfect for the major British categories. We have two rounds of both the British Touring Car Championship and the British Superbike series. Then we host a plethora of club

ABOVE ... *as did the*
MotorSport Vision
Centre at Clark Curve.
(MSV)

events, Historic meetings, F3/GT and so on.

"It's a very popular circuit with the competitors. They like it because it's undulating and has some fantastic corners – both the Indy circuit and particularly the glorious Grand Prix circuit are fantastically challenging tracks to race around. Martin Brundle named Paddock as one of the top 10 corners in the world on the ITV F1 show – and he's right. Drivers also like it because it's very popular with sponsors, having a terrific atmosphere and heritage. And of course the most important thing of all is that Brands Hatch provides the best viewing of any circuit in the country, which makes it an absolutely firm favourite with spectators. Brands Hatch is a major brand name and unquestionably one of the most famous circuits in the world. People love to come here.

"This is quite a difficult business and, overall, I really enjoy the challenge of trying to make it work," he continued. "Often I'll wander about at a club meeting, go in the spectator areas, just bumble around. There's so much you gain from being a punter. Buying a burger, going into the loos, just wandering around. What's the bridge like? What's the PA system like? What's the fence like? What are people saying? Whenever you're out, you'll learn something. People will always come up and chat,

pleasingly often saying now how thrilled they are that we've improved their favourite circuit so much. I don't get many moans, but I do get occasional constructive criticism, which I'm always pleased to listen to. Indeed, I'll often invite it, as it's the best way to improve Brands Hatch. The world is full of people doing quality control and audits but, if you just chat to your customers and ask a dozen or so what they think of the day and how it could be improved, you'll get a pretty good picture of your business. I'd say 70 per cent of people's criticisms are valid.

"After making the MSV media announcement up in one of the Brabham-Stewart suites, my partners and I were posing for the photographers, and I experienced one of those magical moments in life when something profound happens. I was looking out over the track and it just suddenly took me back 30 years to the first time I had been here for my initial trial, driving round and going down through Paddock, and here I was, 30 years on, in charge. I had never, ever dreamed that I'd end up owning it.

"It's a huge honour, I must say. It's also quite a responsibility. I hope the battles we face to keep the place going will never get too much to mean that Brands Hatch can't continue to operate as a race circuit."

2000

■ The Brands Hatch grandstand, which had stood at the circuit since the late 1950s, was demolished in January to make way for a new, modern enclosure.

■ Alain Menu in a Ford Mondeo and Jason Plato in a Vauxhall Vectra took a win each in the season-opening rounds of the British Touring Car Championship on 9 April.

■ The track's 50th anniversary as a car racing venue, on 15–16 April, passed unnoticed. The 750 Motor Club meeting failed to mark the event in any way, and the Brands motorsport manager, Robin Murphy, commented at the time that he was unaware that the anniversary had fallen on that weekend. "The circuit's new owners prefer to keep looking forward," he said.

■ The Lister Storm of David Warnock/Jamie Campbell-Walter won the hour-long British GT round on 4 June, beating the Marcos Mantora LM600 of Calum Lockie/Cor Euser.

■ The 50th anniversary of Brands Hatch was belatedly celebrated on 22–23 July with a pair of 500cc Formula 3 races featuring on the programme. The wins went to the Cooper Mk9 duo of David Woodhouse and John Turner. Dave Hutchinson won the feature BOSS Formula race in a Benetton B194.

■ Wet weather greeted the BTCC runners for the feature race on Bank Holiday Monday, 28 August, but Alain Menu rose to the occasion with a brilliant drive to victory in his Ford Mondeo. Earlier in the day, Matt Neal had won the sprint race in the dry in his privately run Nissan Primera.

■ Anthony Davidson, driving a Mygale SJ00, was the winner of the Formula Ford Festival on 22 October in one of the best races in the event's 29-year history. Second place went to 18-year-old Danica Patrick, who achieved the first-ever podium place for a female racer at the Festival. Commentator Brian Jones was presented with a picture to mark his 25 years of commentating at the event. Before the final, a minute's silence was held in tribute to John Nicol, former boss of the BRSCC and non-executive director of BHL, who had died the day before after a short illness. Nicol had been BHL's motorsports director from 1996–98.

■ In December, it was announced that a 15-year deal had been struck between Brands Hatch and the BRDC for the parent company, Octagon, to take over the running of Silverstone.

BELOW *The British Touring Car Championship has always been one of the most popular categories of racing at the track, usually drawing large crowds to witness close racing. (Author)*

RIGHT *Alain Menu leads the pack in his Ford Mondeo during the August Bank Holiday 2000 BTCC race. (LAT)*

2001

■ The British Touring Car Championship season began with a double-header at Brands Hatch on 16 April. The Vauxhall Astras of Yvan Muller and James Thompson scored a win apiece.

■ In the EuroBoss race on Bank Holiday Monday, 7 May, Tony Worswick set a new outright lap record for the Grand Prix circuit in his Jordan-Judd. The record had been set by Antonio Pizzonia the previous year in his F3 Dallara. Worswick's time was 1m16.170s, 123.96mph.

■ Later in May, it was announced that the Grand Prix loop was to be reprofiled before the start of the 2002 season. Dingle Dell would be realigned to run inside the existing track to provide a bigger run-off area. Hawthorn and Westfield would also be altered in a similar fashion over the next couple of years. The track had to carry out the work in response to demands from the FIM, motorcycle racing's governing body, on safety grounds.

■ Frank Sytner, driving a Cooper Monaco, emerged as the victor from what *Autosport* described as the finest BRDC Historic Sportscar Championship field ever assembled at Brands at the HSCC Superprix meeting over the weekend starting 30 June.

■ Derek Hayes in Manor Motorsport's Dallara won the first of two F3 races on 8 July, but championship leader Takuma Sato, in Carlin Motorsport's Dallara, was unstoppable in the second. Bobby Verdon-Roe/Michael Caine won the British GT championship race with a TVR Cerbera Speed 12.

BELOW *Ferraris as far as the eye can see at the 2001 Ferrari Festival. (sutton-images.com)*

■ About 20,000 people attended a celebration of 75 years of wheeled sport at the track on 22 July. The race meeting was held on the Grand Prix circuit and billed as a Ferrari Festival. It included displays by the Red Arrows and Red Devils display teams and, until mid-evening, the crowd jammed the A20 to its junction with the M25.

■ Tim Harvey/Rob Wilson were the winners at the British GT meeting on 16 September in their Chrysler Viper GTS-R, but second-placed Mike Jordan/David Warnock in their Lister Storm secured the title.

BELOW *A priceless grid of Ferrari sports-racing cars enters Paddock Bend during the 2001 Ferrari Festival on 22 July. (sutton-images.com)*

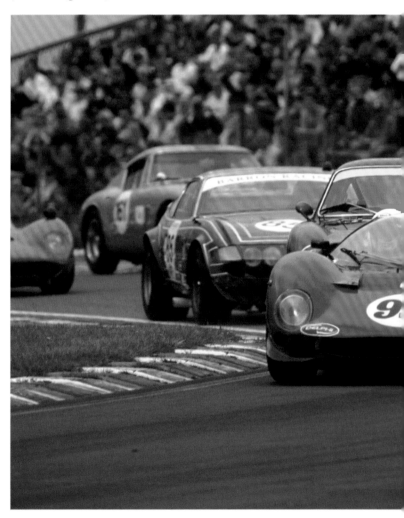

■ There was a dramatic end to the BTCC on 7 October, when the series ended in atrocious weather conditions and with darkness falling. Vauxhall Motorsport team mates Jason Plato and Yvan Muller went into the final rounds only six points apart and Muller took two points for pole position in each race. Anthony Reid (MG ZS) won the sprint race ahead of Simon Graves (Honda Accord), with Plato and Muller third and fourth. Muller now had to win the feature race to take the title, with Plato finishing lower than second. Muller was leading comfortably when an engine fire forced him to retire. Plato finished second behind Phil Bennett in another Vauxhall Astra, and claimed the title.

■ Alan van der Merwe became the first South African to win the Formula Ford Festival on 21 October, driving a works Mygale. The 30th running of the event was held in wet and miserable conditions.

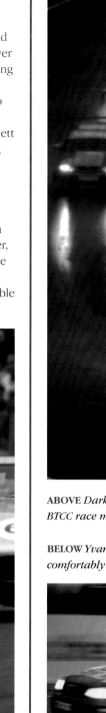

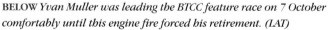

ABOVE *Darkness fell to add to the atrocious conditions during the BTCC race meeting on 7 October 2001. (sutton-images.com)*

BELOW *Yvan Muller was leading the BTCC feature race on 7 October comfortably until this engine fire forced his retirement. (LAT)*

2002

■ The BTCC season kicked off at Brands on Easter Monday, 1 April, as part of a 'Superweekend' of racing. Matt Neal won the sprint event in his Egg Sport Vauxhall Astra, ahead of Dan Eaves in VLR's Peugeot 406. The feature race resulted in a 1-2 for the works Vauxhall Motorsport team, James Thompson and Yvan Muller.

■ The British F3 championship was also on the bill at Easter. Robbie Kerr won the first encounter with Alan Docking's Dallara F302, while Bruce Jouanny, in the Promatecme Dallara, won the second race. The 'Superweekend' also included British GTs, Formula Renault, Renault Clios, Porsche Cup, Formula Ford and World Sports Cars.

■ Peter Hardman put his Aston Martin DBR1 on pole and lapped the entire field to win the Historic Aston race at the Aston Martin Owners' Club meeting over the Bank Holiday weekend of 5–6 May.

■ The third Civil Service Motoring Association Festival over 18–19 May drew 40,000 spectators for a wide mix of racing. The feature BOSS Formula event was won by Klaus Zwart in an Ascari 97.

■ Can-Am cars featured at the HSCC Superprix meeting over 22–23 June, and Frank Bradley raced a March 717 Chevrolet to victories in both Supersport Cup races.

BELOW *Jason Templeman's Renault Clio erupts in flames after an accident during the June 2002 British Formula 3 Championship support race. (LAT)*

■ Robbie Kerr dominated both British F3 races on 30 June in his ADR Dallara-Mugen, claiming two poles, two wins and two fastest laps.

■ The Ferrari-Maserati Festival over 3–4 August had to be switched to the Indy circuit because improvement work on the Grand Prix circuit, required by the FIA, had not been completed. The meeting featured a round of the FIA-sanctioned Thoroughbred Grand Prix championship and the track therefore required a Grade 2 licence, which the loop did not possess. The failure to complete the work on time raised questions as to whether it heralded the end of racing on the long circuit. The feature TGP race was won by Fredy Kumschick in a Williams FW07C and the meeting featured a concert on the Saturday evening, with Eric Clapton and Jools Holland on stage.

■ The BTCC was back for the Bank Holiday Monday meeting on 26 August and Anthony Reid and Warren Hughes took their MG ZSs to victory in the sprint and feature races respectively. A clash between team mates and title rivals James Thompson and Yvan Muller in their works Vauxhall Astra Coupés meant that the championship battle would go down to the final rounds.

■ Pre-event favourite Wesley Barber looked on target to win the Formula Ford Festival on 20 October in his works Van Diemen RF02, but he crashed out of the final, handing victory to team-mate Jan Heylen.

■ It was announced in November that the US-based Champ Cars would be returning to Brands in 2003 for the first time since 1978. It was also confirmed the following month that the track would host the final round of the 2003 British Rallycross championship.

BELOW *Thoroughbred Grand Prix cars make a nostalgic picture during the August 2002 Ferrari-Maserati Festival. (sutton-images.com)*

2003

■ In February, it was announced that the Dingle Dell chicane was to disappear. The corner was to be reprofiled into a right-hander similar to its layout before 1988 when the chicane had been installed, but turning in earlier and taking a slightly different line towards Stirling's Bend.

■ The gravel trap at Paddock was lifted and replaced by asphalt in preparation for the visit by the Champ Cars, because it was deemed to be more effective at stopping a spinning car. The spectator bank was also moved back 3m and debris fencing around the circuit strengthened.

■ In March, the new Dingle Dell corner was renamed Sheene Curve in memory of double 500cc World Motorcycle Champion Barry Sheene, who had died earlier in the month.

■ During the build-up to the Champ Car meeting in May, the bridge at the top of Druids Bend was knocked down by a truck driver, apparently unaware of the height of his vehicle.

■ 'Indycars' returned to Brands Hatch for the first time since 1978 for the London Champ Car Trophy over the Bank Holiday weekend, 3–5 May. The meeting was well publicised and drew a race day crowd of around 40,000. Also on the bill were British Touring Cars, Formula Ford, Porsche Supercup, Renault Clios and Formula Renault. The Champ Car race was won by Sébastien

BELOW *Pole man Paul Tracey's Forsythe Racing Lola B2/00 dominated the London Champ Car Trophy on 5 May 2003 but burst into flames at Paddock Bend after 118 laps. (LAT)*

ABOVE *The London Champ Car Trophy on Bank Holiday Monday, 5 May 2003, drew a large crowd to the circuit. (LAT)*

Bourdais in the Newman-Haas team's Lola B2/00, once pole man Paul Tracey's Forsythe Racing Lola had burst into flames at Paddock Bend after 118 laps while leading. A new lap record for the Indy circuit was established by Adrian Fernandez in his Lola at 38.210s, 112.306mph.

■ In the supporting BTCC double-header, Matt Neal's Arena Honda Civic Type-R nudged Paul O'Neill's Triple Eight Vauxhall Astra into a spin to win the first race, and Yvan Muller in another works Vauxhall finished second. Muller, James Thompson and O'Neill produced a Vauxhall 1-2-3 in the second race.

■ The revised Grand Prix circuit was used for the first time over 5–6 July at the Historic Sports Car Club's 14th annual Superprix. The changes at the new Sheene Curve won approval from most of the drivers. Richard Eyre established the lap record for the

new layout in his McLaren M8F Can-Am car, with a lap of 1m 25.864s, 109.96mph, on his way to winning the Orwell Supersports Cup.

■ In August, it was announced that a Champ Car race the following year was unlikely to take place, despite the success of the May event. The reason given was that CART, the series promoter, was slimming down its calendar for 2004 and the proposed races at Brands and the EuroSpeedway Lausitz in Germany were likely to be cancelled.

■ Yvan Muller had his licence suspended after an off-track altercation with Anthony Reid at the Bank Holiday British Touring Car meeting on 25 August. Warren Hughes in his MG ZS had won the first race ahead of Muller's Vauxhall Astra, which was leading

BELOW *The large gravel trap at Paddock Hill Bend is put to good use by the British GT Championship contenders on 28 September 2003. (LAT)*

ABOVE *Mini racing has always been popular at Brands Hatch. The Mini Se7en Challenge supported the British Formula 3 Championship round in September 2003. (LAT)*

the second race when the Safety Car was deployed. At the green flag, waved with one lap to go, Muller ran wide into Paddock and clashed with Reid's MG ZS as he tried to rejoin the track, allowing Colin Turkington to snatch victory in his MG ZS over Paul O'Neil's Astra. After the race, Muller confronted Reid in *parc fermé*.

■ Twenty years after his father had won the European Grand Prix at Brands Hatch, Nelson Piquet Jr took victory in both rounds of the British F3 championship on 28 September in the Piquet Sports Dallara F303. Will Davison and Robert Doornbos delivered second places for the Menu Motorsport team. The British GT race was won by Martin Short/Tom Herridge with a Mosler MTR900R, thereby clinching the championship.

■ There was a smaller than usual entry for the Formula Ford Festival over the weekend of 17–19 October, but it did not detract from a fine victory by Joey Foster in his Van Diemen RF03.

2004

It was announced on 5 January that Brands Hatch had been acquired by MotorSport Vision (MSV), a new company headed up by former F1 driver Jonathan Palmer.

One of MSV's first moves after buying the circuit was to rebuild the footbridge over Hailwood Hill, which had been demolished after being damaged by a truck the previous May. The run-off area at Druids was also extended. Rates for hiring the circuit were increased, causing concern among some of the organising clubs.

In March, Jonathan Palmer announced that the BTCC and F3 events that year would be run on the Indy circuit rather than the Grand Prix circuit, stating that MSV was unable to subsidise the use of the loop while it was reinvesting in the venue. Planning restrictions meant that the Grand Prix circuit could only be used for 24 days each year and promoted series, such as the BTCC and F3/GT packages, got the circuit hire-free. Palmer claimed that it would cost £20,000 to run these races on the loop, instead of saving the restricted number of days for paying series. He added that any series could use the long track if it paid the hire costs.

The first major meeting since MSV had taken charge was headlined by the British Touring Car Championship over 24–25 April. Visitors to the circuit saw immediate improvements in signage and in catering and toilet facilities. There were three different BTCC race winners: Matt Neal with a Honda Civic Type-R, Luke Hines in a Vauxhall Astra Coupé, and James Thompson, who had run the London Marathon the previous weekend, in another Astra.

RIGHT *Andrew Waller (left), Managing Director of Brands Hatch Circuits Ltd, poses with new owners, Motorsport Vision Ltd partners Jonathan Palmer and John Britten after the sale of the circuit in January 2004. (MSV)*

BELOW *The contours of Brands Hatch are clearly visible in this shot of Touring Cars heading down Brabham Straight on 25 April 2004. (LAT)*

■ EuroBOSS driver Scott Mansell shattered the Indy circuit outright lap record in his Benetton B197 Judd with a lap of 38.032s, 116.06mph, during the CSMA Classic Festival meeting over 22–23 May, winning the race by over a lap. Damon Hill demonstrated one of his father Graham's Lotus 49 F1 cars during the event, which drew a crowd of around 50,000, second only at the track to the World Superbikes. The meeting provided a range of entertainment for all the family, with truck racing, flying displays, a funfair and children's entertainers, and drew people who might not normally attend a motorsport event.

■ During the HSCC's annual Superprix meeting over 17–18 July, MSV boss Jonathan Palmer demonstrated the Canon Porsche 956 with which he had won the 1984 Brands Hatch 1000. Group C sportscars like the Porsche topped the bill, and Gary Pearson raced his Jaguar XJR11 to victories in each of two Group C/GTP events.

■ Matt Neal won the first of the BTCC races on 22 August in his Honda Civic Type-R, while Jason Plato drove his Seat Toledo Cupra to victory in race two. The third encounter provided a dramatic final lap. As the Safety Car pulled off with only one lap left, Plato led from Neal, who hit him on the way out of Paddock, sending both cars sideways. Yvan Muller dived up the inside at Druids in his Astra Coupé, and he and Plato touched. Both ran wide, allowing Robb Huff in his Seat to race past them and take the win.

■ In August, it was announced that the British F3 championship would not feature at any MSV venues in 2005. The promoter of the F3/GT package had been unable to reach agreement with Jonathan Palmer on circuit hire fees.

■ Klaas Zwart in his Ascari 97 Judd was the surprise winner of the EuroBOSS race on 19 September, after Scott Mansell's leading Benetton B197 Judd had spun off with gearbox problems.

■ Nelson Piquet Jr clinched the British F3 title by taking his Dallara F303 to a second place and a win during the 3 October meeting. James Rossiter won the first race in his Dallara F302, but the positions were reversed in the second race. Tim Sugden/Jonathan Cocker won the first GT encounter in their Porsche 911 GT3-RSR, and Nathan Kinch/Andrew Kirkaldy the second race in their Ferrari 360 Modena.

■ Longtime Brands Hatch racer and racing school instructor Tony Lanfranchi died on 7 October.

■ Daniel Clarke swept to victory at the Formula Ford Festival meeting over 15–17 October in his Van Diemen RF04.

■ The first-ever night race in the history of the circuit was held at the Britcar meeting on 20 November. The 90-minute event was won by David Cuff/Mark Smith in their BMW M3 E36.

■ Race Car Live! was held on Saturday 4 December to offer championships the opportunity to showcase their products to competition licence holders. In all, 27 different categories and clubs were represented at the event, which was attended by over 250 licensed drivers plus many spectators.

RIGHT *Nelson Piquet Jr on his way to winning the British Formula 3 Championship in October 2004. (sutton-images.com)*

BELOW *A variety of cars wait their turn to go out on the track during the December 2004 Race Car Live! event. (LAT)*

2005

■ During the winter, the run-off area from the exit of Druids to Graham Hill Bend was extended.

■ In April, MSV applied to register the Brands Hatch Racing Club with the Motor Sports Association as an organising club, indicating its desire to run its own race meetings.

BELOW *The inaugural A1GP race on 25 September 2005 drew a massive crowd and the pit-lane was packed on race morning during the public walkabout. (MSV)*

BELOW *The A1 Team Canada car of Sean Macintosh at the newly reprofiled Westfield Bend during the inaugural A1GP meeting on 23–25 September 2005. (Author)*

■ Modifications were made to Westfield corner in April in order to slow the entry but open up the exit of the bend.

■ Bo McCormick/Calum Lockie won the Britcar race on 16 April in their Ferrari 360 Challenge.

■ Brands Hatch stalwart Gerry Marshall died on 21 April.

■ Formula Palmer Audi topped the bill at the annual CSMA Festival over 15–16 May, with Joe Tandy and Viktor Jenson taking a win apiece in front of a large crowd.

■ Matt Neal and Yvan Muller were the winners at the BTCC meeting on 5 June. Neal raced a Team Dynamics Honda Integra to victories in the first two races, while Muller's Triple 8 works Vauxhall Astra won the third.

■ The revised Westfield bend was used for the first time at the Britcar meeting over 25–26 June. The new lap record was established by a Radical driven by Richard Ince/Austin Kinsella at 1m22.921s, 113.23mph. Both races were won by the Ford Falcon of Adam Sharpe/Mark Cole.

■ Formula 5000 returned to Brands Hatch over 23–24 July at the HSCC Superprix. The VDS-liveried Chevron B37 of Simon Hadfield claimed the laurels in the Derek Bell Trophy race. David Mercer won both Group C/GTP events in his Spice SE90C.

BELOW *Balloons over Brands during the opening ceremony of the inaugural A1GP race on 25 September 2005. (Author)*

■ The *Motorsport News* weekly celebrated its 50th anniversary at the 30–31 July meeting, when Legend cars were among those providing some spectacular racing.

■ In September, the circuit was awarded the FIA Grade 2 licence it required to hold the forthcoming A1 Grand Prix meeting. The work required to obtain the licence had included the realignment of Westfield, a 45m extension to the gravel trap there and the raising of the gravel trap on the exit of Hawthorn to level it out.

■ The 'World Cup of Motorsport' staged its world debut at Brands when the first-ever A1 Grand Prix event took place over the weekend of 24–25 September. A crowd of about 46,000 turned out for a spectacular debut to the new championship, which pitched nation against nation as well as driver against driver, and the event was hailed as a great success. The sprint race was rather processional and was won by the A1 Team Brazil car, driven by Nelson Piquet Jr. The feature race produced a thrilling encounter after the mandatory pitstops, and Piquet passed the Australia car of Will Power around the outside of Surtees. The Lebanon entry of Khalil Beschir flipped spectacularly at Paddock in the second race but the driver was unhurt. Piquet's victories came 22 years to the very day after his father had won the European Grand Prix at Brands Hatch in 1983.

■ It was confirmed in November that the circuit would host a round of the World Touring Car Championship the following year and was also lined up for a round of the DTM.

■ Honda driver Matt Neal clinched the BTCC title at the series finale on 2 October after colliding with Yvan Muller in the second race, sending his championship rival into the pits with a puncture. Dan Eaves won the first race in his Honda Integra R, ahead of Muller's Vauxhall Astra, while Jason Plato won the second in his Seat Toledo, beating Eaves. Third place in the race was enough to clinch the title for Neal. The third and final race was won by Rob Collard's MG ZS.

RIGHT *Formula Ford cars return to the paddock after a race in October 2005. (LAT)*

ABOVE *Big sky over Brands as a pack of Formula Ford cars rounds Graham Hill Bend in October 2005. (LAT)*

■ Entries were up for the Formula Ford Festival over 22–23 October, which was won in dominant style by Duncan Tappy in a Mygale SJ04.

■ The Britcar night race on 19 November was won by Simon Scuffham/Chris Randall in a Prosport LM3000.

■ The second Race Car Live! event was held on 26 November, providing a free motorsport show for the industry.

■ During December, the barriers at Sheene Curve were moved further back.

2006

■ In March, work to extend the run-off at the exit of McLaren caused a midweek Formula BMW test session to be abandoned. The work had left the grass verge soft, and it was feared that an errant car might dig in and flip over.

■ The new MotorSport Vision Racing Club (MSVR) held its first event on 19 March, with races for Formula Ford, T Cars, saloons and sports and GT cars.

■ The British Touring Car Championship began on 9 April with Seat Leons winning all three races. James Thompson took the first two ahead of Tom Chilton's Astra Sport Hatch and Colin Turkington's MG ZS respectively, while team mate Jason Plato won the third. Rob Collard was excluded from second place in the final race for knocking Matt Neal's Honda Integra R off at Paddock, handing the runner-up spot to Turkington.

■ EuroBOSS cars returned to the circuit at the Dunlop Great & British meeting over 29–30 April with victories for Klaus Zwart in the Ascari-Judd and Patrick D'Aubreby in a Benetton.

■ Brands veteran Tony Trimmer won the F5000 Derek Bell Trophy race in his Lola T332 during the HSCC Superprix over 6–7 May.

BELOW *Transporters lined up behind the pits for the FIA World Touring Car Championship meeting on 21 May 2006. (LAT)*

■ Defending FIA World Touring Car Champion Andy Priaulx looked set to give the rain-soaked crowd a home win at the WTCC meeting on 21 May, until his BMW 320si slid off the track. Yvan Muller won the first race, leading Peter Terting and James Thompson to a Seat 1-2-3. Priaulx held the lead of the second race until the Safety Car was deployed, but he went straight on at Paddock on the first flying lap afterwards and eventually finished eighth. Alain Menu gave Chevrolet its maiden WTCC victory in his Lacetti, ahead of Rickard Rydell in another Leon and Thompson. Menu, who had won many races at Brands, rated this as his best victory.

■ On 2 July, the cars of the spectacular, 4-litre V8 DTM touring cars descended on Brands for the first time, and the event was deemed a huge success. Around 21,500 paying spectators attended the meeting, which was dominated by Audi driver Tom Kristensen until he suffered a suspension failure at McLaren while leading comfortably, 17 laps from the end of the race. His team mate, Mattias Ekstrom, took the win, ahead of Mercedes-Benz drivers Jamie Green and Bernd Schneider. Paul di Resta (Dallara F305 Mercedes) and Peter Elkmann (Dallara F306 Opel) won the supporting F3 EuroSeries races.

■ On 27 August, the British F3 Championship returned to the Grand Prix circuit for the first time since 2003. Mike Conway and Oliver Jarvis, driving Dallara F306s for Double R Racing and Carlin Motorsport respectively, took a win apiece. A third place

ABOVE *The spectacular DTM series visited Brands for the first time on 2 July 2006. Here the cars line up on the grid in front of packed grandstands. (MSV)*

ABOVE *Mercedes driver Daniel La Rosa takes his C-Klasse out of the pits after a practice pitstop. (LAT)*

for Conway in the second race stretched his lead in the points table. Chris Niarchos/Tim Mullen co-drove their GT2 Ferrari 430 to victories in both the British GT races at the meeting.

■ At the BTCC meeting on 24 September, Jason Plato, driving a Seat Leon, kept his slim title hopes alive by winning the first two races, ahead of championship leader Matt Neal in his Honda Integra. The third race fell to the works Vauxhall Astra Sport Hatch of Fabrizio Giovanardi, with Neal's team mate, Gordon Sheddon, in second position.

■ Nick Tandy produced a stunning drive in the final of a rain-soaked Formula Ford Festival on 22 October, taking his Ray GR06 from dead-last following a first-lap incident through the field and into the lead before the chequered flag was waved. However, Richard Tannahill in a Van Diemen was declared the winner when Tandy was penalised 10sec for overtaking under yellow flags.

RIGHT *Nick Tandy crosses the line after a stunning drive to win the 2006 Formula Ford Festival, although he was later penalised for overtaking under yellow flags. (sutton-images.com)*

2007

■ Over the winter, the barrier on the inside of Paddock Hill Bend was moved back in order to create extra run-off area on the inside of the track.

■ The world record for the largest number of cars in a parade was broken in January when 313 Lotuses were lined up on the circuit.

■ The British Touring Car Championship kicked off its season at the circuit on 1 April, with Jason Plato taking victory in the first race in his Seat Leon, ahead of BMW 320si driver Colin Turkington and reigning champion Matt Neal, in his Team Dynamics Honda Civic. Plato and Turkington again took the first two places in the day's second event, with Tom Chilton (Vauxhall Vectra) taking the last podium position. In the final encounter, Neal took a surprise win, ahead of Fabrizio Giovanardi's Vectra and privateer Matt Jackson in a BMW 320si.

BELOW *The marshals at Paddock Hill Bend are usually kept quite busy. (Author)*

■ The Team GB car of Robbie Kerr scored a hugely popular home win in the Sprint race at the final A1GP meeting of the season on 29 April. Kerr took the lead at the rolling start from the Team Germany car of Nico Hulkenberg and controlled the race easily, coming home eight seconds ahead of Hulkenberg, who in turn was five seconds clear of Italy's Enrico Toccacelo. It was the first time that a host nation had taken victory at an A1GP meeting. The feature race provided more in the way of entertainment as Hulkenberg and Kerr scrapped furiously over the lead. The pair ran side-by-side through the first two corners with the German just ahead when the safety car was deployed at the end of the first lap. Team Australia's driver, Ian Dylk, had speared head-on into the Paddock Hill Bend barriers after colliding with the Czech Republic's Jan Charouz, taking the South African car of Adrian Zaugg with him. Fortunately, no-one was hurt. Soon after the safety car came back in, Hulkenberg made his mandatory pit stop, handing the lead to Kerr before he too stopped. Another safety-car period followed when Bruno Junqueira (Brazil) crashed at Surtees before the two at the front resumed their battle, with Kerr getting ahead on the run from Hawthorn to Westfield but losing the place at Sheene. Try as he might, Kerr couldn't find a way past and Hulkenberg took victory by just over half a second, with Toccacelo again third. Kerr and Hulkenberg performed celebratory donuts on the start-finish line at the end of a remarkable race.

■ Richard Meins drove his McLaren M23 to victory in the first of the Grand Prix Masters races at the Masters Historic Festival over the Bank Holiday weekend of 27–28 May, ahead of the similar car of Joaquin Folch. The second event on the Monday was cancelled due to heavy rain after the field followed the safety car round for two laps but conditions were deemed too dangerous for racing. Australian driver Wayne Park won both of the World Sportscars Masters events in his Lola T70 Mk3B while David Mercer (Spice SE90C) and Andy Purdie (Porsche 962C) shared the spoils in the Group C/GTP encounters.

■ The second DTM event to be held at the track attracted a crowd of around 18,000 to witness reigning champion Bernd Schneider, driving an AMG Mercedes C-class, take victory after 83 laps of the Indy circuit. Second place went to Audi A4 driver Martin Tomczyk, ahead of Abt team-mate Mattias Ekstrom. The two supporting F3 Euroseries events produced wins for Romain Grosjean (ASM Dallara Mercedes F305) and Edoardo Mortara (Signature-Plus Dallara Mercedes F305). The tight and twisty nature of the Brands Indy circuit, coupled with the 'slicks-and-wings' nature of the cars. made for rather processional races.

■ Forty years of Formula Ford racing was celebrated at the HSCC Historic Festival on 30 June and 1 July, with the John Webb Trophy for Historic FF cars won by Nelson Rowe in a Crosslé 20F. Sixty years of Formula Three racing was also marked with a 37-car entry for the 500cc car race, won by Neil Hodges in a Cooper-JAP Mk8. Highlight of the meeting was a duel between the two Williams cars of Peter Sowerby and Richard Eyre in the FIA Historic Formula One encounter. Eyre led initially in his FW08 but Sowerby got ahead with just three laps to go in his FW07C and took the win.

ABOVE *The slope of the old paddock area is just as apparent in 2007 as it was in the circuit's early days.(Author)*

■ Swedish driver Sebastian Hohenthal scored his maiden F3 victory in the second of the two British F3 rounds at the track on 15 July. The Fortec Dallara-Mercedes F307 driver fought off a last-lap challenge from Atte Mustonen (Double-R Dallara-Mercedes F307), with Marko Asmer in third. Earlier in the day, Asmer had won the first race in his Hitech Dallara-Mercedes F307 from the Double-R Dallara duo of Stephen Jelly and Jonathan Kennard. In the British GT championship, Alex Mortimer/Bradley Ellis took their Dodge Viper Coupé to victory in both encounters.

■ The 750 Motor Club's meeting on 28–29 July was marred by a total of 20 red-flag stoppages over the weekend. Four of the events at the Formula Vee 40th Anniversary Festival had to be stopped twice.

■ The British Touring Car contenders produced carnage in the first of three races at the circuit on 19 August. The Team Dynamics Honda Civic of reigning champion Matt Neal was written off and Neal himself taken to hospital with whiplash, after the BMW 320i of Matt Jackson ran wide at Paddock, triggering an 11-car pile-up on the run-up to Druids as it then spun across the track in front of the pack. Fabrizio Giovanardi in his Triple-8 Vauxhall Vectra won the restarted race from championship rival Jason Plato in his Seat Leon, with Plato's team-mate Darren Turner in third. The second race also produced a win for Giovanardi with Plato again in the runner-up spot, ahead of Gordon Shedden's Honda Civic. In the final race of the day, Colin Turkington in his WSR BMW 320i took victory, with Shedden second and Jackson in third.

■ Andy Priaulx made up for his previous year's indiscretion by taking a crowd-pleasing victory in the second of the day's World Touring Car Championship races on 23 September. Priaulx, driving a Team UK BMW 320si, passed the Team Italy-Spain 320si of pole-sitter Felix Porteiro on the first lap and was never headed, with the Chevrolet Lacetti of Rob Huff in third place. Porteiro had been on pole as result of the reverse grid from race one, which had been won by Alain Menu's Chevrolet Lacetti. James Thompson had pressed him hard all race in his Alfa Romeo 156 but was unable to find a way past. Colin Turkington, in a WSR-run BMW 320si, was third.

■ The annual Formula Ford Festival on 19–21 October ended in controversy for the second year running. The winner on the road, Callum MacLeod driving a Mygale SJ07, was given a two-second penalty for an incident behind the safety car, handing victory to the Ray 07 of Nick Tandy, who himself had been disqualified from a win the previous year. Only six racing laps of the final were completed and red flags brought the race to an unsatisfactory end after just 13 laps in total, following a number of incidents.

BELOW *Steven Kane (left) and Tim Harvey take to the Paddock Hill gravel trap during the Porsche Carrera Cup GB race at the BTCC meeting on 19 August 2007. (Author)*

BELOW *The BMW 320sis of Andy Priaulx and Felix Porteiro battle for the lead of the second WTCC race at the 23 September 2007 meeting. (Author)*

The Bikes

In the 1950s, Brands Hatch became a mecca for motorcyclists from London and the surrounding areas. Its success was due in no small part to the beginning of the post-war boom, as Allan Robinson, who both raced and commentated at the circuit for many years, recalled.

"Brands was motorcycling at its best, really," he said. "Its best – and its crudest. It attracted the Ace café racers, the people who were really the artisans who built up Britain after the war. The Ace café was on the North Circular Road, but there was also Johnson's café down at Brands itself. They attracted thousands of 1950s bikers.

"As people's wages increased, and restrictions and rationing and purchase tax died away, with all the other things that clogged Britain after the war, life became a bit easier. So the artisans – the printer, the train driver, the coalman, the power station worker, the shop worker, the warehouse worker – were earning more. They had been on £4 or £5 a week, and then suddenly they were on £12 a week and then £20 and £30 a week. So that type of person was able to buy new, faster, more exciting motorcycles.

"Because their fathers had never been able to afford cars, the motorcycle was the way in. In 1959, as many as 350,000 bikes were sold new. The industry has never, ever sold that many since. So there were 1.7 million or 1.8 million motorcyclists on roads that were much clearer, and therefore much safer, than they are now. The bike was better on acceleration and braking than the small car of its day – the Standard 10, the Morris 8. They were slow and cumbersome and operating on not very good lights. But the motorcycle was nippy and fast, so 100mph – the 'ton' – was in everybody's reach for £400. And £400 on £20 a week was an achievable hire purchase attainment.

"So you had this huge motorcycle population – and lots of them wanted to go racing. Brands Hatch got the post-war stars coming in – the Ken Bills, the

RIGHT *One of the all-time Brands favourites, Barry Sheene, in 1984. (Michael Hewett)*

Freddie Friths. And then, in the early fifties, Geoff Duke and John Surtees.

"The racing in those days was brilliant," Robinson continued. "They ran it as heats, secondary heats and finals, and then they had a consolation race for the non-qualifiers. So at the end of the day you'd get some horrendous scratching for people who hadn't qualified. And it made for great races. The sidecar races were brilliant because, in those days, the passenger leapt about like a monkey on a stick. And the sidecar was *attached* to the motorcycle, it wasn't built on. Very brave men rode them. Accidents happened and people lay on the side of the track until the race finished, and then the ambulance came and picked them up …

"You fitted a set of tyres at Christmas, changed them in July, and fitted another set the next Christmas. I raced against Bernie Ecclestone at one or two meetings. I'd watched him and, being a motorcycle dealer at that time, he'd turn up on a variety of bikes he'd taken in part-exchange and race the nuts off them. He was all arms, legs and knees and you'd think: 'I'll never get past him!' He was keen

and a very good paddock chap. People could borrow something from Bernie, or lend him something and always get it back. A good sportsman …"

Ecclestone himself also has fond memories of those days. "They were good times," he said. "Certainly on the grass it was different. We used to change an engine from a 350 to a 500 between races because you only had one frame. People always talk about 'the good old days'. When you were there, did you think they were good? Probably not. But you look back and think they were good days. I enjoyed it all.

"I remember Eric Oliver, who was the number one sidecar guy and won everything," he continued. "One day his passenger didn't turn up, and I jumped in the sidecar. It was like travelling with God. I don't know what happened, whether we won or not. That was the sort of thing which made them good days."

Tony Lovett, then a member and now the chairman of the Greenwich Motor & Motorcycle Club, also recalled Oliver turning up to race at the circuit. "Eric Oliver used to arrive in a sidecar outfit

BELOW *A young John Surtees rides as passenger for his father Jack on his 998cc vee-twin Vincent in 1951. (Mick Woollett)*

with a bike on top of it, towing another racing sidecar outfit with three engines in it," he said. "He used to come to a meeting, start off with his 250 engine in his bike and then race the sidecar after that. While he was doing the sidecar race, his father and brother would put a 350 into the 250 and he would carry on like that, winning every race, 250, 350, 500 and sidecar. I've never seen anything like it.

"Lots of them swapped engines, like from a 350 to a 500, but nobody else did sidecars and solos and did 250, 350 and 500. That man went on to be the sidecar World Champion. He was an absolute master. He was like that on the grass track. He didn't do any road racing until the track was surfaced at Brands and it became a road racing circuit."

The facilities at the track, together with safety requirements, were fairly basic in the fifties. "There were corrugated iron shelters in the paddock and loudspeakers that operated on multi-valve operation," explained Allan Robinson. "The microphone would 'click' on a Sunday morning and a voice would say: 'We don't want anybody riding with dodgy boots today, we'll be inspecting dodgy boots, and if you start your engines before 10 o'clock we'll throw you out.'

"The scrutineering in those days was pretty basic, as well. The inspection of kit didn't exist – you had to wear a crash helmet, but there was no standard. The regulations just said your skin had to be protected.

"A typical meeting would consist of 400 bikes in all the classes. Some riders would have two or three bikes, so there would be perhaps 300 riders who'd pay a tenner each to take part. Brands would run a Brands championship which progressed through heats, semi-finals and finals in all the classes, and then a grand final which gave you the winner, who was the 'King of Brands'. The non-qualifiers in each category would have their own races, so there would be failures in each race who would all come together in an idiots' final.

"It's one of the best motorcycling tracks in the world and the short circuit is motorcycle racing *par excellence*. Paddock was, and still is, one of the most challenging corners on a motorbike and the long circuit is a super challenge."

Before the track was surfaced in 1950, the line of the circuit had to be marked out with white pegs for each meeting. "In the early days, when it was a grass track, we used to go down to Brands to do various jobs," said Tony Lovett. "We had to put up stakes and ropes, and then take them all out at the end of the meeting because the farmer used the field for grazing. We went every Sunday, regularly. Not only did we fence it, once it became a road circuit we painted all the white lines and all the black-and-

Fred Clarke

"The regular motorbike commentary team at Brands Hatch was Peter Arnold and Eddie Dow, until Peter tragically died in 1968 and Dow asked me to help out.

"Eddie would do the startline commentary and I would do Westfield. Now, Westfield wasn't used that frequently and the commentary box, for want of a better description, was a potting shed on 20-foot stilts. It was on the outside of the circuit and to gain access to it you had to be a cross between David Attenborough crawling through the woods, and Sherpa Tensing going up a vertical stepladder, with all your equipment strung around your neck.

"These days, of course, we don't use it, although they still use it for cars. With the advent of closed-circuit TV, we just use the commentary box at the startline. The second commentator is utilised before the start, doing interviews.

"The great thing in those days was that the riders didn't change their leathers or helmets. Like football clubs changing their strip every year so their fans buy replica strips, motorbike riders nowadays change their helmets and their leathers with their team sponsors. But in those days, you could guarantee that the rider's helmet would remain the same, year-on-year. So you could literally ignore the numbers on the motorcycles and just recognise the helmet design. I could sit in the commentary box at Westfield and watch them exiting Hawthorn Bend and, bang-bang-bang, give the spectators 40 names as they came into view.

"One of the great characters was Barry Sheene, who was double World Champion, in 1976 and 1977. In those days, Westfield was a straightforward, 90deg right-hander, not a double-apex corner. Whenever I was commentating there, I could guarantee that, at some stage during a race – whether he was leading it, challenging for the lead or whatever, with the bike cranked over to an impossible angle at 90mph – Barry would take his left hand off the handlebar and wave the two-fingered salute, look across and grin up to the commentary box. He knew it would get a reaction from me over the airwaves, and it always did."

white squares around the corners about once a year. All the odd jobs, we used to do.

"It was only the Greenwich club that did all that. We were by far the biggest and we had a big social side as well, so we could call on plenty of people. There were two other clubs, Rochester and Gravesend, which formed the Brands Racing Combine. We used to take turns to run meetings. In those days, you couldn't have a permit every week, you were allocated so many meetings a year, so we had three clubs and we used to run the grass track days every fortnight after the war. We used to get 20,000 people!"

Six times World Champion Geoff Duke made his one and only appearance on a bike at Brands Hatch

in October 1955, riding a Gilera 500-4. "In those days, Geoff Duke was winning everything, and John Hall asked me to get him to Brands," explained Lovett.

"At that time, almost all motorcycle racing was done by amateurs. The only people who ever got any money out of it, other than prize money, were works riders. There was no starting money. My brother and I were running a motorcycle business at Forest Hill and I had a manager, a bloke called Charlie Bates, who was also mad keen on racing. I told him: 'I've got to get Geoff Duke.' He said: 'You pay my expenses over to the TT, and I'll go over there and I'll get him.'

"So he went on holiday and I got a phone call from him. He said: 'I've had words with Geoff Duke and he'll come to Brands, but you've got to pay all his expenses plus £100.' In those days, it was a lot of money. So I had a word with John Hall who said: 'Yes, I'll pay it all.' That was the start of riders being paid appearance money in this country. It was the only time he appeared at Brands but he didn't win – John Surtees had him away there."

In front of packed grandstands, Duke finished third, behind Surtees and Alan Trow. Lovett added: "Once we'd paid Duke, the word went round and we had to pay Surtees, because he was so good

then. Then Derek Minter came along, and they all wanted their money. Professionalism came in."

The advent of appearance money was eventually to prove beneficial to both riders and circuits. The Brands Hatch season used to consist of cars and bikes running on alternate weekends, and the circuit became the venue for a number of International bike meetings, all of which attracted the top riders of the day.

"In those days, factory riders were able to go off and earn extra money by doing International meetings here, there and everywhere," explained Fred Clarke, a long-time Brands Hatch motorbike commentator. "There were meetings all across Europe. At Brands, we had the King of Brands, the Race of the South and the International Hutchinson 100. All were non-championship events, but they attracted top riders who came along and earned extra money. In those days start money, or appearance money, was paid. It's not the case nowadays. Riders picked up appearance money and it was a way of bolstering their prize earnings.

"The first commentary I ever did was at the international Race of the South in 1968," he continued. "It was the final meeting of the year and Giacomo Agostini was there on the MV Agusta. He

Derek Minter

Derek Minter, after whom the back straight between Hawthorn and Westfield is named, won more bike races at Brands Hatch than any other rider.

"I think it was because I studied the circuit – not just walked round it but really looked at the corners, eyed them all up. When I went testing, if I'd had an idea of a new way round a corner, I'd try it there and then. I've even found a faster line along the start-finish straight since I retired. If you come out of Clearways and keep tight to the right, down by the pit wall, you get 300rpm more. And by keeping tight to the inside, you're not using so much road.

"What appealed to me about Brands in the early days was that, when you practised there and maybe found something not quite right, you only had to have a quiet word with George Pennington, who was the manager there, and he would put it right. If you found a bump somewhere or if there was grass overgrowing, it would be fixed by the time you went back.

"I can't remember any single outstanding race. I won so many at Brands, I couldn't think of one that counted more than the others. I even beat John Surtees there."

The occasion recalled by Derek Minter was in 1958, when he beat the reigning World Champion in a race-long duel. The track was wet and the MV Agusta of Surtees was heavy, but Minter was in such great form that he might have won even if the conditions had been more friendly to the Italian 'fire engine'. Surtees pulled in for a brief pitstop but, at half-distance, he got himself back in the lead. Typically, Minter recovered his composure to win the race. Minter was the only rider to beat Surtees that season and this victory is regarded as one of his greatest. It led to him being proclaimed 'King of Brands' by commentator Murray Walker.

Throughout his career, Minter fought against an inability to make quick, effective starts. In a way, that contributed towards his popularity. He would regularly still be push-starting his bike while the others from the front row of the grid were well on their way to Paddock.

After Surtees had moved into car racing, Minter became even more popular. In May 1963, however, he broke his back in a dreadful crash while duelling with Dave Downer for the lead of one of the most dramatic races ever seen at Brands. Minter was riding a 500 Norton, Downer a 650 Norton twin. Downer's bike was clearly faster and he passed Minter on the start-finish line on every lap. Minter came back at him in the corners and ultimately they clashed at Dingle Dell, killing Downer and seriously injuring Minter.

Despite this, Minter returned to racing. Two years later, Brands Hatch having realised that the unofficial 'King of Brands' title was far too good not to be exploited, he was crowned the first official 350cc and 500cc 'King of Brands' on Good Friday 1965.

Derek Minter (11) on his Seeley-AJS leads John Cooper's Norton (1), Dave Gegens on his Aermacchi (12) and the AJS of Peter Williams (16) up Druids Hill on 1 May 1966. (Mick Woollett)

went on to become a World Champion 14 times. It really did attract the *crème de la crème* of the British riders and also a fair selection of the continental riders.

"That meeting and ones such as the King of Brands and Hutchinson 100 stood alone. They were beneficial financially for the riders and they put a bloody good show on for the spectators. They were also part and parcel of the bread and butter of the circuits, which was getting spectators through the gates."

The Hutchinson 100 was organised by BEMSEE, the British Motorcycle Racing Club, and ran from 1968–77. "BEMSEE is the longest-established club in this country," explained Clarke. "They had this unique experiment of running the Hutchinson 100 in an anti-clockwise direction. That was something, to stand there and watch riders coming up Paddock Hill Bend and zapping along Brabham Straight and into Clearways. One of my favourite memories was watching Santiago Herrero, the Spanish rider on the single-cylinder 250cc Ossa, coming up through Paddock. He was one of the leading international competitors at that time and he was also doing Grands Prix. Sadly he was killed in 1970 in the Isle of Man."

In 1971, Brands Hatch played host to the first of the Transatlantic Trophy meetings. A series of match races between top American and British riders, these were held each Easter over six legs at Brands Hatch, Mallory Park and Oulton Park, and ran for 13 years.

"The Transatlantic Trophy races were a major innovation," explained Clarke. "It was initially instigated as a marketing avenue for the brand-new Triumph and BSA triple machines, and it was kicked around in a bar in Los Angeles by a couple of expat Brits, Gavin Trippe and Bruce Cox, with the promoters and representatives of Triumph and BSA. They thought this would be a good idea, first to promote the name of the new BSA Triumph Triple machine, and second as a crowd-puller for the circuits. They took a really big risk, because they had to fly the machines and the riders across, not knowing what reaction there was going to be."

Chris Lowe was a director and the general manager of Motor Circuit Developments from 1964–76, and was instrumental in persuading the Americans over to the UK for the Transatlantic Trophy meetings. "We needed some changes," he explained. "We'd never had any American riders over in England, nor any Harley-Davidsons. I went over to Daytona and made friends with a few people on the organising body, the American Motorcycle Association. They weren't keen on it initially, and I had a hell of a job with some of the teams. The guys at Harley Davidson, strangely enough, were OK about the idea. Initially I think we had five on each side and we ended up with eight on each side."

The John Player Transatlantic Trophy became a regular fixture on the calendar and ran to the same format each year, starting off at Brands Hatch on Good Friday, then moving on to Mallory Park on Easter Sunday and Oulton Park on Easter Monday.

"Brands Hatch was always the first round," said Clarke. "In those days, it attracted a pretty healthy crowd and the first one in 1971 had something like 25,000 spectators. At that very first race, there was a five-man team on each side. The British team was John Cooper, Ray Pickerell, Tony Jefferies, Percy Tate and Paul Smart. The Americans had probably one of the greatest American riders of all time, Dick 'Bugsy' Mann, along with Gary Nixon, Jim Rice, Dave Aldana and Don Castro. I seem to remember Don Emde was also brought over as a reserve rider.

"That was where the Brits always held the upper hand," continued Clarke. "If they had injured riders, they could always call on any Brits who were over here. The Americans only came across with a certain number of riders. If they had injured riders, they were then running with a reduced team."

The second appearance of the Transatlantic match race brought over arguably America's greatest ever road racer, Kelvin Rayborn. "The 1972 series really was one of the highlights of the Transatlantic

BELOW *For several years the British Motor Cycle Racing Club (Bemsee) ran its prestigious Hutchinson 100 meeting the wrong way round the club circuit. Here Phil Read (Yamaha) leads Bill Ivy (Yamaha) in the 250cc race at Druids. (Mick Woollett)*

Trophy," said Clarke. "Kelvin Rayborn turned in what many people say is still the most famous performance of his career. At that stage, I think he was an 11-time AMA champion. He was racing factory Harley-Davidsons but Harley-Davidson wouldn't let him come across with a factory bike, so he brought an old iron-barrelled XR across and won first time out at Brands Hatch.

"Remember, at that stage, very few Americans came across to Europe to do any racing," continued Clarke. "The American nation, as such, was very embryonic, an emerging nation. Latterly, of course, they've come across and won so many World Championships it's untrue – time and time again, they've been world-leading riders. But the series of Transatlantic match races was a wonderful idea in more ways than one. It enabled numbers of American riders to make their first ever sortie out of America to see what Europe was like, and then go on to race in Europe.

"They did bring some wonderful riders across. Go through all the Americans who went on to win World Championships, and invariably they came via Transatlantics. People like Freddie Spencer, for example, and Kenny Roberts. What was interesting was that, over the years, the majority of the series victories went the way of the British team, but the individual star performer was invariably an American.

"Motorcycle-wise, this was the meeting at Brands that people looked forward to. That was the one for which the annual pilgrimage took place, going to Brands and then staying with it at Mallory and Oulton."

Despite its success and popularity as a motorcycle racing venue, Brands has never hosted a motorcycle Grand Prix. "The bike Grand Prix came away in 1976 from the TT on the Isle of Man, where the World Championship points had always been awarded," explained Clarke. "It was felt that it wasn't fair to force riders to go to a circuit that was 37.75 miles long and to make them race for World Championship points. They really needed to serve an apprenticeship in the TT, to go there three or four times to learn the circuit, before they could hope to become competitive. So the British Grand Prix went to Silverstone in 1977 and ran there until 1986. It went to Donington Park in 1987 but there has never been a motorcycle Grand Prix at Brands Hatch.

ABOVE *The start of the second Transatlantic Trophy race at Brands Hatch on 9 April 1971. USA rider Pat Rice (2) on a BSA leads eventual winner Ray Pickrell (10) from the GB team on another BSA.* *(Mick Woollett)*

Stuart Graham

"When I started bike racing in about 1961, I was living in Cheshire, and you tended to operate mostly locally, mainly because of cost. I mean, before motorways, Brands Hatch was a bloody long way. It was a good day's trek to get down there and it probably cost a fiver in petrol. So it was a while before I made the foray down south.

"My first races there were in 1964 on a 350 AGS and a 500 Matchless. I found it to be a specialist sort of circuit, so it was always difficult to beat the locals. In those days, you had the southern set and the northern set. The northern guys operated at places like Scarborough and Aintree, and Oulton Park, Mallory Park and Cadwell Park. Brands was the home base of all the southern activities and was very much where the action was. All the Londoners went to Brands and, being a shortish circuit, there was what we used to call 'the groove'. A lot of those guys had grown up at Brands Hatch and knew the place like the back of their hands, so they were quite hard to beat.

"There were always Brands specialists. Originally there was John Surtees, and then there was Derek Minter, who was known as the 'King of Brands' on the bike scene for a long, long time. Many others were good short circuit men on the national scene. When I became a works Suzuki rider in the mid-sixties, and went to the Internationals at Brands, the big names were people like Mike Hailwood, Phil Read, Bill Ivy and Jim Redman.

"The format was usually heats and finals, from 50cc to 500cc, with races all the way through the day and the big finals for the big classes as the highlights. These were one-off race meetings, not championships.

"It was all part of learning your trade and everybody raced everything. You raced all the classes, or as many of them as you could get bikes for, because there was prize money. Once you became a bit of a star, you got a bit of starting money. So it was making your living – the more races you could do during a weekend, the better it was. You'd be charging around the country, racing on Good Friday, Easter Sunday and Easter Monday.

"Those were the days when all the Grand Prix stars raced at these events. So the bike scene in the sixties paralleled the car scene, where you were able to match yourself against the superstars of the day on fairly similar machinery.

"I loved Brands. The big circuit at Brands was great. The extension loop made it into a proper circuit. Prior to that, it was a great short circuit but the full circuit gave much more satisfaction.

"One of the most difficult or satisfying corners was Hawthorn in its original from. It really was a bloody quick corner – with a quick approach. Paddock was always a daunting corner, and Clearways was very deceptive. Paddock and Clearways are still two corners that have to be treated with a certain amount of respect.

"The place has undulations and camber changes, and all the corners are quite challenging in their own way. Even the 'dreaded Druids', as we used to call it – definitely an easy corner to rush into too quickly and lose an awful lot of time. Because it's such a photogenic circuit, and has been around so long, all the corners are easily recognised.

"It's a racer's circuit. You can get your teeth into places like that. I like proper circuits with big, quick corners that test you a bit – corners that make you feel that, next time, maybe you could go that little bit quicker ..."

"Grand Prix racing has developed away from the two-stroke machines to MotoGP, which uses prototypes, not based on any production machine. We don't have MotoGP at Brands.

"The problem is that there's a vociferous 'green' lobby there with regard to the proximity of the village [to the Grand Prix loop]. The law has changed in recent years. In years gone by, when people moved into an area where there was a nuisance, they basically agreed to that nuisance simply by moving in. Sadly, that doesn't happen now. These days, people can move today into an area where there's a nuisance, and start complaining tomorrow. And they seem to have every right – even if the nuisance, whatever it is, has been there for a hundred years.

"So Brands Hatch has to be acutely aware of the green lobby. I suspect they would have to spend a huge amount of money to make the track comply with the requirements of MotoGP. But the real problem is that, if you love these MotoGP bikes, they're the massed pipe bands of the Honda or Suzuki ensemble. If you hate them, they're bloody noisy. I think the local residents hate them. So I don't think we'll see Grand Prix racing there. I think it's Superbikes at Brands for the foreseeable future."

Superbikes, racing in both the British national and the World series, have certainly become a staple part of the Brands bike scene over the last few years. "World Superbikes started in 1988," said Clarke. "The very first World Superbike round run at Brands Hatch, ironically, was the Irish round. The Irish had been granted the date under FIM regulations but, for whatever reason, financial or otherwise, they couldn't run it, so they sold the rights to Brands Hatch. The World Superbikes were just gaining in strength then. It became one of the major meetings.

"Superbikes were more showroom-based, more akin to the ones people could purchase from showrooms," he continued. "Silhouettes of road bikes, if you like. More identifiable with the bikes you and I could go to our dealer and buy."

Although Clarke has commentated on more than 18,000 individual bike races during his career, one race at Brands stands out in his memory. "In 2000, the World Superbikes came to Brands Hatch twice," he explained. "I think a Spanish circuit couldn't hold their round so, having had the Superbike round at Brands in August, they came back in October. This happened to be the World Supersport meeting, the final round of that championship. And the title hung on the result of this one race.

"Mathematically, any one of four riders could have taken the Supersport title. I'd worked out all the permutations and got them written down, so that I could say who was doing what at any given stage. And I can remember saying that, at one stage or another, each of those four riders was on course to be the World Champion. Every time they changed positions, the crown bounced from one head to another head, to the next head.

"There was a Frenchman, Stéphane Chambon, the defending champion going into that race. There was a former champion, Paolo Casoli, and there were two team mates racing for a team called Alfatechnique, Jörg Teuchert and Christian Kellner. As I recall, Chambon went out of the race early on. But all through the rest of it, the remaining riders constantly slogged it out and constantly changed positions at every corner, and the crown just bounced from one rider to another.

"Two other riders took part in all this – Aussie Karl Muggeridge and British rider Jamie Whitham. They also took turns leading the race. It turned out to be the first ever victory at this level for Muggeridge, and Whitham was second. Teuchert took the championship by finishing third."

Today, the bike racing scene at Brands is as important to the circuit as it has ever been. In John Webb's time, leaving aside the car Grands Prix, motorbike racing represented around 50 per cent of the business, both in terms of track use and spectator attendance. Towards the end of the nineties, when the circuit was not hosting any major International car meetings, the World Superbikes meeting was the biggest event on the calendar. Even today, according to circuit boss Jonathan Palmer, motorcycle racing is even more important than cars.

"Before I acquired the circuits, I really had no idea how much bike sport there was," he said. "Being involved in car racing, rather stupidly I didn't go to bike events. But from the information we were given on buying the circuits, I could see that bikes were a big part of it all. Certainly, since then, the fact is that bikes probably represent 60 per cent of the activity on the circuit, and cars 40 per cent.

"That figure relates to everything," he continued. "With regard to the major promoted events, British Superbikes are even bigger than British Touring Cars, and World Superbikes are bigger than World Touring Cars by a massive amount. The World Superbikes meeting is the biggest event of the year at Brands Hatch, that's for sure. We probably run an equal number of car club events and bike club events, but the bikes probably draw bigger crowds. And we run more bike track days than we will car track days.

"I always say that we have two kinds of customer. One pays to watch people drive cars or ride bikes round the circuit, and the other pays to drive cars or ride bikes round the circuit. From a spectator's point of view, the level of drama is higher in the bike races.

Ron Chandler

"I was racing in the Hutchinson 100. Mike Hailwood was on his factory 350 Honda, and I was on my G50. I got a really good start and was in the lead. Clearways was a really tricky corner going back to front, because it was off-camber. Mike was right behind me when my gearbox locked up there. I lost it and ended up in the Dunlop hoarding.

"My wife saw Mike after he'd won and asked what had happened to me. He said he didn't know – all he'd seen was me disappearing into the Dunlop sign."

Stan Woods

"My first win at Brands came at the Hutchinson 100 in 1973. I liked the circuit much more the 'wrong' way round – Paddock was fantastic, you used to go through it so fast.

"I won the King of Brands twice, but it should have been three times. In 1974, Barry and Franco Sheene were competing there. After I'd won the 500 race, Barry's dad, Franco, said to me: 'Well done, lad, that was a good race – I bet you're tired now, aren't you?' I said I was, and he told me: 'Well, don't go out in the next race, then.' It turned out the next race was the qualifier for the King of Brands, so I didn't qualify!

"When I won my first King of Brands, it was easy, but the next time was more difficult, because it was an aggregate race. The two main races were the 500s and F1s. It was tight between me, Pat Mahoney and Dave Potter. In the final race, the F1, I went through Clearways and completely lost the rear end, ending up on the grass. I got it back and finished third, but I didn't know who had won. All three of us went to the podium and Chris Lowe, who liked to look after the money, came towards us to present the trophies. He had a bottle of champagne under his arm, and some glasses. He poured out a glass for each of us. I asked him if I could spray the rest, but he wouldn't let me."

They overtake more often and, when they have incidents, it looks more spectacular. And from a participant point of view, ultimately it's much cheaper to run a bike than it is to run a car. Track days, for example, are more popular on bikes, and that's not only because they're cheaper to buy in the first place. You've only got two tyres, not four, you've got less fuel to buy, you've generally got less to wear out. And if you do drop it, they're cheaper to fix."

In one sense, then, things have come full circle at Brands Hatch. Motorcycles first broke the silence in the grassy bowl in the early 1930s. Although the circuit became more famous in the intervening period for its car racing, two-wheeled competition is still as popular there more than 80 years later.

Innovations and personalities

The late sixties was a time of innovation at Brands Hatch. In particular, two new single-seater formulae were introduced that were to play a major role in the British racing scene for many years – Formula Ford and Formula 5000. Unsurprisingly, both sprang from the fertile mind of John Webb.

However, it was not Webb who first conceived the idea of a low-cost racing car based on production road car components. That had already occurred to John Tomlinson, an instructor at Motor Racing Stables, a racing school run by Geoff Clarke and based at Finmere Airfield, not far from Silverstone.

The school's running costs were high, since racing engines were expensive and prone to damage by inexperienced drivers. Tomlinson suggested putting a standard engine from an Austin A35 into one of the school's single-seater chassis. The idea worked and the next cost-cutting step was to fit roadgoing radial tyres instead of racing tyres. This saved money, and allowed novice drivers more easily to develop their car control skills.

The concept was further developed in 1965, when the school moved from Finmere to Brands Hatch. Three Formula 3 Lotus 31s were fitted with 1.5-litre Ford Cortina engines and road tyres. The cars proved a great success with the pupils and helped to reduce the school's running costs. They then came to the attention of John Webb.

"The racing school was the catalyst for Formula Ford," he explained. "They had a demand for a low-cost, tuitional vehicle. We had a demand for more single-seater races. There was hardly any single-

RIGHT *The start of the first-ever Formula Ford race, on 2 July 1967. Eventual winner Ray Allen is in the middle of the front row. (LAT)*

seater racing when we started the formula in 1967. From that moment onwards, well over 50 per cent of the race programme became single-seaters."

Webb and Clarke contacted Henry Taylor, who was then the competitions manager at Ford, with the idea of establishing a new, low-cost single-seater formula, in which the emphasis would be on driver ability rather than spending capacity. They took the concept to the RAC's Motor Sports Association and Formula Ford was born.

"Most people still think Ford had something to do with the concept," explained Webb. "My feeling at the time was that it was no use starting a new formula unless it had credibility. You need a decent name – this was long before manufacturers ran their own one-make formulae. In our naïvety, we rang Ford and asked them: 'If we start this, and we use Ford engines, is there any way we could call it Formula Ford?' And to our great surprise they

BELOW Ray Allen, the winner of the first-ever Formula Ford race, takes his Lotus 51 through Bottom Bend on 2 July 1967. (LAT)

replied: 'Yes, and we'll give you 50 engines to start with.' But it was never conceived as a publicity vehicle for Ford. They never interfered with the regulations but they did pay for initial administration and policing."

The first car was based on a tubular spaceframe Formula Junior chassis with a near-standard 1500cc Ford Cortina GT engine, and a four-speed transaxle derived from the VW Beetle. Where possible, the components were based on standard Ford components, including brakes, clutch and wheels. It was agreed that the production single-seaters should cost no more than £1000.

The racing school took delivery of 10 new Lotus 51s, five of which only arrived the morning of the first school race. The first public event was made up of these 10 cars, five Lotus 31s from the Jim Russell Racing Drivers School from Snetterton, three converted Brabhams, a Piper and a converted Mallock U2.

The winner of that first-ever race on Sunday 2 July 1967 was Ray Allen, who was later bought out of the Army in order to pursue a career in motor racing. Claude Bourgoignie, from Belgium, became the first Formula Ford champion that year with a Lotus 31.

Popularity in the category grew rapidly, encouraging many more manufacturers to enter the fray. At the Race of Champions meeting in March 1968, only eight months after the inaugural event, cars from 12 different manufacturers were on the grid for the supporting Formula Ford race. That year, Australian Tim Schenken won 28 of the 33 races he entered with a Merlyn.

Emerson Fittipaldi was another who raced in Formula Ford, as did James Hunt, Jody Scheckter, Nigel Mansell, Ayrton Senna (who dominated the formula in 1981), Johnny Herbert, Damon Hill, Michael Schumacher, Mika Häkkinen, David Coulthard, Eddie Irvine, Mark Webber and Anthony Davidson.

"I never thought it would take off the way it did," said Webb. "I think Ford calculated that something like 10,000 cars were made in the sixties, seventies and early eighties, and there must have been well over 100 different constructors, which created massive employment and component demand. It started an industry that was not linked to Formula One.

"Unfortunately, people who subsequently inherited responsibility for running things like Formula Ford had never updated themselves on its origins and the reasons. They allowed it to become costly and, as it became expensive, it found itself with new competitors, like Formula Renault, Formula Vauxhall, and now Formula BMW. Now they're all fighting for a limited amount of money at the top.

DUNLOP

"To my mind," he continued, "what we now have reluctantly to call the demise of Formula Ford has been due to people who inherited it after I'd gone, who didn't understand the basic reasons for it. They moved it too far away from being a very low-cost formula for the masses.

"Motor racing is a pyramid. At the top are 22 Formula One cars, at the bottom are several thousand of the cheapest possible cars. The inside of the pyramid will always be bigger if the base is bigger. The base determines the mass. That is what I was really trying to do – introduce low-cost motor racing to increase the mass."

For many young drivers, the Formula Ford cars provided a cost-effective introduction to racing, but there was also room at the top of the scale for a big, noisy, ground-trembling class of cars. This was where Formula 5000 came in.

"I saw in the paddock at Silverstone the prototype of a car that Lola had built for a new Formula A series that was starting in America," explained Webb. "It had a great big, 5-litre Chevvy engine, but I knew you'd never sell it in Britain as Formula A. We needed a powerful name, so I suggested Formula 5000. That became a very successful formula. It lasted for a very long time and lent itself to the addition of secondhand F1 cars which, until then, had never been raced. So we had 13 or 14 years of powerful single-seater racing in the UK, before F1-type economics forced it out.

"The first race was at Oulton Park on Good Friday 1969 and it got 30,000 people, which was gob-smacking. The onomatopoeic name worked – it conjured up the feeling of power. It got the response and I followed that through much later when I started a sportscar series called Thundersports – onomatopoeic again."

Webb got together with Nick Syrett, then the executive director of the BRSCC, to create the Formula 5000 category, which rapidly established itself as a 'spectacle formula'. In anticipation of a slow start, it was decided to allow 2-litre single-seaters to run alongside the 5-litre cars for 1969 only. The new category was announced jointly by MCD and the BRSCC in August 1968, with £32,000 sponsorship to come from Carrera, the cigarette manufacturer, under its Guards brand. Each race would have £2500 prize fund with £500 for the winner down to £100 for last place. There was also a £2000 championship fund with £1000 for the winner.

At the 1969 Racing Car Show at Olympia, a number of manufacturers had cars for the new formula on display. Lola had its T142, which sold for £5500 complete with Chevrolet engine, while the McLaren M10A was priced at £7055. In addition, John Surtees announced that he was to become a racing car manufacturer with his TS5. These three became the main manufacturers for the opening season.

The winner of the first four rounds of the championship was Peter Gethin in the Church Farm

ABOVE *The Formula 5000 cars provided a spectacular sight with their high rear wings during their first year of competition in 1969. (LAT)*

Tony Lanfranchi and Gerry Marshall

Of all the thousands of drivers who have raced at Brands Hatch, two will forever stand out as synonymous with the track – Tony Lanfranchi and Gerry Marshall.

During his career, Tony Lanfranchi drove everything from production saloons to Formula One cars, and was the senior instructor at Motor Racing Stables (later Brands Hatch Racing) for many years. On 7 May 1978, after 21 years in motor racing, he was the subject of the sport's first-ever benefit meeting. Appropriately enough, he won the Celebrity Escort race. On the Wednesday evening before the meeting, the BRSCC and MCD organised a 'This is Your Life' for him in the Brands Hatch clubhouse. At the benefit day, the marshals presented him with 22 gallons of beer, and the bar at the back of the main grandstand was renamed the Lanfranchi Bar in his honour.

"He was my idea of the quintessential racing driver," said commentator Brian Jones. "He raced hard, played hard and drank hard, and he was a real playboy. He gambled and he loved the ladies, but his passion was motor racing. He was a larger-than-life character. Despite his name, he was a bluff Yorkshireman. He was not the ascetic fitness fanatic who is today's racing driver. Once he'd finished driving, he was in the clubhouse bar.

"Brands Hatch was very much a social place in those days. The clubhouse bar was mainly run by the beautiful Angie Middleton, who stole the hearts of most of the males who frequented the place. Lanfranchi was running the racing school and he'd come up at lunchtime for a couple of pints. You have to understand, it was a very different environment in those days, and there was a lot more driving and drinking than there is today.

LEFT *Tony Lanfranchi: forever synonymous with Brands Hatch. (LAT)*

BELOW *Tony Lanfranchi drives his Mayfair sponsored Opel Commodore GSE in a Production Saloon race in March 1978. (Author)*

"I associate two particular cars with Tony, the first of which was the Moskvich. This was pure Lanfranchi. He worked out which car he thought had the best chance of winning the British Saloon Car Championship, came up with this Russian car nobody had heard of, and walked away with the championship by winning his class. The other car has to be his 'Mayfair' sponsored Opel Commodore. Motor Racing Stables had an arrangement with 'Men Only' magazine, which promoted the school and presented the awards at the end of the season, and Tony did a deal with its rival, and put its title in huge letters along the sides of his car. It was typical of him – he wanted to deliver for his sponsors and wanted no one to be in any doubt about who his sponsors were."

Lanfranchi's great sparring and drinking partner was Gerry Marshall, another larger-than-life character, in all senses. In a career that spanned 40 years, Marshall won more than 600 races, competing in everything from Formula Ford to Truck racing. But he was best known in saloon cars, and scored numerous race and championship wins in Vauxhalls, especially the Thames TV Firenza 'Old Nail' and the Firenza-based 'Baby Bertha'. He was famous for his sideways driving style and, like Lanfranchi, was the subject of a benefit day at the circuit in 1979, organised by John Webb and the BARC.

Brian Jones remembered: "The most enjoyable drive I ever had in a racing car at Brands was with Gerry, in the wet in a Vauxhall Carlton. He reached angles I didn't think it was possible to get the car back from. His feet were dancing on the pedals like an organist's.

"It was no wonder that, whenever Marshall got out of a racing car, he was steaming – I mean not metaphorically, but literally. At times he was carrying around 20 stone. How he could be quick in a car carrying that amount of additional weight, I just don't know, but this man was a competitor in everything. He and Divina Galica, who was a fitness fanatic and a former captain of the ladies British Olympic ski team, had a race round Brands on pedal bikes, and he beat her!

"After a meeting, Gerry held court in the clubhouse, and subsequently in the Kentagon, and anybody and everybody could talk to him. He had views on every racing driver in the country. They weren't always complimentary. He could be an outrageous critic but he was funny with it.

"He was such a regular at Brands and he was hugely popular. In my view, his popularity stemmed from his entertainment value on the track. Tony wasn't like that – he was popular, too, but his popularity was based on something totally different. For me, Marshall will always be the great circuit entertainer, because he was charismatic to watch. The car would achieve all sorts of attitudes and still he'd get it back. I've never known any driver consistently get a car off the line better than Gerry – even if he started at the back, invariably he'd be at the front by the time they got to Druids."

Matt James, assistant editor of *Motorsport News*, recalled the first time he met Lanfranchi and Marshall. "I was 15 and I was on work experience at the circuit," he said. "At the end of my two weeks, they said: 'We've got a surprise for you.' I was taken over to the control tower and introduced to Tony, who said he'd sort me out with a passenger ride round the track. 'Gerry's free,' he said, 'we'll put you with Gerry.' He could see that this made me a little twitchy. So he handed me a crash helmet and said: 'Now, we've been in the Kentagon at lunchtime and Gerry's had a few so, if he blacks out when he goes round Paddock, bend down and put your head between your knees, and you'll be absolutely fine.'

"I got in an Escort XR3i with Gerry, and it was brilliant. I idolised the guy already and, coming out of the pit-lane, he had his arm out of the window and one hand on the steering wheel. We must have hit about 100mph at the top of Paddock, and he's still got one arm out of the window. They'd told me it would be five laps, and I counted them down. It got to the end of five, and he just carried on. And I just wanted to get out. I was very shaky afterwards. It was my first experience of being in a racing car with anyone and it was a real highlight for a 15-year-old. When I went back to school, all my mates, who had been in the reception desk of the local vet's surgery, asked: 'What did you do?' Well …"

team's McLaren M10. Gethin went on to become the first Guards European F5000 Champion, with Trevor Taylor second and Mike Hailwood third. Gethin and McLaren won the championship again the following year. In 1971, British-domiciled Australian Frank Gardner's Lola triumphed in a 17-race championship, now sponsored under the Rothmans banner, while Dutchman Gijs van Lennep lifted the 1972 crown in his Surtees TS11.

The formula continued to thrive through the early seventies with races held in Italy, Ireland, Sweden, Denmark, Belgium, Austria and the Netherlands, as well as in the UK. It supported non-championship F1 events, such as the Race of Champions, in which F5000 runners helped to boost the grids. In 1973, Peter Gethin made history by taking his F5000 Chevron B24 to victory over the more fancied F1 runners. The Belgian driver Teddy Pilette was the champion that year, driving a Team VDS entered Chevron B24. A season-long battle between Gethin and Bob Evans in 1974 resulted in the latter taking the title in his Lola T332. By this time, Lola and Chevron were the dominant manufacturers.

The following year, 1975, F5000 had a new sponsor in the form of ShellSport, but the biggest change was the eligibility of the new 3.4-litre V6 Ford engine after years of Chevrolet dominance. David Purley became the first driver to win using this engine, driving it to victory at Brands in March in his Chevron B30. Alan Jones also scored victories in a Ford powered March 75A, but Pilette took his second title in a Chevrolet engined Lola T400. It was appropriate, however, that the last-ever 'pure' F5000 race, which was held at Brands that October, should be won by Peter Gethin, who had won the first-ever event in the category.

There was a complete change to the rules in 1976, turning the formula into an 'anything goes' category for single-seaters. The previous season, it had become clear that interest among both drivers and race promoters was on the wane, eroding the international aspect of the formula. Consequently the fields had been shrinking and it was obvious that a rethink was required. It was decided to open up the British championship to all single-seaters with engine displacements of less than 5000cc, apart from Formula Fords. This allowed in F1, F2 and Formula Atlantic cars and produced an exciting season, the champion being David Purley in a Ford V6 powered Chevron B30.

Tony Trimmer in a Surtees TS19 won what was now known as the ShellSport International Group 8 championship in 1977, the last year that 5000cc cars were eligible. The series was replaced the following year by a national Formula One championship.

Many other Webb-inspired formulae came and went over the years – Formula F100, Formula Ford 2000, Sports 2000, Formula Atlantic, Multisports, Formula Turbo Ford, Formula First, Thundersports and Thundersaloons, to name just a few. There was even a methanol fuelled Formula Talbot as an insurance against any petrol crisis. Some enjoyed more success than others.

"I was encouraged by the success of Formula Ford," said Webb, "From the circuit's point of view, it was totally non-commercial – we never took a penny out of it. My next thoughts were, if it works for single-seaters, let's try a two-seater cheap formula. So I went to Firestone and suggested Formula Firestone to them, and they said 'fine'. The buttons were pressed, people started making cars, and then Firestone America decided to pull out of motor racing. So Firestone UK said: 'We've given our word, so we'll still help, but you can't call it Firestone.' The tyre they were making in those days was called F100 so I suggested 'Formula F100'.

"This ran for four or five years, but it was not as popular as the single-seater series. It never did have the promotional push we'd expected from Firestone. But about 40 cars were built and nobody had their fingers burned. The motoring press, because of the contrast with Formula Ford, regarded it as a failure, but we didn't.

"The junior version of Formula A in America was Formula B, which I launched over here as Formula Atlantic. That worked very well for a long time until one of the competitors said: 'I can do it better than you, I can make a lot of money out of this for the competitors.' We said: 'OK, if you're so clever, hire the circuit and do it yourself.' He went broke very quickly. He lost a fortune."

"Formula First was devised by Jackie Epstein and me. Formula Ford was getting so expensive we thought we should do something to bring it back to basics. By then, a Formula Ford car cost about £15,000, with perhaps another £50,000 a year to run it. We got this back to £5000 a unit for Formula First

and sold about a couple of hundred in the end." Two decades later, this is still the standard car for many racing schools.

Brands Hatch was always renowned for the quality and spectacle of the off-track entertainment it provided for the spectators, as well as the on-track action. At the first Grand Prix meeting in 1964, the lunch interval was filled, according to the programme, by: 'A spectacular display by Military Forces of Eastern Command, including a mock attack on defended positions.' At the end of the day, a concert featuring Chris Barber's Jazz Band ran from 6.30pm to 10.00pm with: 'Dancing on the track in front of the main grandstand, beneath the flood-lit band.'

Barber's band became a regular fixture at big events at the circuit and, after the 1968 Grand Prix, spectators could gather round the start-finish line rostrum and enjoy their 'toe-tapping music'.

But the off-track entertainments with which Brands is most associated are the air displays. The

BELOW Peter Gethin takes the chequered flag in his McLaren M10B on 30 March 1970 to win the Guards Formula 5000 championship race. (LAT)

Red Arrows put in their first appearance at the 1966 Grand Prix, together with a jet-propelled 'flying man', while the 1968 British Grand Prix featured the Red Arrows, a P51 Mustang and a RAF 50th anniversary historic flypast, all preceding the main event.

In 1972, Wing Commander K.H. Wallis in the 'James Bond' Wallis autogyro buzzed the circuit at the Grand Prix. At the Rothmans 50,000 that year, drivers competed in a tractor race for the Edgar Jessop Trophy, and Pan's People, the dancers on the 'Top of the Pops' television show, put in an appearance.

A few years later, in 1976, it was the turn of the Red Devils free-fall parachute team and the Blue Eagles Army Helicopter display team to demonstrate their skills before an expectant audience. And Chris Barber was back after a few years' absence to entertain the crowds at the end of the day.

In 1978, the Red Arrows returned again for the Grand Prix, but most people best remember the events of Sunday 13 July 1980. This was the year of

the Harrier MkGR3, piloted by Flt Lt Dudley Carvell. A specially prepared metal pad was laid at Clearways to prevent the aircraft scattering stones and grass onto the track. The Harrier arrived at the circuit from 233 Operational Conversion Unit of the RAF at 11.05am and began its display at 2.00pm.

"The Harrier air display of 1980 was dramatic," recalled Angela Webb, who was then the deputy managing director of MCD and organised all the off-track entertainment. "The recces and preparation for this fabulous aircraft were exact. It cost £1200 to flatten a pad at Clearways for it to land on, and 80 tons of steel was placed by the Royal Engineers in preparation. On Grand Prix morning, an RAF 'whizz-kid' (who had called me 'a mere civilian' in an earlier meeting) arrived with his winged moustache in a sign-written RAF Morris Marina, and based himself in a Royal Navy marquee. His specific job was to radio instructions to the pilot from the ground to ensure that the downthrust didn't cause havoc. Harrier pilots know their level above ground, but they can't see or determine the damage caused from the immense downward thrust. It was even marginal that he would be able to land, because the Harrier was capable of lifting the 80 tons of steel on the pad!

"The pilot, Dudley Carvell, took off from the pad and all went well until he flew a high-speed low pass across the Formula One paddock. The frame tent of Ken Tyrrell's hospitality vehicle was blown apart and the magnificent Essex Petroleum VIP double-decker hospitality bus was damaged, together with their guests' hats. Then, when Dudley started hovering over the trees above South Bank, they began to swing frantically. A whole grandstand on South Bank was subjected to a total blackout with a mass of dust. Trade booths were demolished and T-shirts were flying into the woods. I immediately scrambled my 'A' team of trouble-shooters to the location, fearful of injuries, but all was well.

"Dudley reported back red-faced and was mortified by the damage. It turned out their 'whizz-kid' had positioned himself out of visual contact with the aircraft. The consequences? 'Whizz-kid' drove away from the Royal Navy marquee with amendments to his vehicle, reading 'Royal Fairy Force'. One spectator sent us a letter praising the display because he had only been able to afford the admission fee but, thanks to the Harrier, he also got a race programme. All the traders had their tills open at the time, as well. One said: 'Mrs Webb, they thought it was their birthday, all my £5 notes landing in their laps.' Thankfully, our insurers were magnificent."

Two years later, the Harrier was indirectly responsible for another near-disaster, this time on the eve of the Grand Prix, as former Brands Hatch press officer Robin Bradford recalled. "I think it was

the first year we ever had traffic lights to start a Grand Prix," he said. "We had to have this pad at Clearways for the Harrier and a whole load of squaddies in a couple of trucks came along to build it during the week before the race. They accessed the circuit from the ambulance gate at Paddock, and turned right to drive the wrong way round to get to Clearways. So now they're on the race circuit in their 20-ton Bedford trucks – and suddenly they're racing. One guy is going down 14 gears to pull out and overtake the other one, and he takes out the brand-new lights that have only been hanging there for about 24 hours."

Luckily help was at hand, as John Webb recounted in a letter to *Autosport*. "On the eve of practice," he wrote, "the Brands Hatch Lucas starting lights were struck by a high vehicle and destroyed. A brand-new set was waiting to be installed at Donington and Tom Wheatcroft let us have them, demonstrating the cooperation that exists between the two circuits in the interests of the sport."

That year, the Red Arrows were also back, along with the Marlboro Aerobatic Team and a Royal Navy helicopter. But it was the turn of Concorde to wow the public by making a low pass over the circuit, its landing gear down.

"Angela had the Concorde boys down and gave them a day at the racing school," explained Bradford. "She enquired how low they could fly and was told 1000 feet. 'That's 1000ft above sea level, is it?' she asked. Now, Brands is 350ft above sea level, give or take, so they flew at 1000 ft above sea level, which is why the aircraft was so low. Concorde flew directly over the main straight and everyone in the grandstand looked up. The roof of the old structure rattled, and the St John Ambulance spent the next two and a half hours swabbing little pieces of rust out of people's eyes."

Jill Todd, who worked at the track from 1974–87, assisting Angela Webb with all non-motorsport activities, also remembered the occasion well. She said: "Concorde came over with its landing lights on and I thought: 'My god, he's coming in low!' It was incredible. I thought he was going to land in one of the fields.

"It was just after the Falklands War," she continued. "When the Harrier came in, I was at the back of the main grandstand. The hospitality suites were full and the startline stand was heaving, and as that Harrier came in and hovered in front of the main stand, it turned and bowed, and there were people crying in that main stand. It was one of the

ABOVE *The Red Arrows always put on a spectacular display at the Grands Prix, as shown here in 1982. (Author)*

Ray Allen

"I went to the Racing Car Show at Olympia in 1967 when I was a 23-year-old sapper in the Royal Engineers, because I'd heard on the radio about this simulator. It was the first ever made that sat you in a racing car and you could drive round Brands Hatch. Four of us went up to London in my Triumph Herald and, when we got there, I went straight to the Motor Racing Stables stand and queued for two hours.

"I was the last one on it that night and I beat all the Grand Prix drivers who had been on it, except Graham Hill. Geoff Clarke, who ran the racing school, got me in the back office and said: 'You should come down to Brands and do a proper initial trial.' I replied: 'I can't do that, I'm a soldier.' But he insisted: 'Nobody has driven as quickly as you have, so we'd like to assess you properly.'

"I went home and had a word with my father to see if he would sub me, and he said: 'Here's fifty quid, go and get it out of your system.' I went down to Brands and got an 'A' rating. Nobody gets an 'A' rating.

"So I started to go through the school. I was still in the army so I could only afford 10 laps a week. I used to go down there on a Saturday morning and I passed every class first time. I ran out of the fifty quid when I was only halfway through the school, so the old man gave me another fifty quid. This is 1967, mind – fifty quid was a lot of money. I was earning about six pounds a week.

"I went through and got to the Class 2 tests, which was the very, very difficult one where the senior instructor drives his nuts off the wrong way round Brands Hatch and sets you a target time. You get eight laps, four finding out, learning the circuit, and four to get a ripple on. It was like going to a brand new circuit, finding out where it goes, and going out and doing a qualifying lap.

"Syd Fox set the time and I got within a tenth of a second of it. Syd was shitting bricks that I was going to beat him. Very few people passed that test, because it was bloody difficult. While I was there, one bloke killed himself trying to do it.

"It was great going the wrong way round. I loved it. It was superb. Clearways was a pig of a bend because it had a very fast entry and it tightened right up at the end. So you went flying in there and you had to get your braking and gearchanging done in the corner, and that was difficult, especially in those days.

"I started working at the school in return for laps. I'd do my 10 laps and then I'd work the rest of the day in return for some extra laps.

"When you had become a Class 2 driver, you were allowed to drive the school's Formula 3 cars – the 1-litre screamers. I used to drive one of those quite often on school days, and Geoff Clarke thought the time had come to enter me in a race.

"So I was entered in a Formula 3 race against all the top drivers in the country, and I ended up eighth quickest at the end of practice. I buggered up the start, because those things were a bit difficult to get off the line. They stalled below 8000 revs and you only had power between 8000 and 10,500. I finally got away but Geoff had told me not to overtake anybody, just to get the experience. So there I was, stuck in about in 14th or 15th place with cars all around me – I'd never had cars that close before and it frightened the daylights out of me. But I finished 14th, and I thought it was great fun. Then he put me in a Formule Libre race, and I finished sixth with the F3 car.

"At about this time, the Formula Ford prototypes were being tried out at Brands, and my third race was the very first Formula Ford race. I won it by a country mile.

"Geoff said: 'Right, lad, I want you to drive for me next season.' I told him I'd just been posted to Cyprus. And he said: 'Well then, old boy, we'll have to get you out of the Army.' I asked him how he was going to do that, and he replied: 'Don't you worry, old chap, I've got contacts.' And he bought me out for £250! I've still got the receipt.

"I raced that year in an old Lotus 51 but the Merlyn Mk10 had come out and was a hell of a lot quicker. Tim Schenken was driving the works Merlyn, which was the plum drive, and I could never beat him in this bloody Lotus. I used to tie the thing in knots trying to keep up with him. But then Schenken went on to F3 the following year and his drive was up for grabs. There were six of us up for it, and I got it.

"So I became the works Merlyn driver and then I did Formula Atlantic, then some Formula 5000, and then John Webb got me an F1 drive with Frank Williams in the 1971 Race of Champions. I finished sixth in Frank's March 701. Frank was dead chuffed and offered me a drive for the season. He said: 'The going rate for a driver's first season in F1 is £70,000 but, if you find me £35,000, we'll do the whole season. Everybody will be after you next year because you're quicker than most of this lot.' But, to me, £35,000 was telephone numbers – I'd never even seen that much money in my life. I hadn't got a clue about how to go about getting it and I didn't have a manager.

"John Webb then managed to get me a drive in a semi-works McLaren in F5000. The drawback was that it was sponsored by Pink Stamps, so I had the only pink racing car in the country, and I had to wear a pink bloody anorak.

"Brands has been a bit sanitised now, but Paddock used to be an awesome bend. There was no huge run-off like there is now. In my day, there was about 10 feet and then an earth bank at the bottom of the hill. The bank was sloped and cars tended to get launched, so they later put railway sleepers in there.

"My favourite race at Brands would have to be the F1 race. One weekend I was doing a 10-lap squirt in a Formula Ford car, and the next I was doing a 150-mile race in an F1 car. I'd only had one test session so I was quite proud of myself, going from 100hp to 450hp with wings and slicks. During the race, I had a tussle with Emerson Fittipaldi in the Lotus 56, that jet car. He'd piss away from me up the straights but I'd be all over him in the corners. Every time we got to a straight – whoosh, he was gone. My eyes were watering from the jet fuel.

"Emerson and I used to have some real tussles in Formula Ford. He was a great bloke to drive against. A lot of drivers would try to drive you off the circuit, but he was just magic. I could spend all day an inch away from him at 140mph and know he wasn't going to do anything dirty."

Ray Allen poses in his Pink Stamps sponsored Formula 5000 McLaren with MCD's Jackie Epstein. (John Webb collection)

most poignant moments, it made the hairs stand up on the back of my neck. It was so moving and it went completely quiet."

The variety continued at the Grand Prix of Europe in 1983, with a Westland Lynx, a Hawker Hunter, a Boeing B17 Flying Fortress, a Supermarine Spitfire and a De Havilland Mosquito all taking part.

For the 1984 Grand Prix, Angela Webb, in conjunction with International Air Tattoo, which also organised the world's biggest military air shows at RAF Greenham Common and (later) Fairford, laid on one of the biggest displays seen. There was participation from RAF, Royal Navy and United States Air Force aircraft including the Red Arrows, the Battle of Britain Memorial Flight (Spitfire, Hurricane and Lancaster), a Buccaneer, a Gloster Meteor, a DH Vampire, a Lockheed Hercules, Westland Scout and Westland Lynx helicopters, a Hawker Sea Fury and a Westland Wessex from the Royal Navy, a Fairchild A-10 Thunderbolt, a General Dynamics F-111F, a McDonnell Douglas RF-4C Phantom and F-15 Eagle, a Boeing B-17G 'Flying Fortress' and, last but not least, another Concorde.

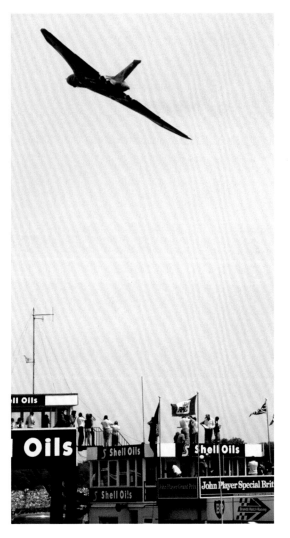

RIGHT *A Vulcan V-bomber deafened the crowd as it flew above the circuit during the British Grand Prix meeting in July 1984. (LAT)*

Concorde had a full load of passengers (all *Daily Mail* readers) and was on an afternoon's supersonic flight to the Bay of Biscay and back. Add to all those the RAF Falcons parachute display team, and it's a wonder there was time for any on-track activity.

A similar packed display, occupying 90 minutes of the lunch interval, took place in 1986 before what was to be the last Grand Prix at Brands, while a mock World War 2 battle was also staged on the Clearways oval.

It was off-track entertainment at its best. "My greatest kick was to appoint and direct the massive air and ground displays at the British Grand Prix during the lunch break," recalled Angela Webb. "It was quite unnerving personally to control the show in front of 120,000 spectators. My challenge to Bernie Ecclestone was to put on a better show than the Formula One race itself. Once we had a USAF Starlifter fly all the way from South Carolina for a flypast, all for no charge. We even tried to beat the Formula One lap record with a Lynx helicopter.

"On the ground, we had simulated battles with aerial explosions, to coincide with the B17 'Sally B' bomber flying through the flak, while Radio Brands played Vera Lynn. We had simulated terrorist attacks on cars. We had military bands, steel bands on low-loaders circulating the track, lawn mower racing, bungee jumping, balloon ascents. My endeavour was to provide non-stop action in all dimensions.

"One of the more useful aspects of my job was to organise the annual Lords *versus* Commons charity race, which inevitably gave us access to some pretty powerful contacts like a young MP named Kenneth Clarke, the Ministers for Sport and, for air displays, the Armed Forces Ministers."

Jill Todd recalled that there was more to the off-track activities than the race day lunchtime air displays. "Angela looked after corporate hospitality," she explained. "And then, Monday to Friday, we used to do all the leasing of the track, the racing school and the non-racing stuff – exhibitions, caravan rallies, clay pigeon shoots. She was responsible for all of these.

"Because it was predominantly a race track, I don't think everyone realised there were other things that went on. We used to do huge caravan rallies with the caravans in the car parks and, from 1974 onwards, we did a lot more non-racing stuff, because they were money-spinners. So if we couldn't lease the track for testing or general practice, we then looked at other ways to diversify.

"The Brands Hatch Grand Prix team worked non-stop for three or four days and we never really slept," Todd continued. "We used to live on site. JW wanted to create a 24-hour village at Brands – he didn't want people to go home. He had the vision to think: 'They're here, so we've got to supply the entertainment, and we've got to supply everything they need so they never leave the circuit.' So that's what we did. We had entertainment in the evenings, discos in the Kentagon, and we had our own Brands Hatch band. They used to start by playing the Fleetwood Mac song, 'The Chain', which was then used by the BBC as the theme for the Grand Prix programmes, and they used to play until midnight or one o'clock.

"At one time we used to have the Kentagon open on Friday and Saturday nights as a nightclub, as well, and that was successful for a couple of years. The locals used to come in, and Ronnie Scott's quintet performed there.

"In all my working life," she added, "the period at Brands was the best. We worked hard and played hard and we were very much a team. JW was a taskmaster and he could blow a gasket, but it was always a joy to go there."

One of the most bizarre incidents ever to occur at Brands happened during one of the lunchtime displays at a Truck Superprix in the eighties, as John Symes recalled. "There's a thing called the Showman's Show," he explained. "It's an opportunity for people who have the sort of acts that you see at county showgrounds to show their wares. So you get 'Co-Co the Clown and his Magic Vehicle' when all the doors blow off, that sort of thing. It was held at an airfield in Cambridgeshire, and Angela and I flew up in the Aztec John used for getting around the circuits. We were looking for something to put into the truck meetings as between-race entertainment.

"We were wandering around and we came across these black bears, and I just knew that we were going to have them. As soon as we saw them, it was obvious Angela fell in love with the bloody things. And I knew they were going to end up at Brands, so I spent a long time talking to the guy and I said: 'We're talking about having a crowd of maybe 30,000, so we're talking about a lot of noise. Are the bears going to cope with that?' He replied: 'Oh yes, no problem.' And I really laboured the point about the noise and the people.

"So these bears came to a truck meeting. They had this 'Bearmobile' vehicle, like a Mini-Moke on steroids, and they'd trained one of the bears to drive the bloody thing. The bear sat there and, instead of a steering wheel, it had a ball and disc and it toddled along at about seven or eight miles an hour.

"At the time, we also had our 'Show & Shine', which was a competition for about 100 trucks in the outer paddock, and their reward was the chance to parade around the circuit in the lunch break. So

now we had about 100 trucks backed up behind the Bearmobile, trundling round the circuit. That was fine until the Bearmobile was making the turn into Druids, and the guy in the lead truck leaned on his airhorn. Well, that just spooked the bear. So the bear stopped the Bearmobile and hopped out.

"Now we had three-quarters of a ton of black bear sitting in the middle of the gravel trap, and that's all he wanted to do. When the trainer tried to approach, the bear just picked up paw-fulls of gravel and threw it at him. All the while the crowd around got bigger and bigger and they laughed all the more, so there was even more noise. The bear stayed put in the middle of the gravel trap, and he wouldn't let the trainer near him. That went on for about 15 minutes or so."

Doug Jennings was following events in Race Control. "I didn't go up there, but I was listening to the radio communications," he explained.

"We need to wind up the bears now, fellers." *They're already bloody wound up – that hooter wound them up.* "What are they doing?" *They're playing in the gravel.* "Can you get them out?" *You*

BELOW *Holding a Truck Grand Prix was another of John Webb's ideas. (Michael Hewett)*

come and get them out – they're bears. "Is their handler there?" *Yes.* "Is he going to get them out?" *No way. He says, when they've finished playing, they've finished playing …"*

Angela Webb took up the story. "When the largest bear, a good 7ft high, jumped off and deposited himself in the gravel trap at Druids, bemused marshals radioed back to Race Control but they were understandably reticent to get involved. The keeper eventually persuaded the bear to rejoin the others, but this lasted for only a few yards before he jumped off again and plonked himself down on the tarmac.

"We were forced into scrambling a Brands Hatch van to the location with the keeper's wife aboard, armed with Polo mints, which were the bear's favourite. Eventually, the bear was cajoled into the van. We all breathed an enormous sigh of relief. But too early – the bear sprang open the doors and was back on the track again. Finally the keeper and his wife got him inside, this time with assistance from marshals to ensure the doors were secure. So now

we had a situation with intrepid 'A' team member Steve Charsley driving the Mini Moke with two bears, and our Brands Hatch foreman, Danny Day, driving the van with a bear's paw on his shoulder, and the keeper and his wife pinned down under the bear's back paws."

John Symes remembered: "Danny often told the story of how he was trundling down the road with this bear in the back and, as he put it: 'I felt the paw and then smelled the smell.' People would say: 'I'm not surprised.' And he would answer: 'Not me, it was the bear.' Sadly, it knackered the bear – I don't think it ever worked again."

The original 'voice of Brands Hatch' belonged to the distinctive figure of John Bolster, who kept the crowds entertained for most of the first decade of motor racing at the circuit. Bolster had been a driver himself before the war, competing in hillclimbs in his 'Bloody Mary' special and driving ERAs in Formula One races from 1947–49. A serious accident during the British Grand Prix at Silverstone in 1949 had forced him to give up racing and turn his hand to commentating, broadcasting and journalism.

With his walrus moustache and deerstalker cap, Bolster was an engaging character who would invariably start his commentary excitedly with the words: 'Hello boys and girls!' His enthusiasm, however, sometimes got the better of him, as Max Le Grand recalled.

"John used to do all sorts of things," said Le Grand. "He had licence to commentate very colourfully on motor racing and it got more and more colourful as the day went on, because we discovered that he was consuming a bottle of champagne. At the end of each race, he would say: 'Right, lick your pencils girls, here are the results.' It was outrageous."

Former MCD director and general manager Chris Lowe also recalled the more colourful side of Bolster's commentaries. "Extraordinary bloke," he said. "He used to turn up in vintage motor cars. One day he said: "That car's like me – piston broke!' And later: "Would the person who's lost a pair of testicles please report to the police office.'

According to Ian Titchmarsh, an occasional Brands commentator, Bolster was finally banned from commentating at the circuit for two indiscretions. Titchmarsh explained: "There was a battle going on between two of the top saloon drivers, Les Leston in a Riley 1.5 and Jeff Uren in a Ford Zephyr. Bolster came out with: 'Oh look, everybody, Leston's passing Uren on the Top Straight!' And then there was a sports car called the Weldangrind, which was built in London, and it turned up at Brands Hatch and John Bolster said: 'I

BELOW *John Bolster interviews winner Jochen Rindt on the podium at the 1970 British Grand Prix. (Phipps/Sutton)*

wonder why it's called the Weldangrind? It must be because they weld all day and grind all night!'

"On the strength of that, he was told he couldn't come back and commentate at Brands Hatch ever again. But, many years later, there was an *Autosport* Escort Mexico race in 1975, and he was allowed back to add to the commentary and he started off just the same – 'Hello boys and girls!'"

John Webb confirmed that Bolster had been asked to leave. "It wasn't me who fired him, nor was I consulted," he said. "I believe it was the BRSCC and John Hall jointly who welded the axe. Even in the late fifties, public opinion on doubtful expressions was still quite severe."

In the 1960s, Anthony Marsh took over as the principal Brands Hatch commentator. Marsh had also previously competed himself in an Alvis Special, and had began commentating in 1954. In 1965, he also took on the role of services manager, looking after the day-to-day running of the circuit.

Marsh did the voiceover for the 1966 John Frankenheimer film, 'Grand Prix', which was partly filmed at Brands Hatch. In 1976, he left to provide the English-speaking commentary at Grands Prix all round the world.

According to former press officer Robin Bradford, the first time Marsh ever used a radio microphone in the pits occurred in the early seventies. "He went up to Jackie Stewart to ask him a question," said Bradford, "but before he could ask it, Jackie said: 'Aye, Anthony, I bet you've never had anything that big in your hand before.'"

Chris Lowe recalled the scrambling events on the infield, when Peter Arnold did the commentaries. "If he needed a number two, we stuck Anthony Marsh on, with malice aforethought," said Lowe. "Marsh knew little about bike riders, so he had to go on their numbers to identify them. Peter stuck him in the box at the top of Paddock Hill infield and of course, once they'd done one lap, their numbers were totally obscured. So the rest of Marsh's commentary was: 'They're coming round again and it's, er, it's, er, over to you, Peter.'"

But the person who has commentated at the circuit longer than anyone else is Brian Jones. "My first commentary as a public address commentator was done in the back of the old grandstand," he explained. "If you looked up from the track at the top of the seating, you would see a glass box, with the timekeepers on the left and Race Control on the right. Sandwiched in between was the commentary box. It was just wide enough to take two chairs – one for me and one for my lap scorer.

"It was a lovely position because you were on the outside of the track, so you had good views of Paddock Hill Bend and, if you lowered your head to peer underneath the lip of the grandstand roof, the Druids hairpin. You could also see Bottom Bend, along Bottom Straight and into the left-hander.

"To get into the commentary box, I used to have to go through the rear door of the main grandstand, up the stairs, along the corridor and past the loo. On my left was Race Control, populated by half a dozen people running the meeting, and on my right were the timekeepers. For many years, Les Needham was the chief RAC timekeeper and his wife used to hold up little notes to the window so that I could see who'd done what, because this was all done by hand. I could see into Race Control and into the timekeepers and they could see me. So I was fed information that way.

"In 1976, they built the timekeepers' box straddling the pit-lane, and on top of that was my small commentary box. It had the effect of blocking out the view of Graham Hill Bend for two-thirds of the occupants of the grandstand, which was a great pity."

BELOW *Veteran commentator Brian Jones has been the voice of Brands Hatch for over 30 years. (LAT)*

Brands Hatch today

Brands Hatch today is very different from the old track of the sixties and seventies, but it retains its unmistakable character. The names of the corners are much the same and the shape of the circuit, although modified over the years with the addition of wide run-off areas and gravel traps, is still virtually as it was when the Grand Prix loop was added in 1960.

But the infrastructure is very different. Gone are the covered grandstands and the scoreboard at Paddock Hill Bend, along with the old Grovewood Suite and the main grandstand on the start-finish straight. Gone too, the old administration block by the back entrance. Today we have the MotorSport Vision Centre at Clark Curve, the Brabham and Stewart hospitality suites, and large, open grandstands on the Brabham Straight.

Gone also are the covered bays of the old, sloping paddock, and there are now twin tunnels beneath the track, linking the paddock to the pits, where a narrow, single-lane passageway used to cope with traffic in each direction. The current pit garages and control tower look very different to their predecessors, but essentially serve the same purposes.

Brands Hatch still provides some of the best viewing to be found at any motor racing circuit in the country. The spectator can still see most of the Indy circuit from any one place, but many vantage points have changed, and some have been lost forever.

RIGHT *An aerial view of the whole circuit. (MSV)*

The spectator banking has been cut back dramatically over the years, especially at Paddock and Druids, to make way for extensive run-off areas in the name of safety. And where spectators used to enjoy uninterrupted views of the action, the circuit is now surrounded by harsh, grey debris fencing, which seems to jar at the senses even more than the raucous bark of a racing engine.

You can still park your car on South Bank, but the tradition of sounding your horn to greet the race winners has disappeared, because time-tight race programmes no longer allow for laps of honour.

On the track, Paddock was tightened in the seventies and the banking increasingly moved back. A car running too wide in the past would come to grief against railway sleepers fronting an unforgiving earth bank, but today it will either end up beached in the gravel or, if the driver is lucky, clatter across, leaving an obscuring cloud of sand-coloured dust in its wake and then scattering small stones as it scrabbles to regain the track.

Graham Hill Bend has been reprofiled in recent times, making it slower and introducing a potential overtaking spot. Out on the long circuit, Westfield and Sheene (formerly Dingle Dell) have also been altered in the name of safety.

Walk the circuit, though, and the ghosts are still there. Paddock is still a dauntingly fast, downhill plunge. Cooper Straight is no more a straight than it ever was. The steep, left-hand climb through Surtees, out into the country, still takes you away from the noise and hubbub and into a temporarily tranquil woodland. You are on your own out here,

alternately plunging down and climbing the sides of the valley, until coming out under the bridge into the colourful and bustling natural amphitheatre of the Indy circuit.

According to John Webb, Paddock Hill Bend, Druids and Clearways corners were named before he arrived in 1954. Hawthorn, Stirling's, Westfield and Dingle Dell on the Grand Prix circuit were named by John Hall, based on the original names on the motorcycle scrambles track. "Hawthorn was a local name and Stirling's was named after Stirlings' pig farm," Webb explained. "Neither was a tribute to drivers. I named Brabham Straight, Graham Hill Bend, Cooper Straight, McLaren, Surtees and Clark Curve."

The old names of Top Straight, Bottom Bend and Kidney corner gave way to Brabham, Graham Hill and Surtees respectively when major alterations took place at the track in 1976. At the same time, Clearways was split into three as McLaren, Clearways and Clark, while Pilgrim's Rise was renamed Hailwood Hill after Mike Hailwood who, like John Surtees, raced at the circuit on two wheels and on four. Two other motorbike riders are commemorated at the track. The old Portobello Straight, which ran between Hawthorn and Westfield, was renamed Derek Minter Straight after the undisputed 'King of Brands'. Dingle Dell corner was re-named Sheene Curve in 2003, in memory of Barry Sheene.

There was a time in the late nineties when Brands was accused of being shabby, but today everything is spick and span, and gleaming in the corporate red-and-black of MotorSport Vision. When the DTM touring cars visited in July 2006, the circuit basked in a heatwave and looked better than it had in years.

A new, albeit temporary, grandstand at the bottom of Paddock Hill Bend provided a spectacular vantage point and three giant television screens on South Bank, facing Paddock, the pits and Clearways, allowed spectators to follow the whole race. The DTM cars looked magnificent on the circuit. At Surtees and McLaren, they twitched as they swept left and then right, spitting flames from each side as the back ends skipped across the hot tarmac.

Behind the pits, the silver transporters glinted in the bright sunshine and the red-and-white of the kerbing contrasted with the grey of the track surface. Just minutes before the start of the race, it was quite surreal to walk through the tunnel underneath Paddock Hill Bend – it was so quiet, yet the air was charged with anticipation.

Yet even an event like this, with spectacular cars and high-profile drivers, illustrated one of the problems facing circuit operator Jonathan Palmer these days: there was not a great deal of on-track overtaking. The reduced braking distances and ever-greater reliance on aerodynamics of the modern racing car has meant that overtaking opportunities in some categories of car racing are few, so some races can be rather processional. Palmer has already said that he would not rule out some circuit changes in the future but that any alterations would be gradual and carefully thought through.

"The problem really is not a circuit one, but of some racecar evolution going in the wrong direction," he explained. "For example, bike racing always produces a lot of overtaking and, on the Indy circuit, the entries into Paddock, Druids and Clearways provide good overtaking opportunities in many car categories, including the BTCC. It's really only in high-grip, low-power categories like Formula 3 and Formula Renault where overtaking can be pretty difficult. Formula Ford has no such problem.

"While we're looking at the possibility of changes," he continued, "I would be reluctant to destroy some great corners just because some of the car categories have chased grip too much. I want Brands Hatch to host the most exciting motor racing in the country, and to be a superb circuit to visit in terms of facilities and everything that anybody would want to have a great day out. But we're not going to be ripping everything down and starting again, that's for sure. It will be evolutionary."

It is good to know that, all being well, the sound of racing engines will continue to echo around this natural bowl in the Kent countryside. That said, however, one of the best times to appreciate the

circuit is not when the cars or bikes are on it, but when it lies dormant in the early evening. When Brands is deserted, it is almost like a seaside town in winter. The pit garages are open, front and rear, so you can see through them. The sun glints on the polished metal of the Armco barrier and the only mechanical noise comes from the M20 motorway in the distance. Out on the long circuit, birds are

BELOW *The Race Control tower is on the right of the track at the start-finish line. (Author)*

singing in the bluebell woods and, in the spring, primroses grow on the banks surrounding the track. It seems incongruous, the peace and quiet, compared with when there is activity on the circuit.

Paddock Hill Bend is steep, whether you are driving or walking, and so is the climb up to Druids, the hairpin at the top of the hill. At the exit, you can see back across to the pits and the entrance of Paddock, before you drop down to Graham Hill Bend. It is a tighter left-hander than it used to be, and the position of the Armco barrier marks the original, faster line of the corner.

The track runs flatter here, taking a gentle left-handed sweep behind the pits complex before tightening at Surtees. If you are taking the line of the Indy circuit, then it is a quick left-right flick through Surtees and McLaren, before the long sweeping right-hander of Clearways and Clark. Stay on the Grand Prix circuit and Surtees rises quite steeply on the exit, leading you up past a marshals' post, over a brow and onto the long loop.

The track kinks right as it flattens out and then straightens towards the vehicle bridge. The branches of an old oak tree, which must have witnessed a few classic races in its time, overhang the gleaming barrier on the left. Only a short distance beyond it is Druids, but you are unaware of

it from here. There is grass run-off area on either side at this point but, at the vehicle bridge, which seems impossibly low as you approach it, the barrier moves in, around the solid and unforgiving-looking supports. Not a place to have an accident, as Johnny Herbert discovered in 1988.

Under the bridge, down Pilgrim's Drop, and suddenly you are climbing again through the fast, uphill right-hander of Hawthorn. On the outside of the corner there is a thin grass strip and then a massive gravel run-off area. If this had been in place in 1971 it would have saved Jo Siffert's life. The gravel crunches under your feet like hard-packed snow. The track levels again along the short Derek Minter Straight, heading towards Westfield. A lot of work has been carried out here recently, the corner reprofiled to allow another, huge run-off area on the outside.

Coming out of Westfield, the track narrows slightly and drops steeply while it is still turning right, down into the dip of Dingle Dell. Then it climbs quickly towards Sheene Curve, a tight right-hander which, again, has been reprofiled recently. Here you can see how close the boundary of the circuit is to the village of West Kingsdown – a house is clearly visible just beyond the marshals' post.

The track takes a slightly different line from Sheene to Stirling's than it used to, allowing another

ABOVE *The pits complex from above. (MSV)*

large run-off area on the left-hand side of the run to the cambered left-hander. Around Stirling's, and in the distance is another, low vehicle bridge. As you emerge from underneath it, the Indy circuit comes back into view.

Ahead of you is the Motorsport Vision Centre on the outside of Clark Curve. On your right, the Indy circuit joins while the track takes its long sweep right through Clearways and Clark Curve and onto the Brabham Straight. The entrance to the pit-lane snakes off to your right. There is fencing along the top of the pit wall to protect team personnel, and a grass strip along the outside of the track. On the start-finish line, you can see how heavily the track slopes and how difficult it must be to get off the line from pole position. And that is something that has not changed over the years.

It has been a long journey from mushroom field to international racing circuit. If you leave Brands Hatch by the paddock gate and turn right down Scratcher's Lane, you can see a rather tenuous link with the past. At the bottom of the hill, a road goes off on the left to Fawkham Green, running under the M20 motorway. There, at the junction, a sign points towards a mushroom farm.

FAR LEFT *The approach to Paddock Hill Bend. (Author)*

LEFT *Paddock is a dauntingly fast, downhill right-hander. (Author)*

RIGHT *The track drops away sharply at Paddock. Note the wide gravel trap on the outside of the corner. (Author)*

FAR RIGHT *From Paddock, the track climbs up Hailwood Hill towards Druids. (Author)*

RIGHT *The hairpin at Druids is the slowest corner on the circuit. (Author)*

FAR RIGHT *From Druids, the track drops downhill again towards Graham Hill Bend. (Author)*

RIGHT *Cooper Straight is really a gentle left-hand sweep behind the pits. (Author)*

FAR RIGHT *The track begins to climb gently in the left-hander at Surtees. (Author)*

RIGHT *Here the Indy circuit sweeps right, through McLaren … (Author)*

FAR RIGHT *… while the Grand Prix circuit climbs steeply through the tightening Surtees. (Author)*

FAR LEFT *The track is still climbing as it sweeps out into the country. (Author)*

LEFT *Ahead, the track kinks to the right. (Author)*

FAR LEFT *An oak tree overhangs the run-off area just before the kink. (Author)*

LEFT *At Pilgrim's Drop, the track plunges downhill under a vehicle bridge. (Author)*

FAR LEFT *Pilgrim's Drop leads to the climb of Hawthorn Hill. (Author)*

LEFT *The track now rises sharply again towards the fast, right-hander at Hawthorn Bend. (Author)*

FAR LEFT *The uphill swoop of Hawthorn Bend. (Author)*

LEFT *The track levels again on the exit of Hawthorn, towards the Derek Minter Straight. (Author)*

RIGHT *The Derek Minter Straight leads into the right-hander at Westfield Bend. Note the extensive run-off area. (Author)*

FAR RIGHT *Westfield has been reprofiled and is tighter than it used to be. (Author)*

RIGHT *On the exit of Westfield, the track plunges downhill again into Dingle Dell. (Author)*

FAR RIGHT *After Dingle Dell, it rises steeply towards the reprofiled Sheene Curve. (Author)*

RIGHT *Previously known as Dingle Dell Corner, Sheene Curve turns sharp right at the top of the hill. (Author)*

FAR RIGHT *From Sheene, the track runs straight towards Stirling's Bend but has recently been realigned to allow a run-off on the left. (Author)*

RIGHT *Stirling's Bend is a cambered, 90deg left-hander. (Author)*

FAR RIGHT *From Stirling's, the track runs gently downhill towards Clearways. (Author)*

FAR LEFT *Under the vehicle bridge at Clearways, the sweep of Clark Curve lies ahead. (Author)*

LEFT *At the exit of Clark Curve, the track drops slightly downhill. (Author)*

FAR LEFT *The entry to the pit-lane peels off on the right of Clark Curve. (Author)*

LEFT *The right-left sweep of the pit-lane entry is designed to slow the cars considerably. (Author)*

FAR LEFT *The pit-lane. (Author)*

LEFT *From Clark Curve, the track climbs gently again onto the Brabham Straight. (Author)*

FAR LEFT *The start of Brabham Straight. The pit garages are on the right, while the Brabham and Stewart hospitality suites can be seen ahead to the left of the track. (Author*

LEFT *Another lap of Brands Hatch is complete. (Author)*

Appendix

CIRCUIT MAPS

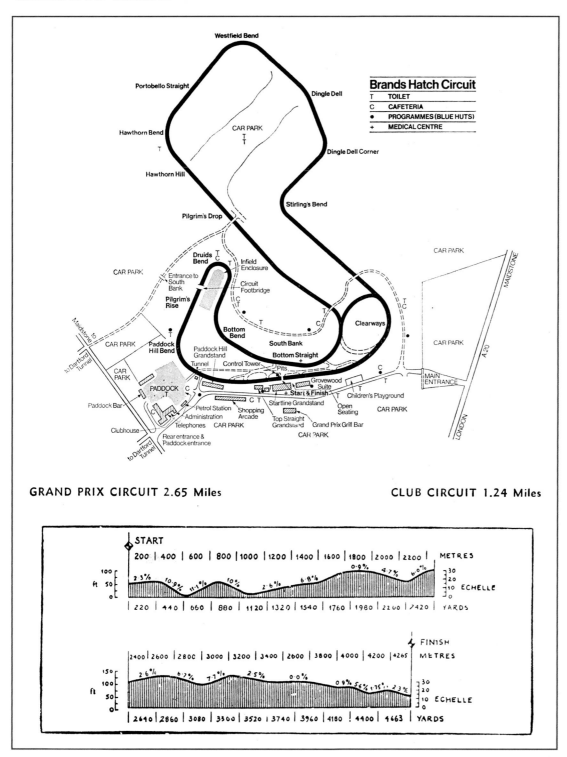

LEFT *Circuit diagrams from the 1960s, showing the layout and gradients of the track.*

Brands Hatch Circuit

T	TOILET
C	CAFETERIA
•	PROGRAMMES (BLUE HUTS)
+	MEDICAL CENTRE

Westfield Bend

Portobello Straight

Dingle Dell

Hawthorn Bend

CAR PARK

Dingle Dell Corner

Hawthorn Hill

Stirling's Bend

Pilgrim's Drop

Druids Bend

Infield Enclosure

CAR PARK

Entrance to South Bank

Circuit Footbridge

Pilgrim's Rise

Bottom Bend

South Bank

Clearways

CAR PARK

Paddock Hill Bend

Bottom Straight

Paddock Hill Grandstand

CAR PARK

Tunnel

Control Tower

Pits

Grovewood Suite

Start & Finish

PADDOCK

Startline Grandstand

Children's Playground

Paddock Bar

Petrol Station

Shopping Arcade

Top Straight Grandstand

Open Seating

Grand Prix Grill Bar

CAR PARK

Administration

Telephones

CAR PARK

CAR PARK

Clubhouse

Rear entrance & Paddock entrance

to Dartford Tunnel

MAIN ENTRANCE

MAIDSTONE

A 20

LONDON

GRAND PRIX CIRCUIT 2.65 Miles   **CLUB CIRCUIT 1.24 Miles**

START

| 200 | 400 | 600 | 800 | 1000 | 1200 | 1400 | 1600 | 1800 | 2000 | 2200 | METRES |

0.9% 4.7% 6.0%

2.3% 10.9% 11.1% 10% 2.6% 6.8%

ft 100 50 0

30 20 10 0 ECHELLE

| 220 | 440 | 660 | 880 | 1120 | 1320 | 1540 | 1760 | 1980 | 2200 | 2420 | YARDS |

FINISH

| 2400 | 2600 | 2800 | 3000 | 3200 | 3400 | 3600 | 3800 | 4000 | 4200 | 4265 | METRES |

2.6% 6.7% 7.7% 2.5% 0.0% 0.9% 5.6% 1.75% 2.3%

ft 150 100 50 0

30 20 10 0 ECHELLE

| 2640 | 2860 | 3080 | 3300 | 3520 | 3740 | 3960 | 4180 | 4400 | 4663 | YARDS |

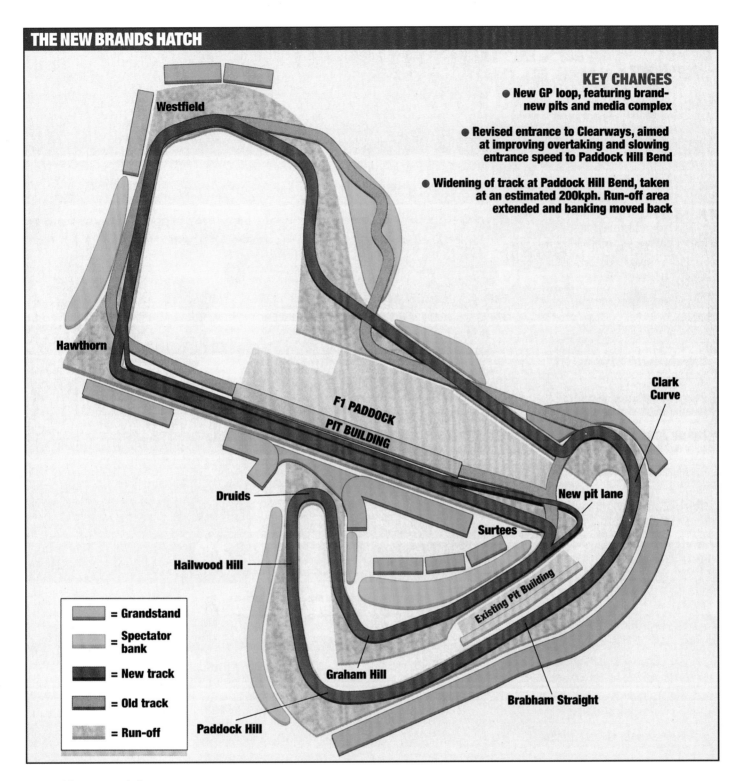

KEY CHANGES
- New GP loop, featuring brand-new pits and media complex
- Revised entrance to Clearways, aimed at improving overtaking and slowing entrance speed to Paddock Hill Bend
- Widening of track at Paddock Hill Bend, taken at an estimated 200kph. Run-off area extended and banking moved back

Westfield

Hawthorn

Clark Curve

F1 PADDOCK PIT BUILDING

New pit lane

Druids

Surtees

Hailwood Hill

Existing Pit Building

Graham Hill

Brabham Straight

Paddock Hill

= Grandstand

= Spectator bank

= New track

= Old track

= Run-off

ABOVE *The proposed changes to the circuit in 1999 included the construction of a new F1 pits and paddock complex and a revised Grand Prix loop. (Autosport)*

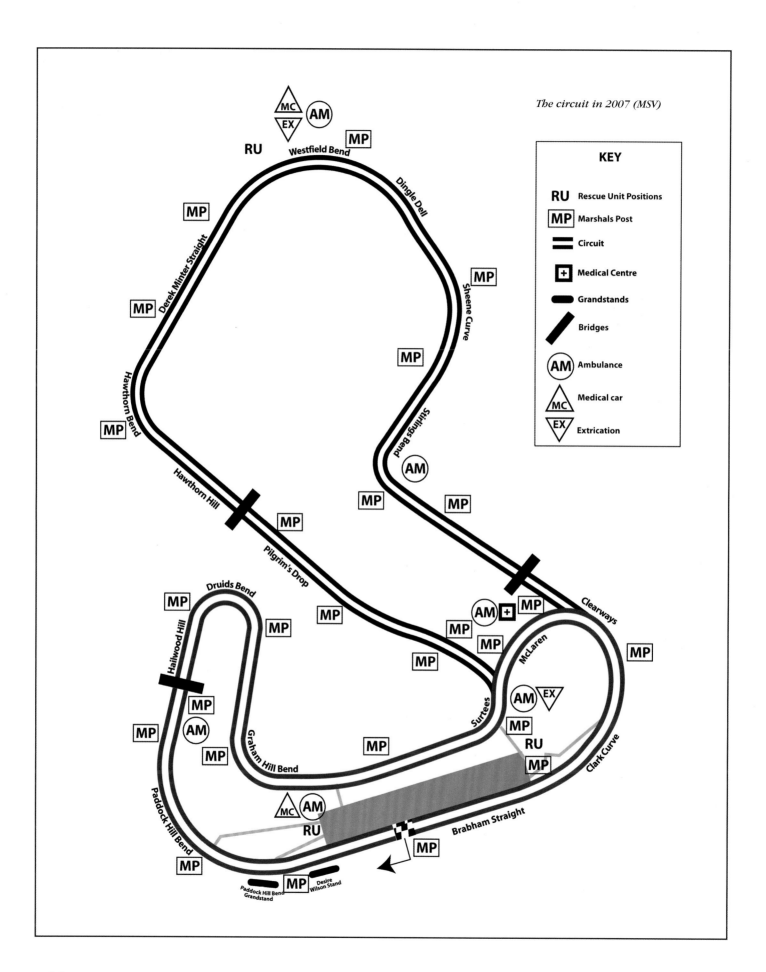

The circuit in 2007 (MSV)

KEY

RU — Rescue Unit Positions

MP — Marshals Post

— Circuit

+ Medical Centre

— Grandstands

— Bridges

AM — Ambulance

MC — Medical car

EX — Extrication

Westfield Bend

Dingle Dell

Derek Minter Straight

Sheene Curve

Hawthorn Bend

Stirlings Bend

Hawthorn Hill

Pilgrim's Drop

Clearways

Druids Bend

McLaren

Hailwood Hill

Surtees

Graham Hill Bend

Clark Curve

Paddock Hill Bend

Brabham Straight

Paddock Hill Bend Grandstand

Desire Wilson Stand

Bibliography

Life at the limit,
by Graham Hill, published by William Kimber, 1969

Jo Siffert,
by Jacques Deschenaux, published by William Kimber, 1972

From Brands Hatch to Indianapolis,
by Tommaso Tommasi, published by Hamlyn, 1973

John Player Motorsport Yearbook 1973,
edited by Barrie Gill, published by The Queen Anne Press, 1973

25 years of Brands Hatch car racing,
by Mike Kettlewell, published by Brands Hatch Circuit Ltd, 1975

Graham,
by Graham Hill with Neil Ewart, published by Hutchinson/Stanley Paul & Co, 1976

Against All Odds,
by James Hunt with Eoin Young, published by Hamlyn, 1977

Brands Hatch – 50 years of motor cycle racing,
by Norrie Whyte, published by Brands Hatch Circuit Ltd, 1978

Only Here for the Beer – Gerry Marshall,
by Jeremy Walton, published by Haynes, 1978

Down the Hatch – the life and fast times of Tony Lanfranchi,
by Mark Kahn, published by W Foulsham & Co Ltd, 1980

Brands Hatch, past, present and future,
by Mark Cole and Mike Kettlewell, published by Brands Hatch Circuit Ltd, 1984

Nigel's Day,
edited by Mike Doodson, published by Brands Hatch Publications, 1986

Formula Ford – a 20-year world success story,
edited by Simon North, published by Brands Hatch Publications, 1987

British Grand Prix,
by Maurice Hamilton, published by The Crowood Press, 1989

Jim Clark – the legend lives on,
by Graham Gauld, third ed. published by Patrick Stephens Limited, 1989

From Brands to Bexhill,
by Max Le Grand, published by Bookmarque Publishing, 1995

Bernie's game,
by Terry Lovell, published by Metro Publishing, 2004

Grand Prix Data Book,
by David Hayhoe and David Holland, fourth ed. published by Haynes 2006

Sundry copies of ***Motoring News***, ***Motorsport News***, ***Autosport***, ***The Autocar*** and ***Motor Sport***, 1950–2007

Index